Mary Taylor Huber is Senior Scholar,
The Carnegie Foundation for the Advancement
of Teaching.

Nancy C. Lutkehaus is Associate Professor of
Anthropology, University of Southern
California.

Gendered Missions

Gendered Missions

Women and Men in Missionary Discourse and Practice

EDITED BY
MARY TAYLOR HUBER
AND
NANCY C. LUTKEHAUS

Ann Arbor

THE UNIVERSITY OF MICHIGAN PRESS

Published in the United States of America by
The University of Michigan Press
Manufactured in the United States of America
♾ Printed on acid-free paper

2002 2001 2000 1999 4 3 2 1

A CIP catalog record for this book is available from the British Library.

Library of Congress Cataloging-in-Publication Data

Gendered missions : women and men in missionary discourse and
practice / edited by Mary Taylor Huber and Nancy C. Lutkehaus.
p. cm.
Includes bibliographical references and index.
ISBN 0-472-10987-1 (alk. paper)
1. Women in missionary work—History. 2. Women missionaries—
History. 3. Missions—History. I. Huber, Mary Taylor, 1944–
II. Lutkehaus, Nancy.
BV2610 .G46 1999
266'.0082—dc21 98-40265
CIP

Contents

Illustrations

Preface and Acknowledgments

This collection of essays is about Christian missionary experience and the gendered discourses and practices that helped set missionaries' expectations about the roles of women and men in missionary work. It is also about the effects that missionary experience had on these discourses and practices themselves. Indeed, this concern with the back and forth between colonial experience and metropolitan ideologies is the hallmark of *Gendered Missions.* We focus most specifically on the changing prospects for professional women in the missions and ask how these shaped, and were shaped by, crucial practical, political, and religious developments at home and abroad. While we focus on the tumultuous period that historian Eric Hobsbawm calls "The Age of Empire" (1875–1914), we consider how gender has been created and debated in later colonial and postcolonial missions as well.

The genesis of this project lies in the late 1970s, when we first met each other as graduate students engaged in fieldwork along the north coast of Papua New Guinea—a region where Roman Catholic missionaries had been active since the late nineteenth century. In thinking about these missionaries, we were both struck early on by the ways in which concepts of gender had informed these individuals' projects and social relationships over the years. And as we soon found out, we were not alone. In the 1980s the topic of gender began to engage many scholars in mission studies and by the early 1990s mission studies itself was being encompassed by the new field of colonial studies.

Interested in broadening our perspective on missionary discourse and practice, we invited an interdisciplinary group of scholars to contribute essays and commentary on other "gendered missions" at the 1993 annual meeting of the American Anthropological Association in Washington, D.C. We were joined in a spirited session by historians Nancy Rose Hunt, Diane Langmore, and Susan Thorne; sociologist Jon Miller; and anthropologists T. O. Beidelman, Dorothy Hodgson, and Rita Kipp. Anthropologists Robert Gordon and Ann Stoler offered insightful and provocative commentary from their respective positions as scholars of African, Melanesian, and Southeast Asian colonial states. We owe a large intellectual debt to these scholars and to our audience, whose questions prompted a lively discussion of ethical issues involved in missionary practice, in the study of missionaries, and in the scholarly representation of missionary work.

As the discussion in our session demonstrated, critical scholarship in sensitive fields like missionary studies requires a particularly careful balance between judgment and analysis. Nor can scholars any longer separate themselves from their subjects, whether culturally near or distant, in the name of science, history, or truth. Indeed, this sense of connection, of mutual implication, between self and other gives a special stamp to much contemporary scholarship in the humanities and social sciences, especially as it involves colonial and postcolonial societies. The essays in this collection may be written by academic scholars about missionaries, but it is important to recognize that missionaries and academics (anthropologists, in particular) both have played significant roles in relations between colonies and metropoles and that gender has shaped and been shaped by the roles that both missionaries and academics have been able to play.

We would like to recognize three people who contributed in special ways to this collection. Ann Laura Stoler encouraged us throughout, sharing with us a prepublication draft of "Between Metropole and Colony: Rethinking a Research Agenda," written with Frederick Cooper to introduce their edited volume, *Tensions of Empire: Colonial Cultures in a Bourgeois World* (1997). Margaret Jolly's careful and provocative review of the manuscript for the University of Michigan Press helped us clarify important points concerning colonial imagery, tighten the introduction, and integrate the essays. And we owe special thanks to Susan Whitlock of the University of Michigan Press for her belief in this project and for skillfully shepherding it through publication.

Finally, we would also like to acknowledge the interest and support of Ernie Vigdor and Jim McBride, who both married into this project (so to speak) and gracefully filled the "stepfather" role.

Introduction: Gendered Missions at Home and Abroad

Mary Taylor Huber and Nancy C. Lutkehaus

Gender issues show no sign of diminishing as topics of discussion and debate concerning the legacy of imperialism. In scholarly arenas as well as in political forums it has become increasingly clear that, whatever else it also may have been, the imperial mission was a gendered mission. This is not only because gender was a frequent idiom for relationships of power in the colonies, the imagery of empire often feminizing its subjects and creating of its agents super-men (Said 1978).[1] Nor is it only because certain colonial policies specifically aimed to control or change relationships between women and men (Stoler 1991). Rather, what gives the colonies special significance in the history and sociology of gender is that the extreme circumstances created by empire so often placed pressure on received understandings about differences between the sexes and their proper roles among colonized and colonizers alike.

The essays collected in this volume aim to illuminate these intricate relations between gender and empire through case studies of Christian missions in Europe, Africa, Melanesia, and Indonesia by anthropologists, sociologists, and a historian. We focus on missions first because missionaries usually worked closer to local communities than other colonial agents, often with a moral agenda that provided a broad critique of local gender regimes.[2] Further, because of their concerns with women, children, and family, missionary groups were more likely than others to include Western women among their workers and thus to face more immediately the destabilizing challenges that colonial experience posed to their own ways of organizing relations between women and men. If, as Rosaldo reminds us, cultural traditions are selected and invented as part of the process of social positioning (1990, 103), then missionary studies provide a privileged site for examining how traditions organized around gender have been negotiated in conditions of rapid social change.

Gender is a capacious, sometimes capricious, term, with a "multiplicity of meaning" in contemporary discussions in scholarly fields, politics, law, medicine, and the like (Hawkesworth 1997). Our essays focus on culturally and historically situated men and women and, most particularly, on how they handled the issue of women's work in their missions in Europe and overseas. In recent years scholars have challenged the view that imperial culture was stable, homogeneous, and resolutely masculinist by examining contributions of Western women at home and abroad (Mehlman 1992; Lewis 1996; Cooper and Stoler 1997). We suggest that, like their sister travelers, artists, teachers, nurses, and social reformers, missionary women complicated the assumptions, habits, and work of their brethren in the very act of helping colonization along. As Fiona Bowie observes in the pioneering volume *Women and Missions: Past and Present,* "what [is] clear is that women have been active participators in the modern missionary movement and that their experience cannot simply be subsumed under that of men" (1993, 18).

Although women's missionary experience has differed from men's, it cannot be assumed that women's missionary experience everywhere has been the same. It is always important in mission studies to recognize how varied missionary organizations have been (Beidelman 1974; see also Huber 1996). Gender, especially, has been construed differently according to missionaries' nationality, denomination, and class affiliations. Our essays consider English Anglicans, Dutch Reformed missionaries from the Netherlands, Swiss Pietists, Norwegian Lutherans, and a Roman Catholic mission with German roots. These groups differed in their emphasis on clerical authority in mission work and on marriage, children, celibacy, and many other social practices and cultural values that shaped relations between the women and men who worked for them at home and abroad. They also changed their own attitudes and policies over time.

The places and periods we discuss in our essays are necessarily limited. Mission ventures in West Africa, East Africa, New Guinea, and Sumatra are included, as are efforts of women in Britain and Norway to support such missions. In all these areas mission work challenged accepted gender roles. The home movement mobilized women as public speakers, fund raisers, organizers, and even policymakers for the missions, while missionaries posted to regions outside or on the margins of the great civilizations had less social and material support to sustain their churches' typical division of labor and authority between women and men. Indeed, most of our essays are set in the late nineteenth to early twentieth centuries, during the early years of these missions' activity, when negotiations about the work of missionary men and women were particularly intense.

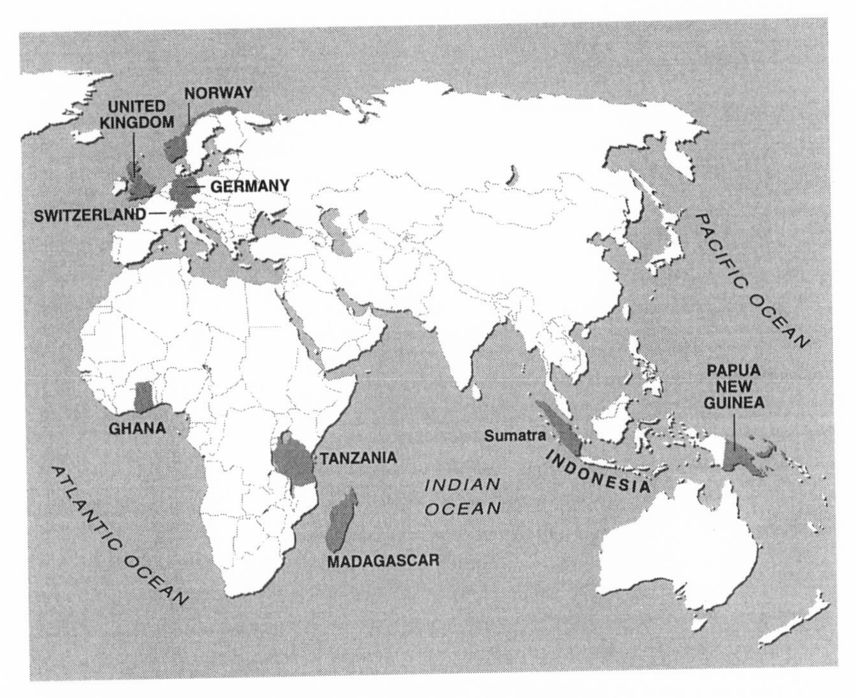

Map showing European countries of origin and overseas locations of missions discussed in *Gendered Missions*. (Map by Carol Cooperrider.)

Our time frame is significant in another way, too. As Ann Stoler and Frederick Cooper have recently shown, over the years colonial Europeans became progressively more concerned with maintaining their identity abroad (Stoler and Cooper 1997; see also Stoler 1995, 95–116). By the late nineteenth century bourgeois practice had become a defining feature of being European for most colonial groups, so that "doing gender right" in the colonies became part and parcel of "doing civilization," of "doing race," and, we would add for missionaries, of "doing Christianity" as well. Gender's importance in missionary life and work, then, was connected with the larger colonial project of which the missionaries were a part. It is beyond the scope of these essays to deal in depth with how mission practice entered into the lives of the indigenous men and women who helped them proselytize or the missionized people themselves. Those of us who venture into later periods of mission history, however, do address these issues, along with the development of official roles for indigenous women and men in the localizing mission/church.

Missionary Studies and Colonial Studies

Every expansionary age in the past has had missionary heroes who captured—even embodied—the imperial imagination and accomplishments of the West. There were St. Augustine of Canterbury and St. Boniface from the early expansion of Christianity into northern Europe; Bartolomé de las Casas and Bernardino de Sahagún in Mexico, Roberto de Nobili in India, and Matteo Ricci in China, from the expansion of Europe in the sixteenth and seventeenth centuries; David Livingstone from Britain's spread into Africa in the mid-nineteenth century; and, from the latter days of twentieth century colonialism, Albert Schweitzer, who gained fame in Europe and America as the very embodiment of Western benevolence. For the postcolonial age one might even cite Mother Teresa, recipient of the Nobel Peace Prize in 1979 for humanitarian work among Calcutta's poorest poor and one of the few women missionaries whose names have become widely known.[3]

There is also a lengthy tradition in Western culture, initiated first in religious magazines, novels, and autobiographical accounts and later through popular film, of the portrayal of missionary men and women. As Susan Thorne reminds us (in this volume), British missionaries who worked in foreign lands and home-based missionary enthusiasts were stock figures in popular nineteenth-century Victorian novels such as Charles Dickens's *Bleak House* (1852) and Charlotte Brontë's *Jane Eyre* (1847). It is also worth noting that the beginning of cinema coincided with the heights of European imperialism and that the most prolific film-producing countries during the early phases of cinema history were also among the leading imperialist countries, in whose interest it was to laud the imperial project (Shohat and Stam 1994).[4] Images of missionaries presented in popular cinema, like those of the novel, have been contradictory. For every mission hero or heroine depicted—such as David Livingstone in *Stanley and Livingstone* (1939) or Gladys Aylward (played by Ingrid Bergman) in *The Inn of the Sixth Happiness* (1958)—there have also been caricatures of overzealous ones, such as the missionaries who appear in movies like *Zulu* (1964) and *Hawaii* (1966). Other classic examples include the various film versions of the sanctimonious Reverend Davidson (an archetypical lustful hypocrite) from Somerset Maugham's popular short story "Rain," such as the 1932 version with Joan Crawford, or Katharine Hepburn's pious missionary brother in *The African Queen* (1951).

More recent films such as *Chariots of Fire* (1981) and *The Missionary* (1986), both British productions, and North American films such as *The Black Robe* (1991), *The Mission* (1986), and *At Play in the Fields of the*

Lord (1992) attempt to present more complex portraits of missionaries. The first two films do so by focusing on individual missionaries and their own conflicting feelings about things spiritual and physical, and about mission projects at home versus abroad, while the latter three films complicate easy judgment by depicting the historical conditions in which missionaries in the New World had to negotiate their mission endeavors. What is clear from all of these filmic portrayals, however, is that missionaries were key players on the imperial scene and that their images, originally created and circulated in writing through the publication of works ranging from Livingstone's *Missionary Travels* (1857) and Stanley's *How I Found Livingstone* (1872) to James Michener's *Hawaii* (1959) and Peter Matthiessen's *At Play in the Fields of the Lord* (1965) have created a rich legacy of missionary figures, both negative and positive, in the Western popular imagination.

Given the political sentiments of much of the postcolonial world, it is questionable whether missionary heroes, male or female, could ever play the cultural role today they once played. It is true that in the United States and Europe there remains a portion of the population that supports Christian mission work in foreign lands.[5] Yet Christianity no longer embodies the West's best self-image vis-à-vis others, and, when it comes to humanitarian causes pursued abroad, missionary circles are generally not from whence today's heroes of human rights, environmentalism, development, or public health emerge.[6] Indeed, Mother Teresa herself has become an ambiguous icon, her Albanian roots and nun's habit evoking an earlier age of Christianity, her goals and methods provoking a widely reviewed critique by Christopher Hitchens (1995) for being out of touch not only with modern Catholicism but also with modern medicine and modern humanitarian concerns.[7]

Criticism of missionaries, present or past, is as pervasive in academic discourse as it is in the wider literary circles addressed by Hitchens's Mother Teresa book. Indeed, any scholar who embarks on missionary studies aiming to contribute to the literature on colonial/postcolonial society (as opposed, say, to missiology or mission history) is likely to encounter dismissive critique and negative stereotypes of missionaries from the start. There is a professional as well as cultural and in some cases personal dimension to the ambivalence with which missionaries are regarded in many fields (Burridge 1991; see also Lutkehaus 1983; Huber 1988, 1996). Anthropology, for example, negotiated its professional identity in part against missionaries, who were considered by many early ethnographers to be biased and amateur observers of native peoples and, sometimes, irresponsible meddlers in native life (Stipe 1980; Stocking

1983, 74).[8] Modern colonial history, too, has established its professionalism in part against what many historians have considered narrow and self-serving accounts by in-house mission historians.[9]

Thus, in recent literature in the burgeoning field of colonial studies, mission studies have played a smaller role than they deserve.[10] In part this reflects a predilection on the part of many scholars to focus on the impact of imperialism on those who were colonized and a related tendency to rely on large generalizations about colonizers without regard to the finer points of geographical, institutional, or historical variation (Stoler 1992a, 319–23). To be sure, there are limits on what a focus on missions, or indeed any particular institution or group, can contribute to our understanding of colonial society and the culture of colonialism. Yet, as scholars of European communities in the colonies have long observed, colonization was never a seamless web, and in any single colony at any particular point in time colonizers of various stripes were pursuing different, even contradictory, interests that played into and upon the interests of various colonized people and groups (Burridge 1960; Huber 1988; Cooper and Stoler 1989; Dirks 1992). "It is becoming increasingly clear," Thomas observes, "that only localized theories and historically specific accounts can provide much insight into the varied articulations of colonizing and counter-colonial representations and practices" (1994, ix).

Even scholars who have engaged with specific colonizer communities, however, seem drawn to projects other than missions. For example, Ann Stoler's pathbreaking work on the intersection of race, class, and gender in colonial Indonesia and Southeast Asia focuses on policies by government and plantation companies (1991, 1992a, 1992b); Jenny Sharpe's exploration of how Western women were used as allegories for empire in British India focuses on secular rather than religious literature (1993); Billie Mehlman's *Women's Orients: English Women and the Middle East, 1718–1918,* though subtitled "Sexuality, Religion, and Work," concerns women travelers—pilgrims and anti-pilgrims but not Christian missionaries in the usual sense of the term. No doubt it is rash to make such a generalization about a literature in which new books are announced daily in university press catalogs. Still, new work does seem less likely to focus on missionaries than on artists and writers (Lewis 1996); travelers (Pratt 1992); anthropologists (Bell, Kaplan, and Karim 1993), and social reformers (Ware 1992; Jayawardena 1995), although Jayawardena does include missionary women among other Western women with reform agendas who worked in South Asia under British rule, as do Ram and Jolly (1998) in their collection of articles concerned with colonial constraints on indigenous forms of maternity.[11]

Nevertheless, enough scholars have persevered to create a growing body of work about missionaries, addressing such important themes in colonial studies as the complexity of colonial societies; the interplay between metropolitan centers and colonial peripheries; the instability of cultural constructions of "self" and "other"; the dynamics of race and gender relations; strategies of inclusion and exclusion; technologies of rule; the production of colonial knowledge; and the limits of reform. To these issues ethnographic and historical studies of missionaries, which of necessity take place on a small scale, offer a more human face—exploring the agency of actors in the colonial drama and the means by which people negotiate the differences, so often highlighted in colonial circumstances, between experience and ideals (Burridge 1978; Beidelman 1982; Clifford 1982; Lutkehaus 1983; Huber 1988, 1994; Kipp 1990; Comaroff and Comaroff 1991; Hall 1992; Miller 1994).

Within this body of mission studies a small but distinguished literature on missionary women, in particular, has now emerged. As a result of the influence of feminist scholarship on disciplines such as history and literature, scholars have paid increased attention to the specific experiences of women missionaries as recorded in their letters, diaries, and other written accounts. Such material allows insight into both the practical and spiritual worlds of these women as well as the gendered dimensions of their lives as missionaries. In addition to biographies of specific missionary women (Lodwick 1995) there has been a growing number of composite portraits of particular groups of women missionaries (Hill 1985; Flemming 1989; Grimshaw 1989; Brouwer 1990; Gagan 1992; Yohn 1995). There has also been increased interest in the communities formed by single women, especially nuns, as exemplars of social forms of sisterhood and alternative lifeways for women outside of marriage and nuclear families (Vicinus 1985; McNamara 1996). Finally, special mention should be made of the landmark collection *Women and Missions: Past and Present,* edited by Fiona Bowie, Deborah Kirkwood, and Shirley Ardener (1993), with thirteen essays covering an encyclopedic set of themes, from the recruitment, position, and achievement of women missionaries to mission impact on indigenous women.

Perhaps the central finding of all this work relates to one of the many ironies of colonialism: the fact that the same enterprises that aimed to dignify and liberate their subjects could also contribute to their denigration and dependence. This is as true of religious missions as of economic, political, and other secular educational and medical missions (Ramusack 1992). Yet the situation is even more complicated when gender is factored in. Religious causes enabled many Western women to go overseas, and women missionaries helped provide many subject women with access to education and opportunities they would not otherwise have enjoyed. Yet neither of these liberating, enlightening moves was without deep shadows, and their intersection, especially, created problems whose implications are just now being explored. For subject women there have been the costs that colonization imposes.[12] For imperial women, including missionaries, there have been the costs imposed by colonizing: as Sharpe has observed, the real question is "not how European women transformed colonialism but how colonialism has left its indelible mark on European women" (1993, 94; see also Ware 1992).

Missionaries, Gender, and Empire

The "Age of Empire," which Eric Hobsbawm dates from 1875 to 1914, witnessed not only a transformation in Europe's relation to Africa, the Pacific, and Southeast Asia but also a reconfiguration of gender in the metropolitan countries and their colonies abroad. As European men were carving up the tropical world, women of the middle classes were beginning to move out from their homes to engage in teaching, nursing, and philanthropy (Davidoff and Hall 1987; Luddy 1995; Thorne 1997). As pressure grew to justify colonial rule, the idea of a "civilizing mission" gained appeal. And, as programs to implement this mission were developed, women found roles in the colonies that helped justify their goals at home. Christian missionaries were specialists in civilizing, as the concept was understood at the time, and many of the women who participated went as wives of missionaries, as professionals employed by the missions, or as missionaries in their own right.[13]

All these developments were facilitated by the fantastic growth of technology in the early and mid-nineteenth century. By the 1870s, Hobsbawm reminds us, the world had become "genuinely global . . . railway and steamship had made intercontinental . . . travel a matter of weeks rather than months" and "the electric telegraph now made the communication of information across the entire globe a matter of hours. In consequence, men and women from the western world . . . travelled and communicated over large distances with unprecedented facility and in unprecedented numbers" (1989, 13–14). With better travel and communications a wider variety of Europeans could take up work in the colonies including, for the first time, a significant number of women accompanying their husbands or volunteering for service in missionary establishments and secular hospitals and schools.

Statistics are not easy to find. Yet a number of scholars have concluded that missionary movements in several nations became increasingly feminized as the nineteenth century wore on. Predelli and Miller (in this volume) note the "feminization of the mission force" during this time in the

United States (Hunter 1984, 14; also Hill 1985, 2); Canada (Brouwer 1990, 5); United Kingdom (Thorne, this volume); and Norway (Tjelle 1990, 105–8). Indeed, in some British and American missionary societies the number of women grew from virtually nil to over 50 percent in the short space from mid- to late century (Williams 1993, 66). Even in the most remote mission fields the proportion of women was high. Of the 327 missionaries who worked in Papua between 1874 to 1914, more than one-third (115 in all) were women, and an additional 46 women (not included in the total) were missionary wives (Langmore 1989, 163). Of course, the numbers vary depending on the mission group, but even in those organizations that allowed them only the most subordinate status women still came.

Behind the choices that led women to the Christian missions in the Pacific, Africa, and Asia were larger demographic, social, and cultural forces. The industrial revolution had already moved production out of homes and left women with domestic roles that were dignified by an ideology that attributed to women a special moral worth (see Beidelman, in this volume). But the mid- to late nineteenth century was a time when young women were thought to have outnumbered young men in the craftsman and middle classes from which most missionaries came (Deacon and Hill 1972).[14] And it was also a time when economic change was making it harder for many middle-class families to afford to keep grown but unmarried daughters at home (Davidoff and Hall 1987). Even married women who did not have to work were looking for ways to participate in public life in meaningful ways (Hobsbawm 1989, 202).

The movement of missionary and other professional women into the colonies cannot be separated from the entry of middle-class women into philanthropy and the professions that took place at the same time (Davidoff and Hall 1987; Luddy 1995). Women needed the colonies, which provided opportunities for professional service rarely available at home, and the colonies needed professional women to make good the humanitarian commitments by which imperial expansion in the late nineteenth century was increasingly justified (Thorne, in this volume; Robinson and Gallagher 1961). By attributing to women virtues crucial to social improvement, Victorian ideology enabled them to be cast in a special role as civilizers. In turn, women's movements for access to education and the professions at home were increasingly justified in imperial terms (Burton 1992; 1994).

Women's heightened role in the colonies was due not only to Victorian views of women but also to a change in the general sense of what "civilizing" was all about. As Sahlins reminds us, the term *civilization* itself was "coined in France in the 1750s and quickly adopted in England, becoming very popular in both countries in explication of their superior accomplishments and justification of their imperialist exploits" (1995, 10). Staying close to Enlightenment roots, emphasis in the early nineteenth century was first placed on political and social reformation as a moral responsibility of imperial rule (Stokes 1959; Hutchins 1967). By the late nineteenth century, however, in what Stoler and Cooper call the "embourgoisement of imperialism," focus had shifted to the moral improvement of colonized individuals. In the name of progress colonists were looking ever more intently into ever more intimate areas of colonial subjects' lives (Stoler and Cooper 1997, 31; Comaroff and Comaroff 1991).

In all of this, of course, Christian missions played a special and often controversial role. As Beidelman observes, "imperialistic colonialism involves a sense of mission, of spreading a nation's vision of society and culture to an alien, subjected people" (1982, 4). And, while many colonial agencies contributed something to that goal, Christian missions were the ones most wholly dedicated to the task. "Missionaries," Beidelman argues, "invariably aimed at overall changes in the beliefs and actions of native peoples, at colonization of heart and mind as well as body" (6). The care and discipline of the soul may have been missionaries' principal concern. But this involved not only conversion but also Christianization—"the reformulation of social relations, cultural meanings, and personal experience in terms of putatively Christian ideals" (Hefner 1993, 3). Missionaries' Christian ideals included not only the formal social teachings of their particular church, but inevitably encoded a whole range of cultural experience that has varied with their nationality and social class as well as over time (Beidelman 1982).[15]

This is not to deny that Christian missionaries from earlier eras of European expansion also inserted themselves into the social arrangements and inner lives of their subjects. Sixteenth-century Spanish missionaries in the Philippines, for example, encoded their own notions of authority and exchange into the catechisms and confession manuals they prepared in Tagalog vernacular (Rafael 1988); Spanish concerns about gender were reflected in the inquisitorial practices of seventeenth- and eighteenth-century Mexico (Behar 1987). The point is that missionaries in the nineteenth (and twentieth) centuries shared much the same cultural heritage as other colonizers and participated in a "civilizing mission" more widely conceived than before. As John and Jean Comaroff have argued, missionaries were vehicles of the West's "post-enlightenment imagination," with its "universalizing ethos" and "hegemonic worldview" (Comaroff and Comaroff 1991, 310).

To observe that missionaries in the late nineteenth century had more far-reaching goals than other colonizing agents, however, is to suggest that there were many areas of mission practice that could subvert as well as support the projects of other colonizing agents. Consider the Catholic mission on the north coast of Papua New Guinea, discussed by two essays in this volume. This mission became one of the most active economic agents in its region during the years between 1900 and World War II, "providing not only sermons and schools for the natives, but sawn timber for government stations and private establishments, transportation services on its steamer, agricultural experimentation, and . . . coconut plantations for its own financial support" (Huber 1988, 48). It claimed partial credit for the pacification of the native villagers, one of the colonial government's early goals; its policies on clothing helped build the market for traders selling women's dresses and blouses and cloth for the sarongs approved for men (Höltker 1946); its schools, plantations, and other industries helped to provide a trained and disciplined work force for New Guinea's struggling business community (Lutkehaus 1983).

Yet, even when colonial agencies like the missions, the government, and business have appeared to work in harmony, one cannot conclude that their interests always converged or that their various civilizing projects—to make Christians, to make taxpayers and loyal subjects, to make money—directly complemented one another.[16] In the case of northern New Guinea the Australian government that succeeded the German administration after World War I was suspicious of the predominantly German Catholic missionaries and jealous of their influence; the business community resented competition from the mission's own plantations, stores, and other business interests; many complained that mission-educated laborers were insufficiently submissive and compliant (Huber 1988; Lutkehaus 1995, 68–72). Indeed, as a later ethnography observes of one strongly Catholic village in the region, "the place of Catholicism in Kragur identity has no simple, predictable relationship to that identity's compatibility with capitalist forms of production and distribution" (Smith 1994, 232).

Along with other colonial agents, and indeed along with many colonized populations, missionaries in colonial situations shared an "interest in creating something new" (Thomas 1994, 106–7; see also Burridge 1960). The missionary projects of conversion and Christianization, however, tended to involve missionaries more intimately with those being colonized than, say, government or business personnel. Missionaries often arrived earlier than other colonizers, typically stayed longer in one region, were more likely to learn local languages, and were—especially—more involved in the critique and reformation of local ways of life. Because the missionary project tended to ally missionaries more closely with local people, missionaries were often looked on with some suspicion by their fellow colonizers; because the missionaries were nonetheless colonizers, they were not always regarded as trustworthy by the people they were attempting to serve (Burridge 1960). To most parties on the colonial scene, in fact, missionaries were quite often—as Burridge so tersely puts it—"in the way" (1991).

Sex and gender, not surprisingly, were persistent points of tension among missionaries, local people, and other colonizing groups. The spread of bourgeois values into imperial ideology during the nineteenth century may indeed have enhanced the interest of colonial authorities in regulating such matters as "[white] male sexual license in the colonies" (Stoler and Cooper 1997, 23). But a far wider range of issues typically was involved in missionary projects. As Jolly and Macintyre (1989) observe, these issues included "sexual relations between indigenous women and foreign men" (which missionaries generally regarded as "immoral or exploitative"); but also "ideals of domesticity" (which missionaries often attempted to impose on local Christians); local marriage practices (e.g., Marquesan polyandry, which offended missionaries there "both because it suggested female power and female appetite"); open expressions of sexuality (which some missionaries attempted to replace with "Christian restraint and repression"); and more, including child-rearing practices, living arrangements, dress, and the like.

It was, in fact, through such concerns that missionaries came to represent both the best and the worst of the civilizing mission itself. From the perspective of other colonizers, who tended to cast imperialism as a manly act, the missionary enterprise was gendered as "feminine" (see essays by Huber, Kipp, and Lutkehaus in this volume). No matter how "muscular" missionaries attempted to be, they were feminized by their ambiguous local alliances and domestic ideals. In its positive valence missionaries embodied the conscience of colonialism, just as women, regarded as the weaker sex, were endowed "at the same time with unquestionable moral superiority, rooted in the ostensibly feminine virtues of nurturing, child-care, and purity" (Burton 1992, 138). In its negative valence, however, missionaries' concern with religion was viewed as soft, in relation to the "hard" economic and political interests of other agents of empire; their emphasis on morality was considered "weak" in comparison with those "strong" enough to prosper without constraint on a freewheeling frontier. Finally, of course, missionaries' typical involvement with women and children and with local domestic life contrasted with the official focus on men and the public sphere that characterized the business community and the colonial state.[17]

Gendered Missions

Within missionary groups ideas about gender played a critical role in organizing work, in giving meaning to missionary projects, and in the messages—often mixed—that missionaries communicated to those they came to save and serve. As a result, women's experience in and with the missions has been in many respects different from men's—not least because it was so often officially unrecognized and unrecorded. Recapturing the contours of women's experience has been a goal of many recent missionary studies, as it has been in the humanities and social sciences more generally.[18] As Bowie notes in her introduction to *Women and Missions: Past and Present,* "In being seen as adjuncts to men, rather than as historical protagonists in their own right, women have been systematically written out of the historical and anthropological records" (1993, 1).[19]

Scholars aiming, with Bowie, to "reclaim women's presence" have shown that in virtually all mission organizations the status and roles of women and men in the mission field differed, as did the special contributions they made through their work and the effects missionary service had on them. Historically, missionary work had been regarded as a clerical, and therefore male, occupation. In most of the mainstream Protestant missionary organizations in the early nineteenth century, women supported the missions as auxiliaries at home collecting funds or in the field as missionaries' wives (Hill 1985; Thorne, in this volume). The domestic and childcare responsibilities of wives, however, often limited their availability for missionary work proper, and in some fields there was such appalling loss of health and life among missionary families that some mission societies stopped sending them abroad. By the last quarter of the nineteenth century even the more conservative missionary societies realized that wives would have to be supplemented by single women for work in mission schools and hospitals as well as for evangelism among local women. This was a decision that caused tremendous argument and hand wringing among mission authorities, but by the late nineteenth century most of the major missionary societies began accepting single women recruits.[20]

At any one time women in the missions served in a variety of capacities. As Diane Langmore has shown for Papua from 1874 to 1914, the London Missionary Society allowed women to come to Papua only as wives, not missionaries, while the Roman Catholic Sacred Heart Missionaries—consisting of celibate orders—allowed women only as missionaries, not wives. At the same time, the Methodists allowed women to come to Papua either as wives or as missionaries, while the Anglicans counted as missionaries all women who joined them, whether as wives or single women on their own (Langmore 1989). In other fields there were women who were neither missionaries nor wives (or daughters and nieces) but, rather, "lay missionaries"—professionals (teachers, nurses, or doctors) or generalists willing to perform whatever tasks needed to be done (see essays by Huber, Kipp, and Lutkehaus, in this volume; see also Ramusack 1992; Swaisland 1993a–b).

This does not count, of course, the even larger number of women engaged in supporting the missions at home (Predelli and Miller; Thorne, both in this volume).

The formal status permitted women in the missions tells only part of the story, of course. Indeed, the extent of ambiguity about women's roles provides another important point of comparison between mission groups. As Langmore (1989) notes, Roman Catholic missionary sisters in Papua had the least ambiguous status, thanks largely to the long history of women's religious orders in the Catholic Church. Women who went to the field as wives seem to have had the most difficult time—especially among groups who expected wives to aid the evangelical effort by actively ministering to women as well as modeling Christian family life (Beidelman, in this volume; Grimshaw 1985, 1989). Even when women were actually designated as missionaries, they were often given subordinate status without the rights held by men (Huber, Kipp, and Lutkehaus, all in this volume; Lodwick 1995). Such was women's lot in mission organizations at home, too, although in some cases women's capacity to raise money for the missions gave them enough power to win the right to formal participation in the councils and congresses in which mission policy was formed (Hill 1985; Predelli and Miller, in this volume).

Many of the essays in this collection explore uncertainties about gender roles in missionary organizations as well as contradictions that arose between expectations about gendered work and the realities of life in the field. Thorne points out that paid employment of women to promote evangelical domestic ideals abroad implicitly violated and thus critiqued those very ideals, although formally the ends were used to justify the means. Beidelman notes that missionary wives, too, were placed in contradictory situations. In the Church Missionary Society (CMS) field of Ukaguru in colonial Tanganyika, he writes, "women were sent out to be stereotyped feminine persons whom they were then thwarted from being." The exigencies of station life, while necessitating their services as accountants, teachers, nurses, and supervisors of staff, took away some of their homemaking roles, and the practice of sending young children home for rearing and education deprived missionary wives of many of the roles of motherhood. A similar contradiction arose, although expressed in different terms, among the Catholic Sister Servants of the Holy Spirit in northern New Guinea. In order to achieve their religious and moral goals the missionary nuns sometimes found it necessary to set aside the feminine qualities expected of them and to assume more masculine behavior (Lutkehaus, in this volume).

A related theme concerns negotiations between men and women missionaries over the roles women might play and the recognition that women might achieve. How this was done, over what issues, when, and with what consequences clearly varied from group to group. Huber examines the efforts of Catholic missionaries in Papua New Guinea to maintain the appearance of separate spheres of work for priests, brothers, and sisters over a period of some eighty years. This task, she concludes, proved especially difficult in the pioneer period, when there was too much work for the missionaries to do, and in the period surrounding national independence, when suddenly there was too little—at least for the European sisters who were displaced from their traditional roles in elementary school teaching and nursing by government efforts to localize personnel.

Patriarchy has had its ways of persisting in missionary organizations, despite challenges from the field.[21] Predelli and Miller note how Basel mission authorities bowed to the formidable missionary skills of an African-Cuban woman who had once been married to an African mission teacher by allowing her to remain with the mission after her unauthorized second marriage to a white missionary. In this case, however, the decision did not lead to systematic change but was, instead, a one-time "capitulation to personal initiative and personal choice." Similarly, Kipp describes the growing bureaucracy of the Dutch Reformed mission as increasingly resistant to influence from the eight professional women it sent to its Sumatran field between 1914 and 1942. Negotiating the bureaucracy required skills and a style that few of these women possessed and made it difficult for them to convince the men of their competence as teachers and nurses and secure the autonomy they needed to fully develop their ministries.

The subordination that mission men tended to expect and demand of mission women was often a cause of consternation and stress and contributed, no doubt, to some of the health problems women suffered and to some of their premature departures from the mission field. Yet negotiations were not always futile, and competent women were not always without sympathizers. Beidelman notes that the Church Missionary Society's central committee was concerned that its women in East Africa not be exploited or their talents improperly used. Indeed, he claims, these women often had support from the center and the problems of authority they encountered were more from the attitudes of individual men than from mission policy per se. Even Kipp's Dutch Reformed missionaries occasionally supported a woman's right to autonomy. She provides two case studies in which a nurse and an administrator "were supported by the board against critiques by their male colleagues," although "the board protected above all the bureaucratic structure it managed," working ultimately to the disadvantage of mission women.

Beyond formal status, the division of labor, and the conduct of work, concepts of gender have helped structure many aspects of missionaries' social and cultural life that we can only mention here. These have included such diverse areas as the organization of mission space, the representation of mission time, the perception and control of danger, access to spiritual and material resources, recreation, dress, music, architecture, and the like (Beidelman 1982).[22] Several authors in this collection explore gendered meanings in mission life by examining the ways in which gender has served to organize reality among missionaries, and between them and the people with whom they worked. They ask: what discourses gave mission practices meaning, how were they gendered, and were there contending systems of meaning that could be used to negotiate alternative readings, conduct, and events?

Although various missions, like the denominations they served, read the great Christian narrative with different emphases and styles, the Christian story, however interpreted, both charted and gave meaning to much missionary practice. Beidelman suggests that the Church Missionary Society's stance in favor of personal fervor and calling over clerical authority and theological training provided a spiritual justification for missionizing that transcended gender. Likewise, its embrace of nonritual evangelical work, such as preaching, prayer, and revival, gave room for those who were nonordained—women and men—to do valued work. Other elements of the "evangelical spirit" inflected the experience of CMS missionaries, too. Beidelman suggests that these missionaries' earnestness about work and rejection of leisure magnified their sense of missionary life as an adventurous sacrificial act and allowed women to take freedoms otherwise suspect or not respectable. A high valorization of suffering and martyrdom strengthened the resolve of women who lost children and justified work that required women to forgo many aspects of domesticity and child rearing. A belief in divine protection inspired women's feelings of safety in dangerous situations and also made mission work into a test of faith.

The intersection of religious ideals and gender ideology has not always worked in women's favor. Consider the Basel Mission Society. As Predelli and Miller observe, the mission was identified with Württemberg Pietism in the nineteenth century, embracing as a social model the traditional agrarian village that Martin Luther had extolled as the Christian ideal. Reflecting these commitments, leadership and the division of tasks inside the mission can best be described as "divinely inspired patriarchy"—a collection of gendered definitions that was used as a template for the Christian communities established in the field. The Society of the Divine Word (Societatis Verbi Divini, or SVD), the Roman Catholic missionary organization described here by Huber and by Lutkehaus, was likewise patriarchally inspired. Although separated in matters of spirit and organization from the larger ecclesiastical and secular societies of which it formed a separate part, its conception of an orderly life as a religious community drew on the social and cultural resources of these larger communities, especially those related to the division of labor by gender and class. These resources gave priests a valorized role in the SVD, while brothers were servants who were to provide material labor to enhance the spiritual services such as preaching and administration provided by the priests (Huber, in this volume; see also Huber 1988, 59–60).

If patriarchy was predominant in the structure of SVD communities both at home and in the field, "maternalism" was prevalent in the associated organization founded for missionary women, the Sister Servants of the Holy Spirit (SSpS).[23] Lutkehaus observes that as their name implies, the dominant image these nuns hold of themselves is one of altruistic service, even servitude. Based on Western and papal notions of patriarchy, "maternal nurturance" and "domesticity" are the gendered forms this service was supposed to take toward priests and native people alike. Despite their best intentions, however, the nuns have not always easily accepted the constraints an imposed maternalism places upon them. Looking more closely at a small community of sisters stationed since 1925 on Manam Island in northern New Guinea, Lutkehaus notes the development over time of a more autonomous and aggressive, or "masculine," style of behavior, manifested in conflicts both with islanders and tensions with male authority, both within the mission hierarchy and the colonial administration. Although their gender curtailed their activities and effectiveness vis-à-vis masculine authority, nonetheless the nuns succeeded in opening new spaces—both literal and imaginative—for Manam women by creating the mission convent as a temporary "all-women's haven" to which they could retreat and, paradoxically, by demonstrating through their own lives alternative visions for women other than marriage and maternalism.

Not all mission organizations allowed women such space for experimentation in alternative modes of living. In the Dutch Reformed mission (Nederlands Zendelinggenootschap, NZG) studied by Kipp, for example, the face-to-face relations of the pioneer period were eroded by increasing bureaucratization and a growing emphasis on technical competence and efficiency rather than traditional religious roles and goals (in this volume; see also Kipp 1990, 1995). The very virtues that women found appealing about mission work—Christian service based on sacrificial love—served them poorly in negotiating a mission bureaucracy that embodied and magnified a "formal rationality" more often associated with men. Kipp argues that women entered the NZG disadvantaged not only by their structural positions in the organization but also by their previous socialization and professional experience. Their "feminine attributes" shrouded their competence and led their work to be underestimated and undervalued. Women were thus prevented from exerting much influence on the mission's operation and style, to the detriment—Kipp argues—of the mission's substantive goals. "That this small bureaucracy proved itself the enemy of feminine virtues is especially ironic," Kipp concludes, "since these virtues are also synonymous with deeply held Christian ideals, namely humility and love."

Humility was not the defining virtue of imperial projects—missionary or otherwise—including what Thorne calls "missionary imperial feminism" at home. The figure of woman degraded by paganism long dominated missionary propaganda, and, as Thorne points out, her "liberation from heathen patriarchy" was depicted as one of the "principal social advantages" that conversion to Christianity would bring about. This mission cause mobilized the largest mass movement of women in Britain in the nineteenth century. But the leaders' goal of creating a "genuinely sisterly sympathy" among women of different classes and races was undermined by relations of domination and subordination that middle-class women brought both to their efforts to mobilize working-class women at home and their work with colonized women abroad (see also Ware 1992). "The missionary language of sisterhood was always already compromised," Thorne observes, "by the unequal social power implicit in the missionary exchange."

Gender Ambiguities and Contradictions

Missionary women were inevitably entwined in the contradictions and ambiguities that their dual position entailed. As Margaret Strobel has argued, European women in colonies around the world "played ambiguous roles as members of a sex considered to be inferior within a race that considered itself superior" (1987, 375). Around this fundamental ambiguity flowed many of the contradictions that contributors to this volume explore: a language of universal sisterhood undermined by unequal social power between women of different classes and races (Thorne); an ideology of church patriarchy compromised by men's recognition of women's usefulness in their causes (Predelli and Miller); ideals of female domesticity contradicted by the exigencies of missionary work (Beidelman); commitment to a gendered division of missionary labor jeopardized by circumstances in the mission field (Huber); a missionary maternalism that provided local women an alternative vision for life than marriage and motherhood (Lutkehaus); "feminine" ideals of Christian love and humility hardened by a bureaucracy that embodied "masculine" rationality (Kipp).

Colonial life during the high tide of empire was particularly productive of contradictions like these. The ideals of civilizing projects were cast so high, the circumstances so uncongenial to "normal" procedure, and the terms of engagement among parties so unequal that means were inevitably at odds with ends. This is not to say that ideals and realities were so well aligned at home but that in the colonies gaps were often more visible and less easily masked.[24] To be sure, many colonials remained blind to the fundamental contradiction of colonialism—what Fernandez succinctly terms "the sacrifice of the natives for the greater good" (1964, 556). But rare was the European who did not realize that colonial circumstances did not place in question conventions that before had been simply assumed. Historian Donald Denoon has argued, for example, "the essence and implications of many Australian ideas became manifest only in those extreme situations which Australians encountered abroad" (1986, 258).

As T. O. Beidelman argued years ago in a pathbreaking essay on the theoretical implications of missionary studies, the extremes of the colonial situation can also highlight broader sociological and historical concerns (1974). Beidelman was particularly interested in what mission studies could contribute to the study of bureaucracy in modern life, but, following his lead, one can also point to other promising Weberian themes. For example, some readings of Weber emphasize how ideals are always placed at risk when a "group decides that something is worth accomplishing" and a "project is put into play (Falding 1968, 26). But no less important is the related Weberian theme—developed in *The Protestant Ethic and the Spirit of Capitalism*—of how cultural contradiction can be a source of social change (Huber 1994).

As the essays in this collection suggest, there have been no easy resolutions to many of the cultural tensions that empire exposed. Not surprisingly, the authors come to somewhat different conclusions on key issues. Were women a humanizing force in the colonies? Both Lutkehaus and Kipp focus on the difficulties women faced in expressing their feminine identity in the mission field. Kipp asks us to imagine what might have happened if the Dutch Reformed mission to the Karo had been an all-female organization and implies that it might have had a very different history if run by "persons socialized to expect self-sacrifice and valorize love." Lutkehaus's study of an all-female organization suggests to her, however, that to have an impact at all the Sister Servants of the Holy Spirit had to adopt a more masculine style than their maternal ideal initially involved.

What were the consequences of ambiguities and contradictions in gender roles in the field? Beidelman concludes that evangelical missions, while highly conservative in their views about gender roles, also embraced a view of "evangelism inspired by the Holy Spirit rather than by theological training," which was friendly to female professionalism in mission work. While Beidelman depicts a case in which the expected hierarchy between male and female missionaries could be modified, Huber presents a situation in which boundaries between male and female missionary work could be easily blurred but not so easily crossed. Though heir to a long tradition of female professionalism, this Roman Catholic mission was also heir to a long tradition of clerical domination. She concludes that, while colonial circumstances could make women's roles negotiable, "hierarchies that colonizers could not express in conventional ways were often re-expressed through other means."

Was there a link between women's involvement in missionary efforts and feminist movements in Europe? The essays by Thorne and by Predelli and Miller address this issue most directly. Both emphasize the professional opportunities missionary work provided for middle-class women in England and in Norway, while both also see limits to the emancipatory value of such "extensions of domesticity" (Predelli and Miller, in this volume). Predelli and Miller suggest that this may explain "the mixed success of NMS women in forming an alliance with other organized Norwegian women, some of whom were clearly feminist in their philosophies." Thorne's conclusion is darker, focusing less on connections between groups of British women than on connections between women of different classes and race. To her the "terms on which missionary-imperial feminism chose to challenge the subordination of middle-class women who promoted it did not, in short, require trans-class any more than it did trans-race sisterhood." It is but a small step, in our reading of Thorne's essay, to see that the limits on missionary feminism were also limits for other styles of Western feminism in the late nineteenth and early twentieth centuries.

Certainly, in regard to gender the contradictions entailed in missionary experience opened up space for social change in the metropolitan social world. The religious cause of Christian missions provided a culturally acceptable forum for middle-class women in Europe and the Americas to gain organizational, fund-raising, and speaking experience in the public sphere. In the cause of furthering Christianity and civilization, the domestic ideal was stretched beyond recognizable limits to provide novel opportunities for missionary women. And, in providing a forum for women to show their importance to the cause they shared with missionary men, missionary projects gave women a claim in their negotiations for political participation, social honor, and even monetary rewards.

As the essays in this collection suggest, however, these gains were not without cost to women themselves nor, because of their imperial setting, to the future of either feminism or of Christianity at home and abroad. Late-twentieth-century feminism is still struggling with issues concerning class, race, and culture in leadership, participation, methods, and goals. Christianity, too, has experienced a loss of evangelical confidence in the wake of decolonization—at least, this was true for the "mainstream" denominations that led the missionary movement during the height of the colonial era. Questions of cultural imperialism persist in Christian forums for discussion and debate, colored indelibly it seems by the colonial context in which Christianity became a world religion.

Missionary Studies and the Postcolonial World

Christian churches have always been transnational institutions, the earthly embodiment of a message believed to have universal relevance. Even those churches most committed to localism in their organization have ways of cooperating with similarly organized groups to join in common—often missionary—causes. Similarly, in the countries where missionaries work, local converts become part of larger church polities. As Christians, they participate in what Benedict Anderson (1983) calls an "imagined community," in this case, a community of other Christians within their region, within their country, and around the world. These imagined communities are grounded not only in belief but also—as Anderson noted for national communities—in a common literature, a common geography, a common time.[25] There are the Bible; a network of local, national, and international centers; a sacred calendar; and there are the travelers—especially the long-distance ones, like missionaries—whose peregrinations tie together the whole thing. Indeed, for most Christian groups the real sign of a mission's maturity is not when the local church it founds becomes independent financially or in regard to church personnel but when it is able to send its own missionaries abroad (Huber 1996; Lutkehaus, in this volume).

Although mission evangelism and the development of local Christianity is beyond the scope of this collection, it is important to emphasize that both Christianity and Christian missionaries have continued to thrive in formerly colonized countries after their attainment of formal political independence. Indeed, in many of the areas covered by these essays Christianity is very much a part of postcoloniality.[26] Statistics on world Christianity are naturally imprecise and subject to multiple interpretation but give some indication of Christian churches' global reach. The International Bulletin of Missionary Research's "Annual Statistical Table on Global Mission" reports that in 1996 Christianity was counted as the religion of just over one-third of the world's population, with Africa, Asia, and Oceania accounting for just under one-third of the membership of all Christian churches (Barrett 1996, 25). Counting missionaries is even more complex than counting Christians. The "Annual Statistical Table on Global Mission" also reported, however, that in 1995 there were 8,100 "pioneer missionaries" working in "frontier missions" in "the unevangelized world," 51,800 missionaries working in "the evangelized non-Christian world," and 332,600 missionaries in foreign countries in "the Christian world." Adding these figures together, we find that there were 392,500 missionaries working across national boundaries in 1995.[27]

Christian mission has thus retained its appeal well past the colonial era, although, instead of traveling the world in the company of businessmen, government agents, and others between metropole and colonies, missionaries now travel in the company of a host of new international workers along more varied routes. In keeping with postcolonial trends in other "industries," missionaries are no longer from metropolitan countries alone. Many mission-sending societies that once recruited in only one or a restricted set of metropolitan countries now recruit internationally, and some, indeed, have had good success in formerly missionized lands. For example, the Roman Catholic Society of the Divine Word, discussed by Huber in this volume, now has 5,729 member priests and brothers, over one-third of whom are from Indonesia, India, and the Philippines, and gets most of its new seminarians (64 percent) from Asia.[28]

Within the SVD's sister organization, the Sister Servants of the Holy Spirit, missionary nuns, too, are being recruited increasingly from places far afield. In 1993 "Indonesian Sisters (SSpS) constitute[d] the second largest national group in the Congregation, taking second place only to Germany." Many of these Indonesian sisters were working in Indonesia itself, but some were going overseas. Since 1987, for example, sisters from Flores have worked in Brazil, Botswana, Ghana, and Europe (Holy Spirit Sisters 1993, 71). Today, there are sisters from Flores at Goroka, Papua New Guinea, as well. Other SSpS mission fields are "behind" Indonesia but moving in the same direction: the first Papua New Guinean sister of the SSpS to be sent overseas departed in 1994 (Lutkehaus, in this volume).

Although the missionary effort is being carried on in a new, postcolonial context, the significance of these developments, especially in regard to gender issues, has yet to be assessed. It is well-known that the formal dissolution of the old colonial empires did not end the domination of former colonies by the West and that there are profound continuities between the colonial and the postcolonial worlds (Thomas 1994; Williams and Chrisman 1994). Certainly, some of the same gender issues that were played out in colonial institutions remain relevant today. If Christian missions in particular continue to offer novel opportunities to women for meaningful work overseas, surely they also continue to challenge conventional definitions of gendered work even while attempting to hold up those conventions as appropriate models for local Christian men and women. Mission churches may now be localized (or at least localizing), in regard to personnel and "culture" (design, costume, music, dance, ritual symbols, oratorical styles, and the like), but transnational workers—regardless of their home port—still bring with them foreign ideas in regard to the gendered work, meanings, and messages that they believe should inform local Christian life.

Still, it is important to be mindful of discontinuities between colonial and postcolonial societies and the context that postcoloniality provides for Christian missions. Indeed, some scholars now see the very distinction between "foreign" and "local" as one that had to be carefully cultivated during the colonial era in order to serve the purposes of colonial control (Said 1978, 1993; Stoler 1992b; Prakash 1995). From the perspective of the present, missionaries from far away may better be seen as part of the translocal stream of persons and money that contribute to what Appadurai calls "deterritorialization" and the creation of "transnational cultures," or "emergent cosmopolitanisms" (1991, 1996). Missionaries' messages about gender, however mixed, may be more or less authoritative or powerful, depending on local circumstances. But for many missionaries—especially the more conservative fundamentalists, who dominate world mission today—the most serious opposition to Christian gender ideals has shifted from indigenous gender practices to images and information from the global media about how to live, work, consume, and play.

Conclusion

"Culture," Nicholas Dirks has argued, was, "in certain important ways . . . what colonialism was all about" (1992, 3). Throughout the age of Western colonial expansion Christian missionaries were important parties in the encounter between the West and people throughout the rest of the world. Through missionary efforts Christianity became a global religion and mission schools, health services, and other cultural technologies helped secure Western colonialism and in some cases transformed or even undermined colonialism's effect. Missionaries not only attempted to play an important role in the cultural prescriptions by which European men and women lived in the colonies, but, as has often been noted, missionaries typically insisted upon a moral critique of local culture and society, encouraging far-reaching change in belief and practice through their insistence that Christianity demands attention to the body as well as the soul (see Huber 1996). We have also suggested that this very breadth of focus brought missionary work beyond the cultural competence of male clerics, making both possible and necessary the increasing involvement of women in missionary work.

As anthropologists, historians, and sociologists have begun to focus more attention on colonialism as a cultural project, the gendered dimensions of colonial discourse and practice have received increasing critical attention as well. As a result, missionaries' effects on the lives and societies of the people they came to convert have come under new scrutiny, and it has been in their role as reformers of "Others," of course, that missionaries' significance in the colonial world has most often been assessed and understood. From this perspective missionary women were no different from missionary men, although the assessment of their achievements has been perhaps more complex.[29] Recent theoretical and empirical work in colonial studies suggests, however, that examination of the effects of colonial experience upon missionaries themselves may be another important area for exploring the complex interconnections between metropole and colony, in particular in regard to the making and remaking of gender (Cooper and Stoler 1989; Stoler and Cooper 1997, 1).

Western women have played important roles in social reform movements both religious and secular throughout the late nineteenth and twentieth centuries—perhaps because predominant gender ideologies attribute to women a "caring" nature but certainly also because women have not enjoyed ready access to political and economic spheres. Yet even in religious organizations, in which women were first able to find public roles, gender hierarchies have continued to operate.[30] As this interdisciplinary collection of essays shows, colonial evangelism brought to the surface ambiguities in missionaries' ideas about gender, and missionaries had to face a range of contradictions between their expectations about gendered work and the realities of life in the field. But the same uncertainties, ambiguities, or points of tension that were so disruptive also offered opportunities for action and opened new vistas for reform. Thus, many of the essays in this volume examine how missionary experience contributed to change among missionary men and women themselves. Colonial experience, it appears, not only made gender negotiable in many missionary organizations but, through them, contributed to the negotiation of gender in other institutions "abroad" and "at home." Exploring the dynamics of these negotiations is one of this volume's contributions to the theoretical and empirical work in colonial studies that emphasizes the interconnections between colony and metropole.

Finally, the contemporary presence of Christian missionaries throughout the world, as well as the changing nationalities of missionaries themselves, attests to the continuing relevance of missionary studies. While the relationship of Christian missions to the proliferation of various fundamentalisms flourishing in the world today has yet to be fully explored, there is no doubt that religious (as well as nationalist) movements are a significant aspect of postmodernity. The essays in this volume suggest the relevance of looking at past histories of colonial missions as a means toward understanding their legacy and role in the dynamics of gender and religion in our increasingly postcolonial world.

NOTES

1. We follow here Joan Wallach Scott's useful distinction between two dimensions of the meaning of *gender:* "Gender is a constitutive element of social relationships based on perceived differences between the sexes, and gender is a primary way of signifying relationships of power" (1988, 42). In *Orientalism* Edward Said argued that gender was used by Westerners to signify relationships of power between themselves and their colonial subjects (1978). As many critics have pointed out, however, Orientalism was not a monolithic or unitary discourse: Western representations of colonial subjects have varied geographically and historically and have been complicated by the fact that representers and represented included women as well as men. Reina Lewis notes, for example, that "debates about the specificity of the female gaze [are] part of a critical movement that has undercut the potentially unified, and paradigmatically male, colonial subject outlined in Said's *Orientalism* in 1978" (1996, 3). Other critics take issue with Said's restriction of gender to metaphor. Anne McClintock agrees with Said that "sexuality as a trope for other power relations was certainly an abiding aspect of imperial power . . . But seeing sexuality only as a metaphor runs the risk of eliding gender as a constitutive dynamic of imperial and anti-imperial power" (1996, 14; see also Stoler 1991).

2. Predelli and Miller (in this volume) borrow the concept of a "gender regime" from Connell (1987). As they say: "Connell (1987, 98–99) employs this term to delineate 'a structural inventory of a particular institution.' It is a concept that recognizes variations according to the specific institutional context, and it does not carry the weight of the more deterministic concept of 'patriarchy.'"

3. Most of these famous missionaries are subjects of a vast literature, and some have received special attention from scholars interested in cross-cultural communication and colonialism. See, for example, Klor de Alva, Nicholson, and Keber (1988) and Todorov (1992) on Bernardino de Sahagún; Spence (1984) on Matteo Ricci; and Fernandez (1964) on Albert Schweitzer. Burridge (1991) provides an appendix of brief but helpful biographies of fifty missionaries, including many of the most well-known.

4. See also Richards 1986, for a discussion of the popularity of adventure films that promoted the virtues of imperialism. Films such as *Stanley and Livingstone* (1939), although an American film, glorified colonialism and the role of missionaries in Africa.

5. See Swanson 1995, for an interesting sociological analysis of the lives of contemporary American evangelical missionaries and the meaning and significance of "the call" in their decisions to become missionaries.

6. It is interesting to note the possible reemergence of missionaries as heroes

or at least honored warriors in the human rights field, especially in Latin America. Liberation theology, though now fallen on hard times, captured attention in the mainstream North American press, and one can also note press coverage of missionaries as victims of right-wing armies and militia (Brett and Brett 1988). In academic circles a debate about missionaries' roles in helping to defend the rights of indigenous peoples in the Amazon was conducted in the pages of the *Anthropology Newsletter* and was followed by a Presidential Session on "Missionaries and Human Rights" at the ninety-third Annual Meeting of the American Anthropological Association in Atlanta in 1995. (See the following exchange in *Anthropology Newsletter:* Cappelletti, May 1994, 2; Turner, May 1994, 48, 46, and Chagnon and Brewer-Carfas, September 1994, 2, on Amazonia; and see the general report in the January 1995 *Anthropology Newsletter,* 3, on missionaries and human rights.) Missionary women, too, may be coming in for a more positive reexamination from a feminist perspective on human rights (Jayawardena 1995).

7. According to Bruno Maddox's brief review of Hitchens's book in the *New York Times Book Review,* the charge, ultimately, is that "Mother Teresa is less interested in helping the poor than in using them as an indefatigable source of wretchedness on which to fuel the expansion of her fundamentalist Roman Catholic beliefs" (1996, 15). A longer review by Amit Chaudhuri in the *London Review of Books* finds Hitchens's charges persuasive but criticizes his one-dimensional portrait of this obviously complex woman (1996, 3–4).

8. But see also the work of historians and anthropologists that has dealt with the complexity of the relationship between anthropologists and missionaries, especially those trained as ethnographers (Burridge 1978; Clifford 1982; Lutkehaus 1983; Huber 1988, 1996).

9. On mission history in particular Strayer observes: "It was of course missionaries and their supporters who initiated formal examination of the subject and thus gave rise to a metropolitan-ecclesiastical school of mission history. Focused on European strategies for the planting of Christianity in Africa, and on heroic missionary efforts to implement these plans, this literature seldom examined the theme of encounter at all. In this respect it resembled the early colonial history which regarded Africa as a stage on which Europeans of all kinds played out both their interests and their fantasies" (1978, 1).

10. By "mission studies" we mean scholarly work focusing on Christian missions and missionaries. Scholarship on Christianity may or may not include serious examination of missions and missionaries. For example, Christianity is now widely recognized as a pervasive and important part of postcolonial life in many African and Melanesian countries. Much of the growing literature on indigenous Christianity, independent churches, and millenarian movements in these regions, however, is only tangentially concerned with evangelists and proselytization.

11. A perusal of indexes to key journals gives a similar result. For example, *Signs: Journal of Women in Culture and Society* published twelve articles on "colonialism" from 1975 to 1995, which focused on such topics as women's mobility in colonial Zimbabwe, women's educational experience under colonialism, a secular colonial reformer in India, the implications of agricultural mechanization on gen-

der relations in Senegambia, reproduction policy in Uganda, and the like. None bore titles suggesting that missionaries receive any special attention. *Comparative Studies in Society and History* lists forty articles on colonialism from 1983 to 1993, but of these only one, by Ann Stoler (1992b), mentioned gender in the title, and it was not about missions. Beidelman (in this volume) notes the relative paucity of "historical study of women missionaries during the Victorian and Edwardian era," and Blackbourn, writing in 1991, regrets that Roman Catholic women's orders and congregations in modern Europe (since the French Revolution) have been "neglected for too long by historians—not least by women's historians drawn to more overtly progressive foremothers," although he believed that there were "welcome signs that this is now changing" (1991, 781). See also Jane Haggis's article on missionary women in Kalpana Ram and Margaret Jolly's volume *Maternities and Modernities* (1998).

12. Again, as a result of an increased focus of attention on the lives of women, scholars have begun to look specifically at the impact of missionaries, both men and women, upon the lives of indigenous women. See, for example, such work as Forbes 1986; Flemming 1989, 1992; Jolly and MacIntyre 1989; Jolly 1991; Haggis 1998.

13. There is a growing literature, especially by women's historians, documenting the phenomenal rise during this period in the participation of women, both at home and abroad, in support of foreign missions. See, for example, Hyatt 1976; Beaver 1980; Kelly 1982; Hunter 1984; Hill 1985; Flemming 1989; Grimshaw 1989; Brouwer 1990; Zwiep 1991; Lodwick 1995; Yohn 1995.

14. The perception that young women greatly outnumbered young men in England may not have been accurate but was widely believed. According to Swaisland, the origin of this "myth of redundancy" was an 1862 analysis of 1851 census data claiming that there were one million women in the population who were being denied the opportunity to marry. Later analyses claimed that this number was vastly exaggerated but had little effect on popular understandings. "Belief in the nightmare continued and inspired much philanthropic activity, including the energetic espousal of emigration for women" (1993a, 72).

15. Mention should be made here of race as well, especially with regard to the significance of the historical and cultural role of black American missionaries in Africa after the Civil War. While these black Christian missionaries shared the belief of their white counterparts that the indigenous religions of the Africans among whom they worked were inferior to Christianity, various scholars have noted the importance of the activities of these black American missionaries in the establishment of the notion of pan-African identity and racial solidarity (Jacobs 1992; Martin 1989; W. Williams 1982). The role of African-American women in these missionary endeavors seems to have paralleled those of their white sisters at the time (Jacobs 1982; Martin 1989, 132). African-American missionaries were also important participants in the earlier colonization of Liberia (Shick 1977).

16. As Margaret Mead sarcastically noted, during the 1930s colonists on the north coast of New Guinea each felt "that the native should be reserved for their special varieties of exploitation" (1977, 124).

17. There is always danger of occluding differences among representers when generalizing about the gender of imperialism in popular culture or of missionaries within it (see n. 1). It is also important to note that masculine and feminine are typically cast as relative positions, so that from one perspective missionaries might be feminized, but they might be masculinized from another. Within the larger Christian community, for example, there is some evidence that missionaries were "masculinized" vis-à-vis other religious workers by virtue of the adventure and hardship of their calling.

18. Not surprisingly, some of the earliest attempts to rescue women's missionary experiences from oblivion came from Christian women themselves. Thus, for example, Winifred Mathews published her book *Dauntless Women: Stories of Pioneer Wives* (1947) by winnowing through the published biographies and autobiographies of male missionaries to extract accounts about their wives.

19. The essay by Kirkwood in the volume introduced by Bowie includes the following demonstration of women's invisibility in missionary history. The official history of the London Missionary Society, published in 1954, includes in its introduction this single statement about missionary wives: "The volume and nature of [their] service is incalculable. Apart from all that a wife's companionship means in a man's work, apart from the distinctive contribution in Christian witness which a missionary's home offers, there has always been rendered by missionaries' wives an immense volume of work at schools, dispensaries and cottage industries, in translation and literary work, in the training of women workers, and in experiments that bear the stamp of a creative originality. To have attempted a record of this work, or even to have named all the outstanding illustrations of it would have been too large an undertaking. With all its inadequacy this single salute to a company which included in many cases the real heroes of the story must be all that can be offered" (Goodall 1954, 13; qtd. in Kirkwood 1993, 28).

20. On the history of recruitment of women in the Wesleyan Methodist Missionary Society, the Church Missionary Society, and the London Missionary Society, see P. Williams 1993. Williams contrasts these "mainline" evangelical groups with the China Inland Mission, whose leader was a pioneer advocate for the recruitment of single women for missionary work. Influenced by the holiness movement that flowed from an 1859 revival, Hudson Taylor thought "nothing was more true than that God empowered men and women by his Holy Spirit to do his work whether or not they had formal status or qualifications" (P. Williams 1993, 46). See also Brouwer 1990; and Gagan 1992, on single Protestant Canadian women missionaries; and Lodwick 1995, on the career of the American Presbyterian missionary Margaret Moniger in China.

21. As Predelli and Miller note in their essay in this volume, "the word *patriarchy* is itself ideologically loaded and problematic. It is unavoidable in the historical discussion of missions, not least because missions have used it to describe themselves." The Basel Mission they discuss, for example, "was defined as a male enterprise, dominated by fatherly (*väterliche*) authority at the center, with the expectation that male missionaries would duplicate that authority in the convert communities they established abroad." In reality, of course, both the letter and the

spirit of this "gender regime" were contested, leading Predelli and Miller to conclude that, in regard to missions, "the term must be framed in a way that allows for paradox, so that both liberating and oppressive forces can be investigated."

22. There is a growing body of work by archaeologists and cultural anthropologists interested in the gendered dimensions of religious life, including the organization of space, time, food, etc. See, for example, Gilchrist 1994; and Curran 1989.

23. In her essay in this volume Lutkehaus uses the term *maternalism* to refer, first, to the role administrators in New Guinea generally ascribed to missionaries in the division of colonial labor (focus on values, use of peaceful methods); second, to the gendered roles of nuns in the Catholic mission effort in New Guinea (nurses, teachers, and helpmates to the priests and brothers); and, third, to the sisters' special responsibilities for the education of indigenous women and the formation of Christian families. Barbara Ramusack focuses on the inequalities inherent in maternal relationships, when using the term *maternal imperialists* to refer to nineteenth-century British women activists who "might be viewed as cultural missionaries preaching a gospel of women's uplift" for India (1992, 132). The intimate tensions of "maternalism" relationships are highlighted by Margaret Jolly: "The symbolic constitution of the relationship between colonizing women and colonized women in the familial mode as that between mother and daughter was a poignant but strategic expression of the tension between superordination and identification, between detachment and agonized intimacy, between other and self" (1993, xx).

24. Gyan Prakash emphasizes a similar point. "Paradoxes and ironies abounded, as did the justification of the gap between rhetoric and practice on the grounds of expediency and the exceptional circumstances of the colonies. These contortions of the discourse were endemic to colonialism not because of the colonizer's bad faith but due to the functioning of colonial power as a form of transaction and translation between incommensurable cultures and positions" (1995, 3).

25. Indeed, some theories of conversion stress the capacity of world religions to incorporate converts into a wider social sphere. As Hefner comments: "For many peoples, it would appear, incorporation into a broader social order brought not just technological and political transformations of traditional lifeways but far-reaching adjustments in the canons of divinity, identity, and social ethics as well" (1993, 3).

26. For Papua New Guinea, for example, see Barker's discussion of conversion to Christianity among the Maisin villagers of Papua New Guinea (1993). Barker sees relations between the village and the eighty-year-old mission station nearby as a "dual culture that has to be understood in the context of a multicultural Papua New Guinea." Barker suggests that "conversion may also be understood as an ongoing process for the converts themselves": the church providing one of the contexts in which villagers refashion "local ways according to imported values and orientations." In this sense the "rhetoric of conversion" can also be seen as a "discourse about the nature of community": by participating in Christianity, "Maisin identify with the common interests, forms, and political values of the larger community in Papua New Guinea" (222–23).

27. This still does not indicate the full extent of evangelism worldwide. The statistics also report 191,200 "cross-cultural home missionaries," defined as "evangelists, missioners, catechists, workers in own countries among other cultures," and notes that 75 percent of these are working in the Christian world, 18 percent in the evangelized non-Christian world, and 10 percent in the unevangelized world. Of the 827,800 "home missionaries (near-cultural)," defined as "religious orders, friars, monks, brothers, sisters, nuns working in their own countries among people of their own culture in outreach situations, 90 percent worked in the Christian world, 9 percent in the evangelized non-Christian world, and 1 percent in the unevangelized world. Pastoral workers (the next category) numbered 3,969,000 people in 1995, while "Great Commission lay Christians," including lay activists and mission supporters of all kinds included another 700 million people (Barrett 1996, 24). See also the editorial "Mission and Statistics: Use with Care," about how such statistics are compiled (1995).

28. The most common nationalities for the SVD are, in order of numerical importance, Indonesians, 1,053 members (18.4 percent); Germans, 921 members (16.1 percent); Poles 651 members (11.4 percent); Indians, 538 members (9.4 percent); Filipinos, 449 members (7.9 percent); U.S. Americans, 402 members (7.0 percent); Dutchmen, 260 members (4.5 percent); Argentineans, 182 members (3.2 percent); Austrians, 142 members (2.5 percent); and Slovaks, 131 members (2.3 percent). The annual periodical *SVD Word in the World, 1993–94* makes the following observation: "It should be noted that the 2,040 Asians (Indonesians, Indians, Filipinos) among the 'top ten' already come very close to the 2,105 Europeans and can readily be expected to take the lead in the very near future" (Piskaty 1993, 10).

29. As Jayawardena sums up the issues for missionaries in South Asia: "Under British rule, women missionaries found space in the public domain and opportunities for achievement denied them at home. While they spearheaded movements for Christianizing and modernizing Asian societies through the education of women, many questions were raised about their motives and the kind of education provided. Was it patriarchal, puritan, riddled with middle-class values and supportive of imperialism, or was it liberating, freeing local women from feudal constraints and traditional social practices oppressive to women? Were Christians keeping women subordinate by creating 'good wives and mothers' or were they championing women's rights to education and promoting ideas of equality? Were they self-less 'angels' helping to alleviate social evils in South Asia or 'devils' subverting local religion and culture and opposing movements for national liberation?" (1995, 21).

30. McDonough argues in his study of changes in the gender ideology of the Jesuits, an exclusively male Catholic order devoted to education and other forms of "apostolic action," that religious communities offer a particularly promising field for "clues about the origins and possible institutionalization of altruism" and for attention to "the variably participatory or hierarchical organizational designs through which 'private' goals are transformed into 'public' goods" (1990, 356).

REFERENCES

Anderson, Benedict. 1983. *Imagined Communities: Reflections on the Origin and Spread of Nationalism.* London: Verso.

Appadurai, Arjun. 1991. Global Ethnoscapes: Notes and Queries for a Transnational Anthropology. In *Recapturing Anthropology: Working in the Present,* ed. Richard G. Fox, 191–210. Santa Fe, N.M.: School of American Research Press.

———. 1996. *Modernity at Large: Cultural Dimensions of Globalization. Public Worlds,* vol. 1. Minneapolis: University of Minnesota Press.

Barker, John. 1993. "We are Ekelesia": Conversion in Uiaku, Papua New Guinea. In *Conversion to Christianity: Historical and Anthropological Perspectives on a Great Transformation,* ed. Robert W. Hefner, 199–230. Berkeley: University of California Press.

Barrett, David B. 1996. Annual Statistical Table on Global Mission: 1996. *International Bulletin of Missionary Research* 20:24–25.

Beaver, R. Pierce. 1980 [1968]. *American Protestant Women in World Mission: A History of the First Feminist Movement in North America.* Rev. ed. Grand Rapids, Mich.: William B. Eerdmans.

Behar, Ruth. 1987. Sex and Sin, Witchcraft and the Devil in Late-Colonial Mexico. *American Ethnologist* 14:34–54.

Beidelman, T. O. 1974. Social Theory and the Study of Christian Missions in Africa. *Africa* 44:235–49.

———. 1982. *Colonial Evangelism: A Socio-Cultural Study of an East African Mission at the Grassroots.* Bloomington: Indiana University Press.

Bell, Diane, Pat Caplan, and Wazir Jahan Karim. 1993. *Gendered Fields: Women, Men and Ethnography.* London: Routledge.

Blackbourn, David. 1991. The Catholic Church in Europe since the French Revolution: A Review Article. *Comparative Studies in Society and History* 33: 778–90.

Bowie, Fiona. 1993. Reclaiming Women's Presence. Introduction to *Women and Missions: Past and Present. Anthropological and Historical Perceptions,* ed. Fiona Bowie, Deborah Kirkwood, and Shirley Ardener, 1–19. Oxford: Berg.

Bowie, Fiona, Deborah Kirkwood, and Shirley Ardener, eds. 1993. *Women and Missions: Past and Present. Anthropological and Historical Perspectives.* Oxford: Berg.

Brett, Donna W., and Edward T. Brett. 1988. *Murdered in Central America: The Stories of Eleven U.S. Missionaries.* Maryknoll, N.Y.: Orbis Books.

Brontë, Charlotte. [1847] 1981. *Jane Eyre.* Reprint, New York: Bantam Classic.

Brouwer, Ruth. 1990. *New Women for God: Canadian Presbyterian Women and India Missions, 1876–1914.* Toronto: Toronto University Press.

Burridge, Kenelm. 1960. *Mambu: A Melanesian Millennium.* London: Methuen and Co.

———. 1978. Missionary Occasions. Introduction to *Mission, Church, and Sect in*

Oceania, ed. James A. Boutilier, Daniel T. Hughes, and Sharon W. Tiffany, 1–30. Ann Arbor: University of Michigan Press.

———. 1991. *In the Way: A Study of Christian Missionary Endeavours.* Vancouver: UBC Press.

Burton, Antoinnette M. 1992. The White Woman's Burden: British Feminists and the Indian Woman. In *Western Women and Imperialism: Complicity and Resistance,* ed. Nupur Chaudhuri and Margaret Strobel, 137–57. Bloomington: Indiana University Press.

———. 1994. *Burdens of History: British Feminists, Indian Women, and Imperial Culture, 1854–1914.* Chapel Hill: University of North Carolina Press.

Chaudhuri, Amit. 1996. Why Calcutta? Review of *The Missionary Position: Mother Teresa in Theory and Practice,* by Christopher Hitchins. *London Review of Books,* 4 January 1996, 3, 5.

Clifford, James. 1982. *Person and Myth: Maurice Leenhardt in the Melanesian World.* Berkeley: University of California Press.

Comaroff, John, and Jean Comaroff. 1991. *Of Revelation and Revolution: Christianity, Colonialism, and Consciousness in South Africa,* vol. 1. Chicago: University of Chicago Press.

Connell, R. W. 1987. *Gender and Power: Society, the Person, and Sexual Politics.* Stanford: Stanford University Press.

Cooper, Frederick, and Ann Laura Stoler. 1989. Tensions of Empire: Colonial Control and Visions of Rule. *American Ethnologist* 16:609–21.

Curran, Patricia. 1989. *Grace before Meals: Food Ritual and Body Discipline in Convent Culture.* Urbana: University of Illinois Press.

Davidoff, Leonore, and Catherine Hall. 1987. *Family Fortunes: Men and Women of the English Middle Class, 1780–1850.* London: Hutchinson.

Deacon, A., and M. Hill. 1972. The Problem of Surplus Women in the Nineteenth Century: Secular and Religious Alternatives. In *A Sociological Year Book of Religion in Britain,* no. 5, ed. D. Martin, 87–102. London: SCM Press.

Denoon, Donald. 1986. The Isolation of Australian History. *Historical Studies* 22:252–60.

Dickens, Charles. 1853. *Bleak House.* London: Bradbury and Evans.

Dirks, Nicholas B. 1992. Colonialism and Culture. Introduction to *Colonialism and Culture,* ed. Nicholas B. Dirks, 1–25. Ann Arbor: University of Michigan Press.

Falding, Harold. 1968. *The Sociological Task.* Englewood Cliffs, N.J.: Prentice-Hall.

Fernandez, James W. 1964. The Sound of Bells in a Christian Country—In Quest of the Historical Schweitzer. *Massachusetts Review* (Spring): 537–62.

Flemming, Leslie A., ed. 1989. *Women's Work for Women: Missionaries and Social Change In Asia.* Boulder: Westview Press.

———. 1992. A New Humanity: American Missionaries' Ideals for Women in North India, 1870–1930. In *Western Women and Imperialism: Complicity and Resistance,* ed. Nupur Chaudhuri and Margaret Strobel, 192–206. Bloomington: Indiana University Press.

Forbes, Geraldine H. 1986. In Search of the "Pure Heathen": Missionary Women in Nineteenth Century India. *Economic and Political Weekly* 31:2–8.

Gagan, Rosemary R. 1992. *A Sensitive Independence: Canadian Methodist Women Missionaries in Canada and the Orient, 1881–1925.* Montreal: McGill-Queen's University Press.

Gilchrist, Roberta. 1994. *Gender and Material Culture: The Archaeology of Religious Women.* London: Routledge.

Goodall, Norman. 1954. *A History of the London Missionary Society, 1895–1945.* London: Oxford University Press.

Grimshaw, Patricia. 1985. New England Missionary Wives, Hawaiian Women, and the "Cult of True Womanhood." *Hawaiian Journal of History* 19:71–100.

———. 1989. *Paths of Duty: American Missionary Wives in Nineteenth-Century Hawaii.* Honolulu: University of Hawaii Press.

Haggis, Jane. 1998. 'Good Wives and Mothers' or 'Dedicated Workers'? Contradictions of Domesticity in the 'Mission of Sisterhood', Travancore, South India. In *Maternities and Modernities: Colonial and Postcolonial Experiences in Asia and the Pacific,* ed. Kalpana Ram and Margaret Jolly, 81–113. Cambridge: Cambridge University Press.

Hall, Catherine. 1992. Missionary Stories: Gender and Ethnicity in England in the 1830s and 1840s. In *Cultural Studies,* ed. Lawrence Grossberg, Cary Nelson, and Paula Treichler, 240–76. New York: Routledge.

Hawkesworth, Mary. 1997. Confounding Gender. *Signs: Journal of Women in Culture and Society* 22, no. 3: 649–85.

Hefner, Robert W. 1993. World Building and the Rationality of Conversion. Introduction to *Conversion to Christianity: Historical and Anthropological Perspectives on a Great Transformation,* ed. Robert W. Hefner, 3–44. Berkeley: University of California Press.

Hill, Patricia R. 1985. *The World Their Household: The American Woman's Foreign Mission Movement and Cultural Transformation, 1870–1920.* Ann Arbor: University of Michigan Press.

Hitchens, Christopher. 1995. *The Missionary Position: Mother Teresa in Theory and Practice.* London: Verso.

Hobsbawm, Eric. 1989. *The Age of Empire: 1875–1914.* New York: Vintage Books.

Höltker, Georg. 1946. Die Kleiderfrage in den beiden Vikariaten Ost- und Zentral-Neuguinea. *Neue Zeitschrift fur Missionswissenschaft* 2:43–55.

Holy Spirit Sisters in Indonesia. 1993. In *SVD Word in the World, 1993–1994,* 71. Steyl, Holl.: Steyler Verlag.

Huber, Mary Taylor. 1988. *The Bishops' Progress: A Historical Ethnography of Catholic Missionary Experience on the Sepik Frontier.* Washington, D.C.: Smithsonian Institution Press.

———. 1994. The Message in the Missionary. Introduction to *The Message in the Missionary: Local Interpretations of Religious Ideology and Missionary Personality,* ed. Elizabeth Brusco and Laura F. Klein, 1–8. *Studies in Third World Societies,* no. 55 (January). Williamsburg, Va.: Department of Anthropology, College of William and Mary.

———. 1996. Missionaries. In *Encyclopedia of Social and Cultural Anthropology,* ed. Jonathan Spencer and Alan Barnard, 373–75. London: Routledge.

Hunter, Jane. 1984. *The Gospel of Gentility: American Women Missionaries in Turn-of-the-Century China.* New Haven: Yale University Press.

Hutchins, Francis G. 1967. *The Illusion of Permanence: British Imperialism in India.* Princeton: Princeton University Press.

Hyatt, Irwin. 1976. *Our Ordered Lives Confess. Three Nineteenth-Century American Missionaries in East Shantung.* Cambridge: Harvard University Press.

Jacobs, Sylvia M. 1992. Give a Thought to Africa: Black Women Missionaries in Southern Africa. In *Western Women and Imperialism: Complicity and Resistance,* ed. Nupur Chaudhuri and Margaret Strobel, 295–308. Bloomington: Indiana University Press.

———, ed. 1982. *Black Americans and the Missionary Movement in Africa.* Westport, Conn.: Greenwood Press.

Jayawardena, Kumari. 1995. *The White Woman's Other Burden: Western Women and South Asia during British Rule.* London: Routledge.

Jolly, Margaret. 1991. "To Save the Girls for Brighter and Better Lives": Presbyterian Missions and Women in the South of Vanuatu, 1848–1870. *Journal of Pacific History* 26:27–48.

———. 1993. Colonizing Women: The Maternal Body and Empire. In *Feminism and the Politics of Difference,* ed. Senja Gunew and Anna Yeatman, 113–27. Boulder: Westview Press.

Jolly, Margaret, and Martha Macintyre. 1989. Introduction to *Family and Gender in the Pacific: Domestic Contradictions and the Colonial Impact,* ed. M. Jolly and M. Macintyre, 1–18. Cambridge: Cambridge University Press.

Kelly, Sister Kathleen. 1982. Maryknoll in Manchuria, 1927–1947: A Study of Accommodation and Adaptation. Ph.D. diss., University of Southern California.

Kipp, Rita Smith. 1990. *The Early Years of a Dutch Colonial Mission: The Karo Field.* Ann Arbor: University of Michigan Press.

———. 1995. Conversion by Affiliation: The History of the Karo Batak Protestant Church. *American Ethnologist* 22:868–82.

Kirkwood, Deborah. 1993. Protestant Missionary Women: Wives and Spinsters. In *Women and Missions: Past and Present. Anthropological and Historical Perspectives,* ed. Fiona Bowie, Deborah Kirkwood, and Shirley Ardener, 23–41. Oxford: Berg.

Klor de Alva, J. Jorge, H. B. Nicholson, and Eloise Quinones Keber, eds. 1988. *The Work of Bernardino de Sahagún: Pioneer Ethnographer of Sixteenth-Century Aztec Mexico.* Studies on Culture and Society, vol. 2. Albany, N.Y.: Institute for Mesoamerican Studies, University at Albany, State University of New York.

Langmore, Diane. 1989. *Missionary Lives: Papua, 1874–1914.* Honolulu: University of Hawaii Press.

Lewis, Reina. 1996. *Gendering Orientalism: Race, Femininity, and Representation.* London: Routledge.

Livingstone, David. 1857. *Missionary Travels and Researches in South Africa.* London: John Murray.

Lodwick, Kathleen. 1995. *Educating the Women of Hainan: The Career of Margaret Moninger in China, 1915–1942.* Lexington: University Press of Kentucky.

Luddy, Maria. 1995. *Women and Philanthropy in Nineteenth-Century Ireland.* Cambridge: Cambridge University Press.

Lutkehaus, Nancy C. 1983. Missionaries as Ethnographers. Introduction to *The Life of Some Island People of New Guinea,* by Karl Böhm, trans. Nancy C. Lutkehaus, 13–69. Collectanea Instituti Anthropos no. 29. Berlin: Dietrich Reimer Verlag.

———. 1995. *Zaria's Fire: Engendered Moments in Manam Ethnography.* Durham, N.C.: Carolina Academic Press.

Maddox, Bruno. 1996. Review of *The Missionary Position: Mother Teresa in Theory and Practice,* by Christopher Hitchens. *New York Times Book Review,* 14 January, 18.

Martin, Sandy D. 1989. *Black Baptists and African Missions.* Macon, Ga.: Mercer University Press.

Mathews, Winifred. 1947. *Dauntless Women: Stories of Pioneer Wives.* Freeport, N.Y.: Books for Libraries Press.

Matthiessen, Peter. 1965. *At Play in the Fields of the Lord.* New York: Random House.

McClintock, Anne. 1996. *Imperial Leather: Race, Gender, and Sexuality in the Colonial Contest.* New York: Routledge.

McDonough, Peter. 1990. Metamorphoses of the Jesuits: Sexual Identity, Gender Roles, and Hierarchy in Catholicism. *Comparative Studies in Society and History* 32:325–56.

McNamara, Jo Ann Kay. 1996. *Sisters in Arms: Catholic Nuns through Two Millenia.* Cambridge: Harvard University Press.

Mead, Margaret. 1977. *Letters from the Field, 1925–1975.* New York: Harper and Row.

Mehlman, Billie. 1992. *Women's Orients: English Women and the Middle East, 1718–1918: Sexuality, Religion and Work.* Ann Arbor: University of Michigan Press.

Michener, James A. 1959. *Hawaii.* New York: Random House.

Miller, Jon. 1994. *The Social Control of Religious Zeal: A Study of Organizational Contradictions.* Rose Monograph Series of the American Sociological Association. New Brunswick, N.J.: Rutgers University Press.

Mission and Statistics: Use with Care. 1995. *International Bulletin of Missionary Research* 19:1.

Piskaty, Kurt. 1993. Divine Word Missionaries in Indonesia. In *SVD Word in the World, 1993–1994,* 9–16. Steyl, Holl.: Steyler Verlag.

Prakash, Gyan. 1995. After Colonialism. Introduction to *After Colonialism: Imperial Histories and Postcolonial Developments,* ed. Gyan Prakash, 3–17. Princeton: Princeton University Press.

Pratt, Mary Louise. 1992. *Imperial Eyes: Travel Writing and Transculturalism.* New York: Routledge.

Pung, Robert. 1968. A Fitting Anniversary. In *The Word in the World, 1968,* 177–80. Techny, Ill.: Divine Word Publications.

Rafael, Vicente L. 1988. *Contracting Colonialism: Translation and Christian Conversion in Tagalog Society under Early Spanish Rule.* Ithaca: Cornell University Press.

Ram, Kaplana, and Margaret Jolly, eds. 1998. *Maternities and Modernities: Colonial and Postcolonial Experiences in Asia and the Pacific.* Cambridge: Cambridge University Press.

Ramusack, Barbara N. 1992. Cultural Missionaries, Maternal Imperialists, Feminist Allies: British Women Activists in India, 1865–1945. In *Western Women and Imperialism: Complicity and Resistance,* ed. Nupur Chaudhuri and Margaret Strobel, 119–35. Bloomington: Indiana University Press.

Richards, Jeffrey. 1986. Boy's Own Empire: Feature Films and Imperialism in the 1930s. In *Imperialism and Popular Culture,* ed. John M. MacKenzie, 140–64. Manchester: Manchester University Press.

Robinson, Ronald, and John Gallagher, with Alice Denny. 1961. *Africa and the Victorians: The Climax of Imperialism.* Garden City, N.Y.: Doubleday and Company.

Rosaldo, Renato. 1990. Celebrating Thompson's Heroes: Social Analysis in History and Anthropology. In *E. P. Thompson: Critical Perspectives,* ed. Harvey J. Kaye and Keith McClelland, 103–24. Philadelphia: Temple University Press.

Sahlins, Marshall. 1995. *How "Natives" Think: About Captain Cook, for Example.* Chicago: University of Chicago Press.

Said, Edward. 1978. *Orientalism.* London: Routledge.

———. 1993. *Culture and Imperialism.* London: Chatto and Windus.

Scott, Joan Wallach. 1988. *Gender and the Politics of History.* New York: Columbia University Press.

Sharpe, Jenny. 1993. *Allegories of Empire: The Figure of Woman in the Colonial Text.* Minneapolis: University of Minnesota Press.

Shick, Tom W. 1977. *Behold the Promised Land: A History of Afro-American Settler Society in Nineteenth-Century Liberia.* Baltimore: Johns Hopkins University Press.

Shohat, Ella, and Robert Stam. 1994. *Unthinking Eurocentrism: Multiculturalism and the Media.* New York: Routledge.

Smith, Michael French. 1994. *Hard Times on Kairiru Island: Poverty, Development, and Morality in a Papua New Guinea Village.* Honolulu: University of Hawaii Press.

Spence, Jonathan D. 1984. *The Memory Palace of Matteo Ricci.* New York: Viking Penguin.

Stanley, Henry Morton. 1872. *How I Found Livingstone.* London: S. Low, Marston, Searle and Rivington.

Stipe, C. E. 1980. Anthropologists vs. Missionaries: The Influence of Presuppositions. *Current Anthropology* 21:165–79.

Stocking, George W., Jr. 1983. The Ethnographer's Magic: Fieldwork in British Anthropology from Tylor to Malinowski. In *Observers Observed: Essays on Ethnographic Fieldwork,* ed. George W. Stocking Jr., 70–120. Madison: University of Wisconsin Press.

Stokes, Eric. 1959. *English Utilitarians and India.* Oxford: Oxford University Press.

Stoler, Ann Laura. 1991. Carnal Knowledge and Imperial Power: Matrimony, Race, and Morality in Colonial Asia. In *Gender at the Crossroads: Feminist Anthropology in the Postmodern Era,* ed. Micaela di Leonardo, 51–101. Berkeley: University of California Press.

———. 1992a. Rethinking Colonial Categories: European Communities and the Boundaries of Rule. In *Colonialism and Culture,* ed. Nicholas B. Dirks, 319–52. Ann Arbor: University of Michigan Press.

———. 1992b. Sexual Affronts and Racial Frontiers: European Identities and the Politics of Exclusion in Colonial Southeast Asia. *Comparative Studies in Society and History* 34:514–51.

———.1995. *Race and the Education of Desire: Foucault's* History of Sexuality *and the Colonial Order of Things.* Durham, N.C.: Duke University Press.

Stoler, Ann Laura, and Frederick Cooper. 1997. Between Metropole and Colony: Rethinking a Research Agenda. Introduction to *Tensions of Empire: Colonial Cultures in a Bourgeois World,* ed. Frederick Cooper and Ann Laura Stoler, 1–56. Berkeley: University of California Press.

Strayer, Robert W. 1978. *The Making of Mission Communities in East Africa: Anglicans and Africans in Colonial Kenya.* London: Heinemann.

Strobel, Margaret. 1987. Gender and Race in the Nineteenth- and Twentieth-Century British Empire. In *Becoming Visible: Women in European History,* ed. Renate Bridenthal et al., 2d ed., 375–96. Boston: Houghton Mifflin.

Swaisland, Cecilie. 1993a. Wanted—Earnest, Self-Sacrificing Women for Service in South Africa: Nineteenth-Century Recruitment of Single Women to Protestant Missions. In *Women and Missions: Past and Present. Anthropological and Historical Perspectives,* ed. Fiona Bowie, Deborah Kirkwood, and Shirley Ardener, 70–84. Oxford: Berg.

———. 1993b. *Servants and Gentlewomen to the Golden Land: The Emigration of Single Women from Britain to Southern Africa, 1820–1939.* Oxford and Providence: Berg and University of Natal Press.

Swanson, Jeffrey. 1995. *Echoes of the Call: Identity and Ideology among American Missionaries in Equador.* New York: Oxford University Press.

Thomas, Nicholas. 1994. *Colonialism's Culture: Anthropology, Travel, and Government.* Princeton: Princeton University Press.

Thorne, Susan. 1997. "The Conversion of England and the Conversion of the World Inseparable": Missionary Imperialism and the Language of Class in Early Industrial Britain. In *Tensions of Empire: Colonial Cultures in a Bourgeois World,* ed. Frederick Cooper and Ann Laura Stoler, 238–62. Berkeley: University of California Press.

Tjelle, Kristin Fjelde. 1990. Kvinder Hjælper Kvinder: Misjonskvinneforeningsbevegelsen i Norge 1860–1910. Master's thesis, Department of History, University of Oslo.

Todorov, Tzvetan. 1992. *The Conquest of America: The Question of the Other.* Trans. Richard Howard. New York: Harper and Row.

Vicinus, Martha. 1985. *Independent Women: Work and Community for Single Women, 1850–1920.* Chicago: University of Chicago Press.

Ware, Vron. 1992. *Beyond the Pale: White Women, Racism and History.* London: Verso.

Williams, Patrick, and Laura Chrisman. 1994. Colonial Discourse and Post-Colonial Theory: An Introduction. In *Colonial Discourse and Post-Colonial Theory: A Reader,* ed. Patrick Williams and Laura Chrisman, 1–20. New York: Columbia University Press.

Williams, Peter. 1993. "The Missing Link": The Recruitment of Women Missionaries in Some English Evangelical Missionary Societies in the Nineteenth Century. In *Women and Missions: Past and Present. Anthropological and Historical Perspectives,* ed. Fiona Bowie, Deborah Kirkwood, and Shirley Ardener, 43–69. Oxford: Berg.

Williams, Walter. 1982. *Black Americans and the Evangelization of Africa, 1877–1900.* Madison: University of Wisconsin Press.

Yohn, Susan M. 1995. *A Contest of Faiths: Missionary Women and Pluralism in the American Southwest.* Ithaca: Cornell University Press.

Zwiep, Mary. 1991. *Pilgrim Path: The First Company of Women Missionaries to Hawaii.* Madison: University of Wisconsin Press.

Missionary-Imperial Feminism

Susan Thorne

The nineteenth century was "the great century" of British Protestantism's missionary expansion abroad.[1] Moribund for most of the early modern period, Britain's churches raced to embrace the foreign mission cause during the decades that bracketed the nineteenth century's turn (Thorne forthcoming, chap. 2). And it is the resonance of foreign missions on their British home front, rather than their activities in the foreign field per se, that primarily concerns me here. For foreign missions would gain a grip on Victorian public opinion that was for long without effective rival. As the Reverend Arthur Tidman, foreign secretary of the London Missionary Society (LMS), put it in 1845, "the Missionary spirit was the characteristic feature" of the religious piety for which Victorian Britons remain renowned (qtd. in Lovett 1899, 2:675).

The enormous popularity of the missionary project in Victorian Britain attracted considerable criticism from those resentful of evangelicalism's growing influence in British political culture. The missionary enthusiast was a staple figure, for example, in the anti-evangelical invective for which the Victorian literati were renowned (Pope 1978, chap. 3; Brantlinger 1986; Comaroff and Comaroff 1991, chap. 2). To Mrs. Pardiggle and Mrs. Jellyby of Dickens's *Bleak House* (1852–53) might be added Pitt Crawley and his oh-so-serious mother-in-law, the Countess Southdown, of Thackeray's *Vanity Fair* (1847), St. John Rivers of Charlotte Brontë's *Jane Eyre* (1847), and even the arch-villain of Eliot's *Middlemarch* (1871–72), Mr. Bulstrode—all characters obsessed to tragicomic lengths with missionary trials and tribulations in "exotic" foreign lands.

This literary indictment of missionary philanthropy was gendered on many levels (Pope 1978, 139). Not only do women figure prominently among foreign missionary enthusiasts portrayed in this literature; even male characters inclined to missionary sympathies are portrayed as "not real men," as Carlyle put it; Dickens called them "weird old women" (qtd. in Hall 1989, 180; Dickens 1848, 117; cited in Smith 1995, 115–17). This suggests, as Nancy Lutkehaus argues more fully elsewhere in this volume, that the missionary project was itself gendered "feminine," regardless of the biological sex of the missionaries involved. This was not the inevitable expression of feminine qualities intrinsic to the mission project but, rather, a historically specific moment in British mission and imperial history. As Catherine Hall has recently argued, debates about colonial policy were frequently waged in a language of "competing masculinities" (Hall 1989; Segal 1990). An evangelical model of masculinity held sway for much of the early nineteenth century, predicated on religious piety, moral seriousness, and a civilizing mission at home and abroad (Davidoff and Hall 1987). It was this model of masculinity that our literary critics of missions were seeking to contest by portraying its missionary manifestations in stereotypically feminized terms. Missionary attentions to the colonized were disparaged as a misplaced application of maternal energies that should be confined to "home." Intellectuals indignantly entreated "loud-sounding, long-eared Exeter Hall" (the building in London where most of the major missionary societies held their annual public meetings) to attend to home needs first.

> wilt thou not perhaps open the dull sodden eyes to the "sixty thousand valets in London itself who are yearly dismissed to the streets" . . . or to the hunger-stricken, pallid, *yellow*-coloured "Free Labourers" in Lancashire, Yorkshire, Buckinghamshire, and all other shires! These Yellow-coloured, for the present, absorb all my energies. (Carlyle 1843, 278)

Dickens put it with his usual directness: "the work at home must be completed thoroughly, or there is no hope abroad. To your tents, O Israel! but see they are your own tents! Set *them* in order; leave nothing to be done *there*" (1848, 134).

The consequences of the foreign missionary movement's reversal of these priorities are revealingly manifested in the missionary antiheroine's disregard for the familial responsibilities on which her virtue as a woman is clearly considered to depend. Note the gendered slippage here between the British Empire's national home front and the geographical space of the middle-class home. The unkempt and unhappy children, drunken servants, and emasculated husbands of the Mrs. Jellybys who purportedly dominated the evangelical world were the inevitable consequence, according to evangelicalism's critics, of the British public's unseemly fascination with missionary work abroad and its consequent neglect of more deserving beneficiaries at home.

These still familiar caricatures obscure both the piety and the power on which missionary philanthropy was predicated. But they do draw our attention to the myriad levels at which missions were getting "class-ed" as well as "race-d" in the process of being gendered as feminine undertakings. And it is precisely this complex intersection of gender, race, and class in the foreign missionary project that concerns me here. How many evangelical women accompanied Mrs. Jellyby on her missionary rounds? Were British women's missionary involvements as subversive of Victorian gender conventions as their enemies feared? Did evangelical women use missions to escape their confinement to a separate domestic sphere or to ease their sojourn therein? How did missionary women, moreover, view the colonized targets of missionary interventions? Were they the "friendly" subverters of racial hierarchy as well, as their critics claimed? And, finally, what was the relationship between women's involvement in the foreign missionary crusade and evangelicalism's not inconsiderable missionary crusade closer to home?

Gender

The gendering of missions as feminine registered, on the most obvious level, the social fact of evangelical women's large-scale involvement in the foreign missionary crusade. British women were mobilized on behalf of foreign missions in larger numbers over the entire course of the nineteenth century than on behalf of any other claimant to their attention, with the possible exception of the closely related antislavery movement (Midgley 1992). By the end of the nineteenth century British women were contributing more than 70 percent of the funding for foreign missionary operations (Mandler 1990, 20; Prochaska 1980). And by the early 1890s the number of female missionaries serving abroad was rapidly approaching the number of men, and female applicants far exceeded their male counterparts (Williams 1993, 43). Indeed, the missionary movement may be said to have comprised in Britain as it did in the United States the single largest social movement in which Victorian women participated (Hill 1985).

Women's support was solicited and forthcoming, moreover, from the outset. Most of Britain's major missionary organizations were founded during the decades that bracketed the nineteenth century's turn.[2] The Baptists were first to field a formal organization; the inaugural meetings of the Baptist Missionary Society were held in Northamptonshire in 1792 (Stanley 1992). The London Missionary Society, which was officially nondenominational but would effectively be the missionary auxiliary of Britain's Independent or Congregational Churches, was founded shortly thereafter in 1795 (Morison 1844). The Church Missionary Society was established by Evangelical Anglicans in 1799 (Stock 1899). The central missionary committee of the Wesleyan Methodist Church had been sending missionaries abroad since the 1780s; a separate foreign missionary society was not established, however, until 1813 (Findlay and Holdsworth 1921).

Each of these organizations actively courted female support, and evangelical women responded enthusiastically. Although they would remain invisible in the upper echelons of missionary administration throughout the nineteenth century, women played a prominent role at the local level, in the provincial "auxiliary" movement (auxiliaries were local branches of national missionary organizations, which were usually based in London) (Prochaska 1980; Stanley 1979). Women also labored in the foreign mission field itself from the very earliest days, if not yet as professional missionaries in their own right then as wifely assistants to missionary husbands. These latter repeatedly testified that they were able to devote themselves to their ministerial duties in large part because their wives attended to the more social needs of their target population—teaching children, nursing the sick, delivering babies, teaching domestic arts, etc. (Cunningham 1993). And, as Huber points out elsewhere in this volume, the frontier conditions in the foreign mission field required practical adjustments to principled adherence to the separation of spheres that further expanded the missionary mandate of missionaries' wives in the mission field (see also Kirkwood 1993, 25).

What distinguished the missionary involvements of these mothers of the Victorians from those of Mrs. Jellyby was the degree of institutional autonomy and professional recognition they were, or, rather, were not, accorded. Early women's auxiliaries were explicitly described as subsidiary adjuncts of their male counterparts. It was the officers of the proximate male auxiliary who planned the extraordinarily popular anniversary meetings, wrote the auxiliary's reports, forwarded their district's receipts to the London office, spoke on behalf of missions at public meetings and in their chapels, churches, and affiliated Sunday schools, and otherwise publicly associated themselves with the increasingly popular mission cause. Women's involvement was largely confined to the more private and behind-the-scenes tasks of serving tea, sewing fancy goods for sale at missionary bazaars, and collecting subscriptions door-to-door, an intensely personal affair in which women's purportedly maternal powers of persuasion over society's weaker beings—children, other women, and especially the lower classes—were believed to stand them in good stead (Carr 1914, 8; Leeds Auxiliary Minute Books, 30 August 1830). And, while the missionary labors of missionary wives was extensive, it was also entirely voluntary. Nowhere was the missionary work that married women did acknowledged as professional or paid. Men and men alone were deemed fit to minister.[3]

The early mobilization of evangelical women on behalf of the foreign mission cause was therefore more in keeping with the Victorian gender convention of confining women to a separate domestic sphere, appearing in public, if at all, solely in a voluntary capacity and as helpmates to their husbands. It was not until the middle decades of the nineteenth century that British women's involvement in the mission cause began to acquire a more controversial, because independent, cast. A great leap forward in what were arguably feminist directions (in the sense of challenging women's exclusion from paid employment) was signaled by the founding, independent of the mainstream missionary organizations, of the Society for Promoting Female Education in the East (SPFEE) in 1831 and the Indian Female Normal School and Instruction Society in 1854, to promote the professional deployment of single women in the foreign mission field (Williams 1993, 44–45).

This breach of Victorian conventions of domesticity and the confinement of women to a separate private sphere was justified by the growing importance accorded to the conversion of heathen women in the foreign mission field. Civilizations were increasingly held to be more or, usually, less receptive to Christianity, and their softening was increasingly believed to depend upon reaching the women therein. Heathen women, like their metropolitan counterparts, were the most important influence on their entire family's capacity for piety. It was they who would support or discourage their husbands through the sacrifices and suffering entailed in receiving Christ into their lives, particularly in societies that were otherwise hostile. The family was, in other words, the central determinant of a civilization's openness to the Gospel, and it was women therein who held the key to the heathen family's Christian potential. Unfortunately, such women were often beyond the male missionary's effective reach.

It was the women of England alone who would be able to "find their way into the zenanas[4] and rescue the unhappy section of humanity they found there" (*Leeds Mercury,* 3 October 1890, 5; see also Beidelman, in this volume; Kirkwood 1993, 25; Stanley 1992, 231–32). The mainstream missionary organizations began establishing their own committees to oversee the dispatch of single women missionaries during the 1860s and 1870s. Delicacy if not dispatch required that female applicants be interviewed by women and that those accepted be taught and to some extent supervised by women as well. Committees of "Ladies" were formed for these purposes in connection with the Wesleyan Methodist Missionary Society in 1858; the Baptist Missionary Society and the Society for the Propagation of the Gospel in 1866; and with the London Missionary Society in 1875 (Williams 1993, 55; Stanley 1992, 229; Kirkwood 1993, 32). Their success was such that in the course of a single generation the societies with which they were affiliated were sending out almost as many women as men.[5]

Most British women would stay home, however, in both senses of that word; they would remain in England, and they would not engage in paid employment outside of their home. But their involvement in the mission cause intensified considerably in response to foreign missions' gendering. Men, they were repeatedly told, could not be depended upon to do what was necessary to promote the interests of this most worthy cause. As the SPFEE's founders complained, "one missionary report after another, filled with interesting information, will scarcely be found to contain an allusion to the condition of the female population. The information which a ladies' society may acquire would bring that affecting condition before the public" (Anon. 1831, 3). And this these ladies' societies did. British women were besieged from all sides by reminders of their special responsibility to their "heathen" sisters in the foreign mission field.

> You who are the noblest product of Christian civilisation, sheltered, honoured, loved by father, husband, son—can you be content to sit at ease in Zion whilst millions of your sisters suffer untold shame and anguish? . . . Nothing but the spread of the Christian ideal of womanhood will break the fetters of India's women. Can you do nothing to help? (Anon. 1899, 3–4)

Children' literature similarly encouraged British girls to support missions because of their responsibility as girls to girls in other lands, remarking on how "pleasant" it was "to see little English girls stretching out their hands to help their little Hindoo sisters" (Brown 1879, 36–39).

And they responded on a large scale. Local women's missionary auxiliaries directed their energies ever more exclusively toward the "special object" of missions to women, sending sewn and other goods, letters, prayers, and money directly to individual women missionaries in the field. These auxiliaries also began organizing separate meetings for the cause of female missions, which were addressed by women themselves—female missionaries for the most part but also the leading women activists in the locale. And the intensity of women's connection with missionary operations abroad, the fact that they enjoyed a more intimate and "living relationship" with the foreign field than their male counterparts, was the subject of considerable contemporary comment, within the missionary movement as well as without (LMS, *Chronicle of the London Missionary Society,* June 1885, 180).

Thus were foreign missions gendered on their metropolitan home front as well, predicated on evangelical women's identity as women. British women's increased involvement in the missionary crusade in the foreign field as well as on its home front did not translate at any point, however, into institutional control. Despite the enormity of their contribution, women wielded relatively little influence within missionary organizations, which were founded and administered by men and men alone.[6] For most of the nineteenth century women were without representation in the parent organizations that formulated missionary policy. Women were not eligible to serve on the Board of Directors of the London Missionary Society, for example, until 1891; they were not eligible to sit on the General Committee of the Church Missionary Society until 1917 (Williams 1993, 65). At no point in the nineteenth or even in the twentieth century can it be said that women had control over or even an equal voice in formulating missionary policy.

Nor did this gendered missionary discourse explicitly challenge British women's subordination. To the contrary, missionary propaganda aimed at British women utilized the indictment of "heathen" patriarchy to celebrate the prevailing state of gender relations on the missionary home front; for "to think of the difference" between heathen women and their British Christian counterparts, argued one missionary speaker on a British platform in 1883, "was to excite feelings of grateful wonder" (*Leeds Mercury,* 3 October 1883, 7). Missionary outreach to women abroad was expressly designed to extend to so-called heathen women precisely those advantages that Victorian women reputedly enjoyed on their domestic pedestals. British women had been "elevated to their rightful station and dignity, the equals and beloved associates of men . . . by the heavenly principles of 'the glorious gospel of the blessed God,'" argued another, and it was this Gospel that held the key to reversing "the present degradation of their sex in pagan and Mohammedan countries." Thus, "if all Christians are bound to exert themselves in this cause, surely the obligation which rests on Christian women is fourfold! They, far more than men, owe to Christianity their present free and happy state—while it is on their sex that, in other lands, the hard bondage of heathenism presses with the heavier weight (Thompson 1841, xv, lxxviii–lxxix).

Missionary discourse thus projected the problem of women's oppression outward, to the empire; the obvious implication of the missionary critique of heathen patriarchy was that Britain's Christian homes were truly a fulfilling as well as safe haven. "Wives, who are happy in the affectionate esteem of your husbands—mothers, who enjoy your children's reverence and gratitude—children, who have been blessed by a mother's example, and a mother's care—sisters, who have found in your brothers your warmest friends—Christian women, who feel that you can lend to society its charm, and receive from it a loyal courtesy in return—protected, honoured, and loved"—these were the subject positions to which the missionary movement appealed (Thompson 1841, xvii–xviii).

At least on the surface. When scrutinized more closely, Dickens may not have been altogether paranoid in sensing that the missionary movement's tributes to the virtues of domesticity were, if not hollow, then more ambiguous than apparent at first glance. I do not wish here to minimize the limits to women's authority in the missionary movement more generally, which are examined in a variety of denominational and national contexts elsewhere in this volume (Predelli and Miller; Huber; Kipp). What I do want to suggest, however, is that there were chinks in the ideological armor of Victorian rationales for women's subordination that the gendering of missions exposed to view (Huber, in this volume). Even, perhaps especially, the most celebratory descriptions of Victorian gender relations invited by their excess critical reflection about the reality they claimed to represent. The passage quoted earlier addressed those whose "minds are intelligent and cultivated," whose "lives are useful and happy," as well of course as those who "can look for a blessed immortality beyond the grave" (Thompson 1841, lxxviii–lxxix). Cultivated intelligence and useful lives were certainly far removed from the leisured and ornamental existence toward which respectable women were increasingly encouraged in this period (Davidoff and Hall 1987, chap. 9). Such gaps between social reality and missionary discourse may have encouraged a critical attitude toward the very gender conventions missionary propaganda purported to uphold (Cunningham 1993, 93–94).

Such a reading is supported by the actions of women missionary supporters themselves, actions that belied rhetorical celebrations of the gender status quo by implicitly and sometimes explicitly challenging the familial foundations of the domestic ideal. Marriage itself, the ultimate purpose and central relationship of ideal Victorian woman, was called into question, not only by those "independent women" who flocked to missionary opportunities for paid employment in the second half of the nineteenth century (Vicinus 1985) but by many of their married counterparts as well. In the years before going out on their own became an option, female missionary enthusiasts deliberately and openly sought entry into the field by marrying missionary candidates. These marriages were often arranged by sympathetic ministers, taking place after only a few weeks' acquaintance. The mission cause would remain the central preoccupation of many of these women after their marriages and even after the arrival of their children, most of whom seem to have been sent back to Britain at an early age (Thompson 1841; Beidelman, in this volume; Cunningham 1993; Hall 1992, chap. 9). This was perhaps the most extreme repudiation in practice, if not principle, of the Victorian feminine ideal. Motherhood was the primary purpose for which evangelicals believed God had created women in the first place, and it was in the rearing of their children that women enjoyed their principal opportunity of religious as well as personal fulfillment; it was largely in relation to (their) children that women could spread the Word (Poovey 1988; Davidoff and Hall 1987).

Even more dramatic was the challenge to the premises of separate spheres posed by the paid employment of women in the mission field. An early pamphlet urging women's involvement in the cause alluded to the gravity of this innovation in British gender relations but concluded that the missionary ends more than justified the "un-gendering" means required:

> To what extent, and under what circumstances, Christian women may even now engage in personal service among the degraded of their sex in foreign lands, must be left to the consciences of individuals, and to the Providence of God to determine. "Let every one be fully persuaded in her own mind." There is far less ground to question whether we ought not to embrace opportunities of preparing for such employment, in contemplation of the possibility of a divine call to the work. To make His Gospel known to every creature under heaven is the great duty of the Christian church; and nothing but obstacles interposed, or pious duties appointed by God Himself, can absolve us from taking our part in the diffusion. Ought we not all, therefore, to be ready to do so, in case those obstacles be removed? (Thompson 1841, xiv–xxv)

Male missionaries' gendered inadequacy to the task of converting heathen women was not the only justification mounted for European women's professional missionary employment. Missionary propagandists sometimes turned the conventional assumption of the fundamental difference in men's and women's "nature" on its head to argue that women possessed qualities that made them singularly adept at mission work.

> There is a patience of endurance, a buoyancy of hope, and a fervour of devotion . . . so well adapted to the work of foreign missions, as to make it manifest that women are to sustain an important part of this honoured enterprise . . . If less capable of what is bold and hazardous in action, profound in thought, or laborious in investigation, [women enjoyed a] tenderness of feeling, a depth of compassion, a quickness of perception, and a forgetfulness of self, which are commonly found to less extent elsewhere. They appear also generally to manifest a greater facility for the acquisition of languages, as far as the mere power of con-

> versation is concerned; and they can sooner adapt themselves to the prejudices, and win their way to the hearts, of those on whose welfare they are bent. (Thompson 1841, xx)[7]

The seriousness with which British women pursued a missionary avocation framed in these ways suggests that the Victorian cult of domesticity encountered more subterranean resistance than is often acknowledged. This is further suggested by the more derogatory reflections on Victorian gender relations that occasionally erupted to the rhetorical surface. Rationales for employing (British) women in the mission field were implicitly and sometimes explicitly critical of the alternatives available to women on the missionary home front. As early as 1841, Jemima Thompson, an advocate of female missions, sounded a noticeably bitter note when reflecting on the pointlessness of British women's ornamental lives.

> All human beings, whether they are men or women, require an object for which to live; i.e., not merely the grand object of preparation for the future life, but a subordinate and immediate one for the present. Women, a little removed from the humbler classes of society, commonly labour, in this respect, under a disadvantage not experienced by men. The latter have some profession on which to enter, as soon as what is usually denominated education is completed; but women, at that period, for the most part, have none. Many girls leave school at sixteen or seventeen, and spend several of the most valuable part of their lives in a kind of restless indolence. Had they before them some great and benevolent object, such as taking a share in the regeneration of the world, they would be much happier, and much more amiable. Their mental powers, instead of being frittered away, would be increased,—their moral character would acquire a higher tone,—they would be more, rather than less, fitted for the enjoyment of domestic life in after years,—and many of the regrets of a death-bed would be avoided. (Thompson 1841, xxv–xxvi)

Jemima Luke, a staunch supporter of the London Missionary Society and the Society for Promoting Female Education in the East, explained her own missionary enthusiasm in similar terms, as a decision not to settle for "the luxurious ease of a beautiful country—home, reading interesting books, writing chatty letters to friends, receiving and paying calls, doing Berlin woolwork, and making wax on paper flowers as then in vogue, and knitting babies' socks and anti-macassars for bazaars," a life that she considered to be a waste of "an excellent constitution, untiring energy, and years spent in mental cultivation" (Luke 1900, 107).

The mission cause does seem to have sanctioned the obvious desires of at least some Victorian women to invest their energies outside home and family, in public endeavors that they themselves explicitly likened to the professional employments of men. Such women may not have wielded the emasculating power of Dickensian shrews, but they did utilize their gendered missionary piety to advance their position in relation to at least some of the men in their lives. Thus did Elizabeth Ann Wilshere, who as Mrs. Robert Barry Taylor would serve the London Missionary Society in British Guinea, go beyond the gentle moral suasion allowed her gender to the point of self-righteously instructing her older brother Edward (she was then ten years old) to "seek, above all things, to be conformed to the image of Christ . . . nothing short of perfection must be your standard. It is true that we can never attain unto it in this world; but from beholding it in the Lord our Righteousness, we shall go on from strength to strength" (Thompson 1841, 219). Mary Ann Chambers was similarly less than demure when she wrote her brother Hiram on the eve of her marriage to the Reverend James Coultart, with whom she would soon depart for his mission station in Jamaica:

> Should this, my dear brother, be the last letter I am permitted to write you, forget not that a sister, who loves you very tenderly, entreats you to consider it an unspeakable privilege to be called to convey the glad tidings of the gospel to perishing sinners. Labour, dear H., in your study; labour in the pulpit; and, above all, labour in prayer to God for the conversion of the souls of guilty men. Let your life be a continual sermon. O! forgive me, if I have gone too far: I cannot, I would not pretend to teach you; but I feel so anxious that every power may be spent in glorifying so kind, so gracious a God, and in extending his kingdom. (Thompson 1841, 14)[8]

The missionary project also provided British women with the institutional space in which to engage in activities traditionally the purview of men: to act collectively, handle money, organize meetings, and, most important, it seems to speak in public on behalf of the cause. It is not surprising in this regard that the initiative for separate women's organizations seems to have come from women themselves and to have been initially resisted by men who saw no need for the multiplication of further organizations. Male missionary advocates were reluctant no doubt to lose the unacknowledged labor that female collectors had long provided. Such fears appear to have informed the resistance of the London Missionary Society's Board of Directors to the formation of separate Ladies' Auxiliaries in 1870 (London Missionary Society Archives, Board Minutes,

1 February 1870); the board was forced to capitulate in 1875. Women, conversely, reasonably recognized that the presence of men in their organizations deprived them of both bureaucratic control and the social space in which to speak. This was in fact one of the costs of reintegrating male and female missionary operations in the opening decades of this century. When the Leeds Auxiliary of the London Missionary Society opened its committee to women in 1906, "the diffidence of lady members in joining in discussion at the meetings" was a concern raised by one of the first women members, who also complained about "the apparent hurrying of meetings to an early conclusion without full opportunity being given to each one to express their opinion" (Leeds Auxiliary Minute Books, 19 October 1906).

Missions were one of the few such spaces available in evangelical churches, whose nineteenth-century history was characterized by the silencing and exclusion of women from positions of influence (Valenze 1985; Anderson 1969; Juster 1994). This is the context in which we are to understand the repeatedly acknowledged importance that ladies' auxiliaries attached to having women speakers address their meetings. The enthusiasm of female audiences, gathered to hear a speaker of their own sex, suggests the sense of personal empowerment which these women derived from even vicarious involvement in this breach of separate spheres.[9] To be sure, gestures were almost always made to the latter's continuing purchase; female missionary enthusiasts testified over and over again to how difficult it is to bring themselves to speak. When opening a women's missionary bazaar in Newcastle, for example, Mrs. Arthur Coote admonished her audience that "it was time the ladies were coming forward to speak on such occasions as the present. (Applause.) She knew how difficult it was for ladies to do so, she knew how difficult she felt it at first, and she had great sympathy for those who tried (hear, hear, and laughter) but it was their duty to help in such good works. (Applause)" (*Newcastle Daily Chronicle,* 26 September 1883, 4). Indeed, at least one female missionary deputation who had never spoken in public before suffered a nervous breakdown under the strain (London Missionary Society Archives, District Secretaries Reports, 31 December 1899, Home/Odds, box 16, folder 1). But part of the transformative power of the missionary project was its sanctioning of transgressive behavior as religious exceptions to gender rules. It was, after all, the pious woman's "duty" to overcome her "natural diffidence" in order that she might better serve the mission cause; and scores of women embraced the opportunity to do so with open arms.[10]

The organizational, political, and interpersonal skills that evangelical women learned through their involvement in the mission cause would serve them in good stead in the political activities on behalf of women's causes in which many evangelical women became involved in the late nineteenth and early twentieth centuries. The connections between British women's political activities and their religious involvements, missionary or otherwise, have not received the scholarly attention that they warrant. The still widespread assumption among British historians is that religious and feminist causes attracted different "kinds" of women (which appears to have been the case with respect to many denominations; see, e.g. Predelli and Miller, in this volume). Peter Williams has argued, for example, that the "most able" British women, put off by the limits to women's autonomy in the persistently male-dominated mission field, gravitated toward secular and political involvements *instead* (1993, 59–65). That they might have considered a missionary career in the first place, however, suggests that many professional and/or feminist women were from evangelical backgrounds. And for the vast majority of British women even the limited opportunities of the foreign mission field far exceeded those available at home (Cunningham 1993, 93–94; Beidelman and Huber, both in this volume). The likelihood is that missionary work and political feminism were differing expressions of similar impulses that were at the very least precursors of political feminism and that women moved from one to the other application with relative ease. Evangelical women played an important role, for example, in Josephine Butler's campaign against the Contagious Diseases Act in the 1870s (a campaign that was, interestingly enough, also launched in India) (Walkowitz 1980; Burton 1994). The Ladies Committee of the London Missionary Society condemned the British government's "license of sin" in a resolution put before the society's Board of Directors on 7 June 1888. And at least some evangelical women were involved in the frontal assault on traditional gender roles waged by the women's suffrage movement.

Louisa Spicer Martindale (1839–1914) is an instructive example. As the eldest daughter of James Spicer, a successful London stationer and sister of Albert Spicer, chairman of the London Chamber of Commerce, and long-time treasurer of the London Missionary Society, Martindale dedicated herself at an early age "to the cause of women as well as to the cause of religion." In addition to serving as a director of the London Missionary Society, in which capacity she frequently hosted furloughed missionaries in her home, Martindale was a moving force in the Brighton Women's Liberal Federation from 1891 as well as being active in the National Union of Women's Suffrage Societies. Not only did Martindale not perceive any conflict between her missionary and feminist commitments; she saw them as positively related to one another. Martindale gave lectures to British women's groups on the condition of women in India, admonishing her audiences "that if they did not desire votes for their own sakes, they ought, at any rate, to work for them on behalf of their Indian sisters for whose life and freedom they had a deep responsibility" (1944, 43).

Race

But what kind of sisterhood was it? As Antoinette Burton has reminded us, British feminism emerged in an imperial context and was, as a result, "profoundly influenced by the imperial assumptions of its day" (1992, 138). The same can be said about the missionary movement more generally as well as its woman's wing. Indeed, I have tried to suggest that foreign missions were a vital if underexamined institutional link between the British feminist movement and developments in the empire. For those feminists who were also evangelicals—and Hilda Martindale was certainly not the only Victorian suffragist to be active in church or chapel affairs or at the very least to have been brought up in an evangelical family—this influence was felt first and perhaps primarily in the context of their involvement with foreign missions. And this missionary connection between British feminists and the empire helped to establish the imperial coordinates of Western feminism's conception of global sisterhood. Missionary tracts appealed explicitly to women's solidarity across "racial" divides by condemning the patriarchal abuse of heathen women in the colonies. Missionary literature abounded with "heart-rending details" of female infanticide, child marriage, forced prostitution, polygamy, widow burning, and the like, bound to move the "spirit of every reader . . . by the deplorable debasement to which females are reduced in the nations of the heathen" (Thompson 1841, lxxviii).

These observations expressed without doubt the genuine sympathy on the part of many missionaries and their metropolitan supporters for the plight of Third World women (Kirkwood 1993, 37). This was not necessarily compromised by British women's ability and willingness to make rhetorical use of heathen women's suffering in ways that benefited the cause of British women's "feminist" advance (Burton 1994). In my own research I found juxtaposed to a report on a recent missionary meeting, an exchange in the correspondence columns of the *Sheffield Daily Telegraph* in which "A Mere Man" who had criticized the Pankhursts was chastised by a "Globe Trotter" who invoked the missionary imperial indictment of heathen patriarchy to domestic feminist ends. "The crushing of womanhood" (which is how opposition to the suffragettes is herein framed) "has brought down nations" in the East, was her ominous warning. British audiences would be well advised, she went on, " to hear what the women [in Britain] have to say, before it comes too late" (*Sheffield Daily Telegraph,* 20 November 1907, 5).

There was, however, an ever-present and too often realized danger that British women would acquire a personal and self-interested investment in the unequal social power inscribed in the missionary gift. Missionary feminism rendered British women's religious piety as well as their political interests dependent upon their Hindu sisters' *needing* help—which is to say, their piety and their politics were predicated on the projected absence in the colonized woman and/or her society of some quality, strength or virtue which the missionary project implicitly ascribed to their English benefactresses (Burton 1994). The missionary-reforming "concern" for heathen women was thus inclined toward what could be an extremely critical assessment of their moral state; however much social conditions were held responsible, British missionary enthusiasts clearly viewed their colonized "sisters" as deservedly damned:

> Were these poor creatures, as their own masters suppose them to be, "without souls," humanity would plead for the alleviation of their present misery. But when we consider the short term of their earthly life but as an imaginary point in their eternal existence, and regard eternity as stamping perpetuity on that moral state in which heathenism leaves them and death finds them, we shall feel that their condition in the present life is far from being the most powerful argument for attempting their deliverance and renovation. (Thompson 1841, xvii–xviii)

The "gift" of missionary benevolence thereby validated colonial social hierarchies, for in the words of the last article cited, "Hindoo girls need a great deal of helping up before they can get even half as high as English girls are." Whatever benefits colonized women may have accrued from missionary interventions (Brownfoot 1990), British women almost invariably emphasized their own dominance in the missionary gift exchange. They were, at the very least, elder sisters or, more often, maternal substitutes who "cared" from the great distance of space, culture, and power inscribed in their discourse of moral character. This distance sometimes found expression in outright hostility. The LMS's *Quarterly News of Women's Work* frequently aired field missionaries' ostensibly "natural" feelings of disgust for the peoples among whom they worked. A Miss Rowe wrote from her new station in Canton, South China, that while "the natives were invariably civil and pleasant . . . I feel as Ezra and Nehemiah and Zerubbabel did in the midst of a people that had backslidden and forgotten their first love, and grown careless in every way." Although assuring her readers she will "stick to them until my heart breaks, or my body gives out," she concludes her communication with a bizarre fantasy:

> I do not say of them, as a missionary once declared of a certain African tribe, that a second deluge sweeping them off the face of the earth would be the best thing that could happen to them; but a fiery persecution would, I am convinced, be a fierce and salutary trial of the faith that is in them . . . That would test them, purge out the dross, and bring the pure gold to light. (LMS *Quarterly News of Women's Work,* October 1894, 110; October 1895, 107)

That relations of power were being imaginatively furthered by this missionary-feminist discourse is further suggested by the frequency with which British women's "maternal" concerns for heathendom found expression in orphan motifs. For one of the chief regrets expressed about the debilitating sufferings of heathen women is their consequence for indigenous home life. Such degraded women, it is presumed, could not contribute to their family's moral development; indeed, they are themselves the greatest brake on progress.

> We are over and over again told that it is the women who are the obstacles to Christianity and progress in every direction. A man is often very brave outside his own house, and talks of progress and reform on platforms and public halls, but when he enters his own house his courage evaporates; he cannot contend against the women of his household, especially as they would all unite to prevent any innovation affecting caste rules or customs. But let us educate the girls, let them be taught as their brothers and husbands are, and reform will become easy. (Lewis 1893, 16)

Heathen women were rendered incapable of being real mothers as well as virtuous wives by the abject conditions of their existence; "rare" were the mothers who "really had their children's best welfare at heart (LMS *Quarterly News of Women's Work,* January 1893, 19). "There was no home life in India, there being no mothers in the real sense of the term." So the Leeds Ladies Auxiliary of the London Missionary Society was informed by LMS missionary Miss Barclay in 1897 (*Leeds Mercury,* 30 September 1897, 6). Reverend H. W. Weatherhead, a CMS missionary in Uganda, complained along similar lines in the *Church Missionary Review* in December 1907:

> Family life in a Christian sense did not exist, and even among Christians the new ideas of parental responsibility are making but slow head-

> way. In close connexion with this is, of course, the lack of discipline and self-control and our boarding schools are largely for the purpose of remedying this defect. (Qtd. in Pirouet 1982, 237)

Heathen children's only hope was commonly believed to lie in their removal from their parents—in order "to 'be good'" heathen children "have to flee from their mothers" ("A Talk about Some Betsileo Girls [Whom We Are Trying to Save from Their Surroundings]," LMS *Quarterly News of Women's Work,* January 1894,15–17)—and be "adopted" by sympathetic missionary substitutes who alone could provide proper moral guidance. Among the regular duties of missionary wives as well as female missionaries was the establishment and supervision of institutions for housing those children in the surroundings who were identified as "orphans" (Cunningham 1993, 92). "If we could give to orphan girls, or to the daughters of our very poor members," argued one female missionary, "even a short experience of what a happy Christian home should be . . . we should do for them a work which we cannot do at present (Davies 1892, 108–9). And, as we have seen, even converted parents were not safe from missionary designs on the empire's children.

> It is very hard for those who have become Christians to throw off at once the influences which have bound them so long with a power more than human . . . We need to get the children of Christians away from their influences during the years in which impressions for good or evil are so easily made. If some of these tender years are spent in Christian boarding-schools, then the chains of fear which have bound the parents, and whose traces are still visible, can never in the same way, or to the same extent, influence the minds of their children. (Extract from a letter from Mrs. Bridle of Canton to the *Quarterly Paper of the Wesleyan Ladies' Auxiliary,* reprinted in the LMS *Quarterly News of Women's Work,* January 1894, 31)

That female missionaries and their British supporters might want to steal the children of their colonized sisters was a domesticated extension of the imperial state's displacement of indigenous political authority in the empire. Caring and control went hand in hand for imperial trustees, missionary sisters, and mothers of young children alike. For the genteel and respectable evangelical women of the mid-Victorian period, however, such "intimate" relations, however coercive, were only possible in relation to the more "civilized" heathen societies such as China and especially India (which is where the majority of female missionaries were sent in the nineteenth century). "Hindoo girls are not like negroes or Malays," argued

Jemima Luke, a prominent missionary advocate, when urging single women to acknowledge and accept their racial responsibility for the children of the foreign mission field. "Many of them are graceful, beautiful and affectionate, and as capable of intellectual development as English children" (1900, 153). These were the features that enabled the woman missionaries' "adoption" of Eastern children, an imagined community from which the reputedly more primitive peoples of Africa and the Pacific were, perhaps fortunately for their sakes, sheltered, at least for most of the nineteenth century.[11]

Class

The missionary compulsion to displace colonized parents was rendered all the more ironic by the dispatch with which their "own" children were repatriated away from their happy Christian homes, an irony that recalls Dickens's indictment of the "telescopic" character of missionary philanthropy by portraying evangelical characters' homes as chaotic and neglected. Evangelical churches did not, however, ignore the missionary home front. To the contrary, the "feminization" of foreign missionary discourse in the second half of the nineteenth century coincided with the evangelical public's mounting anxiety about the purported irreligion of the British working class. In the aftermath of the religious census of 1851 (the century's first and only religious census, which revealed that less than half the eligible population in Britain attended religious services on census Sunday) the number of missionary organizations targeting the British working classes mushroomed.

Historians are just beginning to acknowledge the connections between evangelicalism's home and foreign missionary operations. Valentine Cunningham's insightful observation that "as the great nineteenth-century missionary ventures became a more and more prominent features of British religious and social life, so the sense grew that Britain too was a mission-field in ways that simply mirrored the overseas ones" (1993, 100–101; see also Beidelman, in this volume) is an accurate assessment of the relationship between the home and foreign missions fields during the first two thirds of the nineteenth century (Thorne 1997). During the closing decades of the nineteenth century, however, foreign missions began to figure in home missionary operations in a more "social imperial" manner as well. The concept of social imperialism has been used most notably by German historians to describe the efforts of political elites in the Wilhelmine period to utilize foreign and especially colonial affairs as a means of defusing domestic social tensions (Eley 1987). British missionary organizations were also well aware of the domestic uses of their missionary imperialism, and they deployed imperial drama in a self-conscious effort to instill specific "social" virtues among subordinate groups at home. Beginning in the 1880s, these virtues were increasingly constructed against the mounting challenge of socialism. A social gospel had evolved out of the churches' efforts to incorporate the working classes and the poor, but contemporaries warned that the church must be on guard lest "Christ becomes the schoolmaster to lead them to Socialism, or to some other political activity." Foreign missions, it was believed, channeled working people's interest in the social question along healthy lines: "it is not to stir the emotions and leave the matter there," it was argued, "but to cultivate the will and let the impression of love be followed by the expression of service" (Anon. 1911, 10, 67). Foreign missionary allusions were increasingly deployed in support of the religious public's efforts to convince an increasingly organized and class-conscious working class to identify with and participate in the national community of organized religion. Though targets of (home) missionary outreach themselves, working people were simultaneously invited to join their middle-class superiors in foreign missionary benevolence on ostensibly equal terms. This, at any rate, was the gist of foreign missionary propaganda, much of which explicitly targeted working-class women. In fact, the vast majority of working-class church and chapel goers were women and, to an even greater degree, their children (Chadwick 1986, 163, 171–73; Laqueur 1976).

An underlying theme in missionary literature had to do with the amelioration of the sorts of un-Christian social resentments that threatened to destabilize the religious as well as national community. Such resentments were countered not only by the juxtaposition of the benefits enjoyed by British women to the horrific treatment endured by their colonized counterparts but also by allusions to the conciliatory ideology of cross-class sisterhood espoused by the latter's foreign missionary benefactors. I will close with an extended description of a missionary pamphlet, "Mrs. Pickett's Missionary Box," which typifies the missionary-imperial-feminist prescription for the resolution of class tensions in British society (Eddy n.d.). The narrator, Mrs. Pickett, runs a boarding house and speaks in a broad ungrammatical dialect, which suggests she is from a working-class or lower-middle-class background. Certainly, at the outset of the story she was pointedly resentful of the women missionary activists in her community, who are from obviously middle-class backgrounds. The story opens with Mrs. Pickett recalling her irritation when invited to a missionary meeting by her young niece Mary:

> *I'd got to have hard feelings against every on't looked's as if they got along easier'n me, an' I'd most give up going to church at all . . . I says*

> [*to Mary*], *"Pretty doin's 't would be for me to go traipsin' off to meetin's an' leave the i'nin' an' the cookin', an' sit alongside o' Lawyer Stapleton's wife, Learnin' about—what? Folks had better stay at home an' see to their work," says I.*

The contrast between the piously humble churchgoing niece and her bitterly hard-hearted aunt is marked. Mary went to the meeting alone but returned with a missionary box for her aunt, inscribed "What shall I render unto the Lord for all His benefits to me?" Mrs. Pickett harumphs that she hasn't any benefits to spare the heathens but later asks what "them geese" talked about at the meeting. Mary proceeds to describe the plight of widows in India, to which her aunt responds:

> *"Well, if I be a widder, I'm thankful I'm where I kin earn my own livin', an' no thanks to nobody, an' no one to interfere!" Then Mary she laughed and said that was my fust benefit. Well, that sorter tickled me, for I thought a woman must be pretty hard up for benefits when she had to go clear off to Injy to find them . . . An' next meetin', Mary she told me about Japan, an' I thought about that till I put in another because I warn't a jap.*

The final step in Mrs. Pickett's conversion to the missionary cause confronted Mrs. Pickett's social resentments with the plight of heathendom and her love for her family:

> *An' one day—I'll never forget that day . . . she was a'tellin' me about Turkey, an' she told how some missionaries heard a little girl sayin' how the smallest thing in all the world warn't any smaller than the joy of her father when she war born. Them words went right through me. I was standing over the i'nin' board, an' Mary was opposite to me, but all of a sudden, instead of her, I seemed to see my husband's face, that had been dead ten year, an' him a-leanin' down over our little baby, that only lived two weeks, the only one I ever had. Seemed to me I couldn't get over it, when that baby died. An' I seemed to see my husband smilin' down at it, an' it lyin' there, all soft and white—she was a white little baby, such a pretty baby!—an' before I knew it, I was droppin' tears all over the starched clothes, an' I turned round an' went an' put another penny in that box, for the look on my husband's face when he held her that time . . . An' before I went to bed I went out in the dinin' room, an' I put in a little bright threepenny-piece for my baby, because I couldn't bear to count her jest like everythin' else, and I found myself crying because I hadn't enough money jest then to spare anythin' bigger.*

That night Mrs. Pickett dreamed about her mother and father and their love for her and woke up saying, "Oh Lord, I am a wicked, ungrateful woman!" From then on she couldn't find enough pennies with which to count all her blessings, until the box was full and she decided to take it to the missionary meeting herself. Where, of course, "there was singing' an' everythin', jest as there always is, only it was all new to me, an' everyone seemed as glad to see me as if I'd been as rich as any of 'em." Mrs. Pickett testified before all to her changed heart, whereupon the ladies put their arms around one another, cried, and praised God.

Truly was it claimed that the missionary project was indeed "a great and imperial work" (London Missionary Society Archives, Board Minutes, 23 January 1906). Not only would the empire be the richer for the education of future Mrs. Picketts into the mothers of a missionary-imperial "race" (Davin 1978). Such international benefits of missionary agitation were also intimately linked to the progressive goals of political conciliation and social order on the home front.

The primary mechanism through which domestic social benefits were believed to result from foreign missionary expenditure was in the creation of a community of missionary philanthropists among the socially diverse constituencies of organized religion. Audiences of poor and working women were not only admonished to forgive the wealth and admire the philanthropy of their social and political superiors who dominated the women's missionary movement. They were also invited to join this prestigious community of philanthropists by supporting missions themselves.

Here as elsewhere, however, missionary feminist rhetoric and women's missionary practice were at odds. Those middle-class women who were willing to put their social respectability at risk in feminist efforts to renegotiate gender relations proved less adventurous in their interactions with poor and working women. The sort of intimate physical contact across class lines experienced by Mrs. Pickett was precluded in most women's auxiliaries by the imposition of membership dues sufficiently high to exclude working-class women. Evangelical churches were, furthermore, effectively segregated along class lines throughout the nineteenth century; chapel missionary auxiliaries, therefore, were largely homogeneous in social terms. And, where cross-class contacts did occur, working-class women were perpetually reminded of their subordinate status, in circumstances that, if they did not shake their faith in God, would certainly have removed any illusions concerning the sincerity of middle-class women's professions of "sisterhood" (Thorne forthcoming, chaps. 5 and 6). The relations of domination and subordination inscribed upon the missionary project through which so many middle-class women sought escape from their "frivolous" private lives cast their shadow across these missionary efforts to forge gender solidarity across class as well as racial divides, constituting a missionary legacy from which Western feminism still suffers.

Missionary Imperial Feminism

It is tempting to dismiss the authoritarian and exclusivist trajectory of missionary imperial feminism as simply the unfortunate residue of dominant ideologies for which dominated British women were not themselves responsible. Certainly, imperialism and the racial arrogance that it spawned predated women's arrival on the colonial or missionary scene, where "women were more frequently the subjected territory across which the boundaries of nationhood were marked out than active participants in the construction of nations" (Hall et al. 1993, 162). At the same time, however, Hall and others remind us that imperialism provided white women in Britain with unprecedented opportunities for negotiating the terms of their own subordination, negotiations that gave these missionary feminists a direct and positive interest in maintaining middle class hegemony, white supremacy, and the imperial status quo.

The entire edifice of missionary "feminism"—the employment opportunities, the valorization of (British) women's skills and virtues, the institutional and social space for self-assertion, collective action, and aggressive challenging of male prerogatives—rested on the existence of a degraded female Other in the colonies and at home. The missionary rationale for women's escape from the separate sphere, in other words, actively depended on the subordination of their heathen sisters. It was perhaps for this reason that British women missionaries and their sponsoring organizations rejected the applications of non-European women to become missionaries themselves. The application of one such lady born in Bombay "with some native blood in her" was forwarded to the LMS Ladies Committee in 1876 by Reverend Alexander of Manchester; in refusing her offer, the committee stipulated that it sends out "only English ladies of thorough English education at present" (London Missionary Society Archives, Ladies Committee, 8 March 1876). The missionary presumption that the best means of reaching female and male heathens alike was by displaying examples of pure Christian character and lifeways convinced most "white" missionaries that their physical presence was indispensable. As one medical missionary modestly described her own impact on her heathen observers, "for a foreign lady, who is so scrupulously clean in her own person and surroundings, to be willing to cleanse and bind up the loathsome sores of the dirtiest of Chinese women, without any other expression but that of tender sympathy, is surely one of the most practical lessons in Christianity which we can set before the Chinese" (Pearson 1892, 69). No indigenous woman could substitute for the European woman's example; indeed, there is a persistent undercurrent of resentful criticism in this literature of converts' pretensions to the contrary.

The question we should be asking then is not whether British women who supported missions were complicit in colonial or class oppression or resistant to patriarchy but, rather, as Antoinette Burton has reminded us so forcefully, why and how they were both and at the same time. The terms on which missionary-imperial feminism chose to challenge the subordination of the middle-class women who promoted it did not, in short, require trans-class any more than it did trans-race sisterhood. To the contrary, the construction of middle-class women's professional capacities as a missionary vocation may well have precluded it.

NOTES

1. Kenneth Scott Latourette (1937–45) devoted three of the seven volumes of his *History of the Expansion of Christianity* to the nineteenth century, which he refers to as "the great century" of Christian mission.

2. High Church missionary outreach predates the 1790s. The Society for the Promotion of Christian Knowledge was founded in 1699; the Society for the Propagation of the Gospel in Foreign Parts was founded in 1701. But, by comparison to the missionary exertions of the next century, their efforts were "sporadic and haphazard," and they were primarily concerned to minister to the European population in the colonies. It was not until the 1790s that the British Protestants began focusing their missionary energies primarily on the indigenous peoples of the "heathen" world, thanks in large part to evangelical initiative.

3. Women were briefly allowed to minister during the tumultuous 1790s and 1800s, but they were quickly silenced, their presence defining social marginality and cultural chaos (Valenze 1985).

4. Zenanas were the rooms to which high-caste Hindu women were secluded from contact with men outside their immediate family. The word derives from the Persian *zan,* which means "woman" (Stanley 1992, 228 n. 90).

5. According to M. Louise Pirouet (1981), the CMS recruited only 87 women as against 902 men between 1804 and 1880. Between 1880 and 1900, however, the CMS recruited 125 women as against 197. When the active presence of missionary wives is factored in, the female presence in the foreign field is seen to be predominant. My own findings with regard to the London Missionary Society are much the same. The LMS hired only 3 women missionaries prior to 1875 (Cunningham 1993, 91). By the 1890s, however, women were here too approaching if not exceeding parity. Between 1890 and 1894, for example, the London Missionary Society dispatched almost as many women (50) as men (67) to the field and was apparently receiving far more applications from women than from men (London Missionary Society Archives, Board minutes, 23 February 1892). Women far out-

numbered men at the society's missionary summer schools held in 1911, much to the organizers' disappointment (London Missionary Society Archives, Funds and Agency Committee minutes, 1911). The society's anxiety about the preponderance of women in its ranks is evident in the proposal of a publication entitled "Missions: A Man's Job," by the London Missionary Society's Literature Committee, 27 June 1916. (See also Williams 1993).

6. Although Peter Williams suggests that Hudson Taylor's China Inland Mission was exceptional in this regard (1993, 46–50).

7. For similar commentaries on maternalist rationales for German women's missionary as well as political activism, see the essays by Huber and Lutkehaus in this volume.

8. The Coultarts left for Jamaica on 14 March 1817; Mrs. Coultart died of fever within five months. Hiram Chambers, Mary Ann's brother, served in India with the London Missionary Society from 1820 until his death, in 1826.

9. Some ministers refused to allow such "innovations" within their chapel (see London Missionary Society Archives, Home/Odds/box 9/folder 2/December 1889).

10. Such as one Mrs. Halley, an Australian woman who, after visiting her missionary daughter in China, became so excited about the mission cause "as to enable her to overcome her nervousness in speaking; and, since her return to Melbourne, she has spent a great deal of her time in addressing ladies' meetings, and telling of China's need for more workers" (Hamer 1893, 120).

11. The vast majority of female missionaries dispatched by British missionary organizations during the nineteenth century were sent to the more "civilized" mission fields of China and India, and this was particularly true of the London Missionary Society, on which my research focuses (Langmore 1989, 164).

REFERENCES

Anderson, Olive. 1969. Women Preachers in Mid-Victorian Britain: Some Reflexions on Feminism, Popular Religion and Social Change. *Historical Journal* 12, no. 3: 467–84.

Anon. 1831. *Appeal of the Society for Promoting Female Education in China, India and the East.* MS. London: British Library.

Anon. 1899. *"Is It Nothing to You?" A Record of Work among Women in Connection with the London Missionary Society.* MS. London: British Library.

Anon. 1911. *The Challenge of the Modern Situation.* London Missionary Society, now Council for World Mission, Archives. School of Oriental and African Studies, London.

Brantlinger, Patrick. 1986. Victorians and Africans: The Genealogy of the Myth of the Dark Continent. In *"Race," Writing and Difference,* ed. Henry Louis Gates Jr., 184–22. Chicago: University of Chicago Press.

Brontë, Charlotte. [1847] 1981. *Jane Eyre.* New York: Bantam Classic. Reprint of 3d ed., London: Smith, Cornhill.

Brown, Miss. 1879. "Bungar," the Little Hindoo Girl. *Juvenile Missionary Magazine of the London Missionary Society.* February.

Brownfoot, Janice N. 1990. Sisters under the Skin: Imperialism and the Emancipation of Women in Malaya, c. 1891–1941. *Making Imperial Mentalities: Socialisation and British Imperialism,* 46–73. Manchester: University of Manchester Press.

Burton, Antoinette. 1992. The White Woman's Burden: British Feminists and "The Indian Woman," 1865–1915. In *Western Women and Imperialism: Complicity and Resistance,* ed. Nupur Chaudhuri and Margaret Strobel, 137–57. Bloomington: Indiana University Press.

———. 1994. *Burdens of History: British Feminists, Indian Women, and Imperial Culture, 1854–1914.* Chapel Hill: University of North Carolina Press.

Carlyle, Thomas. 1843. *Past and Present.* London.

Carr, Joseph. 1914. The Story of the Sheffield Auxiliary to the London Missionary Society, now Council for World Mission, Archives, Pam. 78, Blue Box 22A. School of Oriental and African Studies, London.

Chadwick, Rosemary. 1986. Church and People in Bradford and District, 1880–1914: The Protestant Churches in an Urban Industrial Environment. Ph.D. diss., Oxford University.

Comaroff, Jean, and John Comaroff. 1991. *Of Revelation and Revolution: Christianity, Colonialism, and Consciousness in South Africa,* vol. 1. Chicago: University of Chicago Press.

Cunningham, Valentine. 1993. "God and Nature Intended You for a Missionary's Wife": Mary Hill, Jane Eyre and Other Missionary Women in the 1840s. In *Women and Missions: Past and Present,* ed. Fiona Bowie, Deborah Kirkwood, and Shirley Ardener, 85–108. Oxford: Berg.

Davidoff, Leonore, and Catherine Hall. 1987. *Family Fortunes: Men and Women of the English Middle Class, 1780–1850.* Chicago: University of Chicago Press.

Davies, Helen. 1892. Day School Work in Hong Kong. *Quarterly News of Women's Work* (October [London Missionary Society]): 108–9.

Davin, Anna. 1978. Imperialism and Motherhood. *History Workshop* 5:9–65.

Dickens, Charles. [1852–53] 1985. *Bleak House.* London: Penguin Classics.

———. 1848. The Niger Expedition. In *Miscellaneous Papers,* vol. 1. London: Chapman and Hall.

Eddy, Miss. N.d. "Mrs. Pickett's Missionary Box." Lamp Series, no. 4, London Missionary Society, now Council for World Mission Archives, Pamphlet Collection. School of Oriental and African Studies, London.

Eley, Geoff. 1987. Defining Social Imperialism: Use and Abuse of an Idea. *Social History* 3:265–90.

Eliot, George. [1871–72] 1956. *Middlemarch: A Study of Provincial Life.* Boston: Houghton Mifflin.

Findlay, G. G., and W. W. Holdsworth. 1921. *The History of the Wesleyan Methodist Missionary Society,* vol. 1. London: Epworth Press.

Hall, Catherine. 1989. The Economy of Intellectual Prestige: Thomas Carlyle, John Stuart Mill and the Case of Governor Eyre. *Cultural Critique* 12 (spring): 167–96.

———. 1992. *White, Male, and Middle Class: Explorations in Feminism and History.* New York: Routledge.

Hall, Catherine, Jane Lewis, Keith McClelland, and Jane Rendall. 1993. Introduction to "Gender, Nationalisms and National Identities," a special issue of *Gender and History* 5, no. 2: 159–63.

Hamer, Mrs. 1893. Our Australian Auxiliary. *Quarterly News of Women's Work* (October [London Missionary Society]): 118–21.

Hill, Patricia R. 1985. *The World Their Household: The American Woman's Foreign Mission Movement and Cultural Transformation, 1870–1920.* Ann Arbor: University of Michigan Press.

Juster, Susan. 1994. *Disorderly Women: Sexuality, Politics and Evangelicalism in Revolutionary New England.* Ithaca: Cornell University Press.

Kirkwood, Deborah. 1993. Protestant Missionary Women: Wives and Spinsters. In *Women and Missions: Past and Present,* ed. Fiona Bowie, Deborah Kirkwood, and Shirley Ardener, 23–42. Oxford: Berg.

Langmore, Diane. 1989. *Missionary Lives: Papua, 1874–1914.* Center for Pacific Island Studies, Pacific Monograph Series, no. 6. Honolulu: University of Hawaii Press.

Laqueur, Thomas Walter. 1976. *Religion and Respectability: Sunday Schools and Working Class Culture, 1780–1850.* New Haven: Yale University Press.

Latourette, Kenneth Scott. 1937–45. *The History of the Expansion of Christianity.* New York: Harper and Brothers.

Leeds Auxiliary Minute Books. London Missionary Society Auxiliary Records. Dr. Williams Library, London.

Lewis, Annie M. 1893. Women's Work in Bellary. *Quarterly News of Women's Work.* January. London Missionary Society (LMS).

London Missionary Society (LMS). Archives. Council for World Mission Archives, School of Oriental and African Studies.

———. Assorted years. *Chronicle of the London Missionary Society.*

———. Assorted years. *Juvenile Missionary Intelligencer.*

———. Assorted years. *Quarterly News of Women's Work.*

Lovett, Richard. 1899. *The History of the London Missionary Society, 1795–1895.* 2 vols. London: Oxford University Press.

Luke, Jemima. 1900. *Early Years of My Life.* London: Hodder and Stoughton.

Mandler, Peter. 1990. Introduction to *The Uses of Charity: The Poor on Relief in the Nineteenth-Century Metropolis,* ed. Peter Mandler, 1–29. Philadelphia: University of Pennsylvania Press.

Martindale, Hilda. 1944. *From One Generation to Another, 1839–1944: A Book of Memoirs.* London: Allen and Unwin.

Midgley, Clare. 1992. *Women against Slavery: The British Campaigns, 1780–1870.* London: Routledge.

Morison, John. 1844. *The Fathers and Founders of the London Missionary Society.* London: Fisher, Son, and Co.

Pearson, Annie. 1892. Work among the Native Women in Peking. *Quarterly News of Women's Work* (July [LMS]).

Pirouet, M. Louise. 1982. Women Missionaries of the Church Missionary Society in Uganda, 1896–1920. In *Missionary Ideologies in the Imperialist Era: 1880–1920,* ed. Torben Christensen and William R. Hutchinson, 231–40. Denmark: Aros.

Poovey, Mary. 1988. *Uneven Developments. The Ideological Work of Gender in Mid-Victorian England.* Chicago: University of Chicago Press.

Pope, Norris. 1978. *Dickens and Charity.* New York: Columbia University Press.

Prochaska, F. K. 1980. *Women and Philanthropy in Nineteenth-Century England.* Oxford: Clarendon Press.

Segal, Lynne. 1990. *Slow Motion: Changing Masculinities, Changing Men.* New Brunswick, N.J.: Rutgers University Press.

Smith, Faith Lois. 1995. J. J. Thomas and Caribbean Intellectual Life in the Nineteenth Century. Ph.D. diss., Duke University.

Stanley, Brian. 1979. Home Support for Overseas Missions in Early Victorian England, c. 1838–1873. Ph.D. diss., Cambridge University.

———. 1992. *The History of the Baptist Missionary Society, 1792–1992.* Edinburgh: T and T Clark.

Stock, Eugene. 1899. *The History of the Church Missionary Society,* vol. 1. London: Church Missionary Society.

Thackeray, William. 1950 [1847]. *Vanity Fair.* New York: Random House, Modern Library.

Thompson, Jemima. 1841. *Memoirs of British Female Missionaries: With a Survey of the Condition of Women in Heathen Countries and Also a Preliminary Essay on the Importance of Female Agency in Evangelizing Pagan Nations.* London: William Smith.

Thorne, Susan. 1997. "The Conversion of Englishmen and the Conversion of the World Inseparable": Missionary Imperialism and the Language of Class in Early Industrial Britain. In *Tensions of Empire: Colonial Cultures in a Bourgeois World,* ed. Frederick Cooper and Ann Laura Stoler, 238–62. Berkeley: University of California Press.

———. Forthcoming. *Congregational Missions and the Making of an Imperial Culture in Nineteenth-Century England.* Stanford: Stanford University Press.

Valenze, Deborah. 1985. *Prophetic Sons and Daughters: Female Preaching and Popular Religion in Industrial England.* Princeton, N.J.: Princeton University Press.

Vicinus, Martha. 1985. *Independent Women: Work and Community for Single Women, 1850–1920.* Chicago: University of Chicago Press.

Walkowitz, Judith. 1980. *Prostitution and Victorian Society: Women, Class and the State.* Cambridge: Cambridge University Press.

Williams, Peter. 1993. "The Missing Link": The Recruitment of Women Missionaries in Some English Evangelical Missionary Societies in the Nineteenth Century. In *Women and Missions: Past and Present,* ed. Fiona Bowie, Deborah Kirkwood, and Shirley Ardener, 43–69. Oxford: Berg.

Piety and Patriarchy: Contested Gender Regimes in Nineteenth-Century Evangelical Missions

Line Nyhagen Predelli and Jon Miller

A special perspective on religion and gender is provided by the evangelical missionary movement of the nineteenth and early twentieth centuries. Commerce and colonial expansion opened vast areas of the world to Western influence, and creating missions to send women and men out into that "heathen darkness" enjoyed widespread popularity in the churches of Europe and North America. Piety and patriarchy were interwoven principles in the governance of these organizations. Indeed, if only missionary rhetoric were examined, a case could be made that the individuals whose shared religious commitment sustained this social movement simply absorbed and faithfully reproduced a collection of traditional "biblical" understandings about gender.

Reality is more complicated. Protestant missions have not been simply patriarchal or patriarchal in simple ways. Even where there is a strong public expression of consensus about the "proper spheres" for men and women, the underlying understandings are emergent social accomplishments, which means that they are created and enacted by men and women who must live together in the daily round of practical activities.[1] In this continuing process the accumulation of cultural tradition and public prescriptions concerning authority and power can marginalize a category of people—in the usual case, women—but understandings about gender evolve, necessarily, as circumstances and pragmatic realities change. Moreover, the agile evasions, smart resistance, and shrewd politics of marginalized individuals and groups can also produce mutations in established structures of control. Missions are not free of these dynamics. However doctrinaire they may have tried to be, their attempts to preserve patriarchal domination have always been limited by the material indispensability of women's participation and by the resulting day-to-day necessity of absorbing women's energy and adjusting to their presence.[2] It is our thesis that the historical record of these organizations will be marked by contest and change as often as by acceptance and accommodation. It is not, in other words, a record of unanswered male dominion.

Our contribution to the understanding of these gender confrontations is based on research in the archival records of the Basel Mission, a Pietist organization based in Basel, Switzerland, and on the history of the Norwegian Missionary Society (NMS), the overseas evangelical arm of the established Lutheran Church in Norway. Both of these organizations had mission stations in many areas of the world in the 1800s, and both remain active and influential in missionary circles today. In Basel our research has focused on the mission's involvement in the West African country of Ghana (formerly the Gold Coast), where the ties established over a century and a half ago continue in the present (see Miller 1994). We will offer several examples of the give-and-take of gender relations in this organization, both at home and in Africa. The exceptions to simple patriarchy that we discovered involved individual women and men who either seized or were given leeway to cross the boundaries of prescribed rules of gendered behavior.

Our research on the Norwegian Missionary Society concentrates on the ways in which the large number of women's local missionary associations in the nineteenth and early twentieth centuries negotiated their relationship with the NMS and how the agenda of these religiously committed women at one point became interwoven with that of the secular women's movement in Norway.[3] In contrast to the Basel Mission, where isolated individuals challenged established expectations with little impact on the overall structure, the NMS case illustrates how the organizational need for women's resources and the articulation of women's collective demands effectively changed the reigning gender regime.

The nineteenth-century Protestant missionary movement in which these two organizations participated was certainly male dominated in the sense of organizational control, but it is inaccurate to describe it as a movement in which the labor of men was ever predominant, let alone sufficient. Whatever their founders may have intended, missions such as these soon learned that they must rely heavily on the energy and personal commitments of women in all that they did. Hunter writes of the "feminization of the mission force" that took place in the United States in the late nineteenth century (1984, 14; see also Hill 1985, 2), and Brouwer, looking at Canada, has found that, "well before the turn of the century, single women missionaries and missionary wives outnumbered their male colleagues in many overseas fields" (1990, 5; see also Mitchison 1977, 58). In Great Britain, too, the women's missionary movement was the largest social movement of women in the nineteenth century (see Thorne, in this volume; Williams 1993). A parallel development took place in Norway, where the women's missionary movement came to be the mainstay of the Norwegian Missionary Society, whether measured by the number of participants, the coordination of local mission support groups, or the raising of money for missionary projects at home and abroad (Tjelle 1990, 105–8; Jørgensen 1992, 78–79).

The demographic picture that emerges from this is plain: women and men shared the work of the missionary movement throughout all of its phases. Nevertheless, we lack a satisfactory answer to this key question: In what precise ways, with what intentions, and with what lasting consequences, at home and abroad, have missions absorbed the energies of women and men? The stereotype is that patriarchal relations were simply reproduced inside the missions because the societies from which missions emerged were patriarchal in legal form and social practice. Like many stereotypes, however, the grain of wisdom in this one leads to premature closure if not examined critically. To begin with, the word *patriarchy* is itself ideologically loaded and problematic. It is unavoidable in the historical discussion of missions, not least because missions have used it to describe themselves. But in some usage the term conjures up unrealistically static and deterministic structures of oppression in which men are omnipotent and women are fundamentally and irretrievably subjugated. We do not accept this description because it diverts attention from the active agency used by women to advance and protect their own interests.

On one level, certainly, the early missionary movement embraced conservative views of women's participation in public life (see Beidelman, in this volume). On another level, however, it provided opportunities, as Peter Williams (1993), among others, has observed, for women to participate in regions of civil society that were otherwise beyond their reach. Women were able to acquire practical training and administrative skills, and in this way many of them gained a measure of actual independence from the culturally prescribed roles of mother and wife. Brouwer has found that Canadian Presbyterian women missionaries in India "developed a desire for power and authority not only in their dealings with converts and mission employees but also in their relationships with their male co-workers" (1990, 160). Bowie also has emphasized the attraction of "opportunities for independent action and challenges which would stretch the woman's missionary abilities" (1993, 6). Even though the mobilization of their energy in this way was often an unanticipated development, it affected the general status of women in society, by "play[ing a part] in changing cultural assumptions about what women can accomplish" (Hill 1985, acknowledgment). Because the missionary movement was such a visible one, changes that began within it left marks on the division of labor and relations between women and men in the family, in the churches, in other kinds of voluntary organizations, and in the larger societies in which missions originated as well as those in which they pursued their evangelical goals.

Given that the people who carried the missionary movement forward have often figured significantly in the changing of traditional relations between women and men in society, the word *patriarchy* must be used advisedly to describe the organizations in which they worked together. The term must be framed in a way that allows for paradox, so that both liberating and oppressive forces can be investigated. A conceptual connection that serves this purpose is to merge the idea of patriarchy with the notion of *gender regime,* which we have taken from Connell (1987) and which we find useful for describing the changing and paradoxical nature of the positions of women and men in religious missions. Connell employs this term to delineate "a structural inventory of a particular institution" (1987, 98–99). It is a concept that recognizes variations according to the specific institutional context, and it does not carry the ideological weight of the more deterministic concept of "patriarchy." What emerged over time in the missions we have examined were *contested gender regimes* or, perhaps more realistically in nineteenth-century contexts, *contested patriarchies.* In the latter hybrid the retention of *patriarchies* keeps the meaning close to the usage of that earlier time, but *contested* signals that, then even as now, the dominant arrangements were challenged directly or indirectly, in general or in particular ways, and on a continuous basis, by those participants with the least power.[4]

To be sure, recognizing contest and resistance is not sufficient for concluding that the missionary movement was, as such, a feminist movement or that the women who took part in it were guided by feminist concerns. That question has not been settled. Implied in the notion of feminism is an open commitment to changing the material and ideological structures of gender oppression, with a view to raising the status of women. In order to assess whether or not the nineteenth-century women's missionary movement had links to feminist ideals, we should use a standard of evaluation proper to the time and place of our inquiry. Susan Thorne's straightforward definition of feminism as "those activities which challenged . . . women's confinement to a separate and essentially private social sphere" is a useful point of departure (Thorne, in this volume).[5] In order to determine whether specific missions and missionary women fit this definition, we must examine the discourse and actual behavior of the organizations and their members.

In this connection Alice Hageman has asserted that "Protestant women interested in missions in the latter half of the nineteenth century did not ally themselves with those others of their time struggling for the rights of women in the United States" (1974, 174). Beaver, on the other hand, did not hesitate to call the Women's Foreign Mission Movement, which consisted of American Protestant women, "the first feminist movement in North America." He has also insisted that the mission movement "stimulated the rise of various other streams in the nineteenth-century struggle for women's rights and freedom" (1980, 11). Beaver's views have been challenged (most directly by Hill 1984, 194), but the possibility of the feminist implications of the women's missionary movement has also been advanced by Grimshaw (1983, 494) and, again, by Susan Thorne (in this volume), who makes a case for a direct link between the women's missionary movement and the feminist movement in Britain.[6]

That women in missions, like those in secular society, have sought and found strategies for resisting entrenched gender relationships, however, does not imply that they have had free rein for the use of their energy and creativity. To the contrary, missions—including the ones we describe here—have typically placed constraints on women's activities that have far exceeded those placed on men, and they have often confined women's activities to a rather limited sphere (see Haas 1994; Williams 1993; Brouwer 1990; Grimshaw 1989; and Hunter 1984). While it is true that women taking active part in the missionary movement have sometimes defined their own terms of participation, more often they have been limited by factors rooted in cultural prescriptions and in the rules and modes of organization present at a particular time and place. Some missions have been an outlet for creative, bright, and independent women and thus have attracted such individuals, while in others submissive and rule-bound women have been comfortable with confining hierarchical structures. In the latter regard consider Peter Williams's observation (1993, 66) that Protestant missions were too male-dominated to be able to attract "the most privileged, able, ambitious, and liberated women of the period" and Wendy Mitchison's assertion (1977, 70) that Presbyterian women in Canada, who were dependent on men for the administration of their affairs, were for some time attracted to the missionary society by the fact that they themselves did not have to be in charge.

In short, women have approached missions with a variety of expectations and have had ambiguous experiences of liberation and constraint, opportunity and restriction, in those organizations. Like men, they have joined missions not only for reasons of altruism, faith, and sense of divine calling but also under the influence of a wide array of other motivations. These range from family tradition, marriage, spinsterhood, and family death to economic advantages, social mobility, and the spirit of heroism, adventure, and independence (see Hunter 1984; Brouwer 1990; and Gagan 1992). Whatever their openly expressed motivations,[7] it is clear that women have used missionary work in many ways, not just as an outlet for their specifically religious zeal, energy, and creativity but also as the means to fulfill themselves in much broader ways by putting their own abilities to work. Moreover, we must look beyond the immediate personal experiences of individuals to ask about the intended and unintended implications of their activities, seen in the aggregate, for their societies at large. And, finally, questions about gender relations within missionary organizations and within their originating societies must at some point give way to questions about how missionaries have altered the lives of women and men in the cultures that were the objects of their evangelical zeal. Whatever mission work meant for the missionaries themselves, they generally agreed that Christianity was the proper vehicle for improving the conditions of "heathen" women. Helen Barrett Montgomery, for example, saw the task of the women's missionary movement as one of implementing "an organized campaign for oppressed womanhood and childhood in non-Christian lands" (1910, 21), and Shirley Garrett (1982) talks about a "missionary feminist ideology," which had profound effects on the status of native women in the missionary field.[8] To address questions at any of these levels—individual, organizational, or societal (at home and abroad)—requires careful case studies that include missions of various persuasions active in a variety of cultural contexts.

We offer our research on the Basel Mission and the Norwegian Missionary Society as a contribution to that larger effort. Whether these partial histories suggest a progressive evolution toward equity in gender relations in missionary organizations is a question about which readers can reasonably disagree (just as present-day members of both missions do). A definitive judgment on that issue remains just beyond our grasp. What is indisputable, however, is that the initiatives of women have from time to time profoundly changed the rhythm of interaction in both of these organizations.

Gender Relationships in the Basel Mission

In 1785 a circle of prominent Württemberg Pietists came together in Basel, Switzerland, to create a Bible study group known as the German Society for Christianity,[9] which in turn created the Basel Mission in 1815. The leadership of both the society and the mission came from the economic, political, and religious elites of the Basel region and from the circle of prominent Pietist theologians in Germany. In contrast to the men in the leadership, who referred to themselves quite openly as a "patriarchal" and "aristocratic" group, the ordinary male missionaries—that is, the ones who were trained in the mission seminary and posted abroad to Russia, Persia, India, China, and Africa—came disproportionately from farm and craft families in the villages and small towns of Württemberg and German-speaking Switzerland. The leaders and the male rank and file of the mission thus shared a common culture but occupied widely different positions in the social hierarchies of the time. What bound them to one another was the intensity of their shared identification with the Pietist religious movement.

Women were not included in seminary training and ordination, and those single women and wives who became involved in the mission community abroad were, as we shall see, from a slightly higher social level than the ordinary male missionaries. The exclusion of women from ordination is typical of the period covered by the investigation, which is roughly the century preceding World War I. Whenever there was talk in the mission of "bringing the Gospel to the heathen," it was clear that the carriers of the "good word" were men. With one prominent exception, which will be discussed later, the leadership of the organization during the same interval was resolutely and self-consciously monopolized by men.

There was thus little ambiguity in the expressed norms governing the positions of women and men, either in the broad cultural traditions of southern Germany and German-speaking Switzerland or in the narrower collection of religious beliefs that provided the evangelical impetus for the Basel Mission. The mission was defined as a male enterprise, dominated by fatherly (*väterliche*) authority at the center, with the expectation that male missionaries would duplicate that authority in the convert communities they established abroad. If reality could be read directly from shared cultural prescriptions and stated organizational policy in any simple way, straightforward biblical "patriarchy," in spirit and in fact, should have ruled in the Basel Mission with little effective challenge. Strategic departures from that straightforward cultural theme, however, were already evident in the period of the mission's creation.

The Promise and the Threat of Effective Female Leadership

When they established the mission in 1815, the founders lodged its leadership in a self-perpetuating circle of men, called "the Committee," that usually had about twelve, sometimes fewer, members. Only one woman, Juliane von Krüdener, was intimately involved in the founding and early financial support of the mission. Frau von Krüdener (as she is almost always referred to in the archival record), widow of a Russian diplomat, came from an aristocratic Russian family and was thought to be a confidant of Czar Alexander I. She converted from Russian Orthodoxy to Protestantism and became by all accounts a charismatic and effective evangelist who moved freely among the highest social circles throughout Europe. In 1815 she was resident in Basel, after some years in Paris, and was an important participant in the daily affairs of the German Society for Christianity. The records of the committee's earliest meetings reveal that the men who constituted that body spoke of von Krüdener among themselves with respect and acknowledged her extraordinary success in attracting financial contributions to the mission. Her presentation of a collection of jewelry, for example, which she was able to entice as gifts from wealthy Pietist women of the region, was seen as a pivotal event in the founding of the mission. The men in the leadership also credited her with bringing a number of influential people to Pietism and to the mission cause, including some who later became members of the mission's controlling elite. However "biblically" those men defined the term, *patriarchy* did not lead them to exclude this resourceful woman from open and meaningful participation in the formative stages of the mission, which was a religious enterprise that was gaining visibility far beyond the immediate Basel area.

In the end, however, Juliane von Krüdener's very effectiveness alarmed those of the civil and clerical authorities of Basel who were not involved in the mission. These men saw her as a peripatetic and enigmatic outsider. It worried them that a powerful and potentially separatist religious movement like Pietism should number among its vanguard a person who was not of their own familiar social network, and they were especially concerned that such a movement might come to be dominated by a woman.[10] Authorities pressed von Krüdener to sever her ties to the German Society for Christianity and the Basel Mission and leave the city. In the face of this opposition she returned eventually to Russia. Joining her entourage when she left Basel were some men who were among the important early mission enthusiasts, including one member of the organization's first official governing committee. After her departure no woman served in a central policymaking position in the Basel Mission for the next hundred years.

Juliane von Krüdener's curious story deserves more attention than we are able to give it here. It shows that influence could be gained by a resourceful woman at a time and in an organization in which the desirability of male hegemony was not even open to debate. Her success, while it lasted, was the product of her own ingenuity and of the pressing need for the resources she brought to the mission. At the same time, her experience demonstrates how quickly that influence could be lost, even by a person with von Krüdener's talent, when it threatened to put the mission at odds with powerful outside secular authorities. To be sure, the leadership continued to recognize the usefulness of women's energy and skill, and female members of the elite families that launched and led the mission were always visible in important subcommittees and support roles in the seminary and central administration in Basel. Marriage to a daughter of one of the mission patriarchs often preceded a man's entry into the organization's inner circle of leadership, with all of the prestige and personal gratification that came with that membership. Fund-raising groups for the mission, which proliferated throughout Europe in the nineteenth century (it was a popular cause in Lutheran and Calvinist church circles), relied heavily on the volunteer efforts of women, who collected the contributions from ordinary Pietists that were increasingly important to the survival of the organization.[11] These kinds of involvement are by no means insignificant, but in the main and on a day-to-day basis mission practice relegated females to the background, no matter how important their individual and collective contributions were, and the committee could (and did) summarily expel male seminarians and missionaries if they interacted with women in unauthorized ways.

After Juliane von Krüdener's withdrawal from Basel, members of the Swiss urban bourgeoisie prevailed numerically in the tight circle of men who continued to govern the mission, but representatives of the Pietist theological elite of southern Germany, especially from Tübingen University, actually held the key policymaking positions. The inspector, for example, who was in charge of daily administration, was usually a German theologian. The Swiss members of the circle continued to describe themselves as an "aristocracy," and the leadership as a whole, Swiss and Germans together, defended the "divinely inspired patriarchy" of the organizational regime over which they presided. Moreover, when it came to prescribing the outlines of family, community, work, and worship for the convert villages that were planned for the African mission stations, it was the Lutheran ideal of the self-sustaining, patriarchal agrarian village that provided the template. The ordinary missionaries (recall that only males could be ordained) came in large numbers from just such villages and farms in Württemberg. Because of this, they were prepared both by tradition and by religious belief to inhabit such an order in their own lives and to reproduce it in the convert communities they were charged with creating in the field.

The Indispensability of Women Abroad: Work and Marriage

This Pietist ideal in the mission was rarely challenged openly on either ideological or theological grounds, but some twists and turns of practical accommodation are visible in the archival record. The traces of these adjustments are especially visible in the evolution of the rules governing marriage and mate selection for the ordained male missionaries. Different missions approached this matter in different ways. The leadership of the Church Missionary Society (CMS), for example, the large and influential Anglican mission whose practices were watched closely by other evangelical societies, believed that marriage had a steadying influence on missionaries because it enabled them to live normal family lives and kept them from being tempted into sexual improprieties in the field (see Piggin 1974; C. P. Williams 1976). Missionaries were often married before they were posted abroad for the first time.

In Basel, by contrast, the leadership's attitudes toward marriage reflected the view that women represent temptation and men are corruptible. Their policies were initially much more narrowly drawn than those of the CMS. In the early years the committee actually considered it desirable to have the missionaries remain single, in part because they thought it would be less expensive to support single missionaries in the field and easier to move them from one station to another as the need dictated. More important, however, was the supposition that women represented uncertainty for men destined for the religious life. It was feared that marriage would compete for their energy and concentration and thus compromise their religious zeal. Strict rules regulated contact with women from the time the male recruits entered the seminary. Movement in and out of the Mission House (which was the site of the administration and the seminary) was closely monitored, but the isolation of the compound was nothing like that of a monastery or cloister. Seminarians were sure to encounter female domestic servants, wives of mission teachers, and visiting mothers and sisters of fellow seminarians. Unplanned contacts also occurred in church, in the community at large (where the young men had some freedom of movement), and on the frequent occasions when prominent mission supporters summoned students to their homes as guests. The leadership strongly discouraged unsupervised interaction with women in all of these circumstances, but encounters inevitably did occur and were a persistent source of concern. Where mission authorities discovered unapproved contacts, an attachment that appeared to be a serious one, or a truly grave transgression such as an unsanctioned betrothal, summary dismissal of the offending seminarian was the usual remedy.

Similar concern surrounded contact with native women in mission communities abroad, where the rules for the missionaries were even stricter (for examples of transgression of such regulations, see Hyam 1990, 103–6). Official policy discouraged casual relations between male missionaries and Africans in general, including personal friendships and informal interaction (as opposed to firm and somewhat aloof "paternal guidance"). Such unscripted relationships, it was thought, undermined both religious and temporal authority. Where native women and male missionaries were involved, the strictures were especially severe. To limit casual contact with native women, the committee ruled that unmarried male missionaries were to have only male servants. All traffic with single women, including natives, Europeans (schoolteachers or nurses), or even the intended brides of other missionaries, was strictly governed. If a missionary encountered a woman alone in a room, he was to leave if possible; otherwise, he was to see that doors and windows were left open. In the outdoors men walking near where native women might rest or bathe must call out before approaching in order to avoid contact with women who were, by European standards, less than fully clothed. Sexual contact between missionaries and native women was grounds for immediate defrocking and dismissal. It is only speculation, but the absence in the archival record of any commentary about sexual contact between European women and native men suggests that such contact was simply beyond consideration.

As Waltraud Haas points out, it was only reluctantly that the governing committee relaxed its position on such matters to the point of allowing missionaries to marry at all (1994, 25). Being out of conformity with the practices of more influential missions like the CMS played a part. On several occasions the severity of Pietist discipline brought unwelcome attention to the Basel Mission's policies. Because it often relied on the goodwill and active assistance of larger, politically connected societies like the CMS, the Basel Mission had to be concerned with projecting an image of reasonableness. Ultimately, however, it was Pietist belief itself that exposed the contradictions of male exclusivity in the mission and brought women's indispensability into sharp focus. This paradox requires some clarification.

In the Pietist worldview evangelical success meant more than just growing tallies of converted individuals. In the end success had to be measured by the development of permanent Christian enclaves, or communities, outside of which true and lasting conversion was thought to be impossible.[12] In these Christian communities the stability of the family was fundamental. Single male missionaries were obviously ill suited to serve either as the model or as the repository of wisdom for such family-based settlements. They would have no families of their own to use as a point of reference, and they were not well prepared either by inclination or by training to minister to the women and girls who would be part of the native Christian settlement. Women as wives of the missionaries, as fellow workers alongside the ordained men, and as teachers for native girls and women in the emerging Christian community were simply indispensable for the creation and sustenance of such settlements. No degree of commitment to an all-male evangelical enterprise could be reconciled with that simple necessity, and, once that was recognized, the marriage policy changed.

The committee began to permit missionaries to marry but under carefully supervised conditions. Examination of the written and unwritten criteria for spouse selection, formulated in 1837, make it clear that marriage was always complicated by concerns about social class identity and racial separation. It was possible for a man in good standing to apply for permission to marry after two years in the field. He could suggest who his marriage partner might be, and often that choice would fall on the widow of a colleague who had died (as many did) in service in the field. In the absence of such an opportunity, however, the general expectation was that the committee would conduct a search at home for a bride of suitable background, character, piety, and commitment to the mission's cause. As with most important matters defining the missionary's relationship to the organization, the committee spelled out the reasoning in detail:

> Because the wife of a missionary is called not only to share the sacrifices and dangers of the mission life with him but also herself to perform her share of the Mission's work, it is also necessary to require of her that she possess the physical, spiritual, and motivational capabilities appropriate to the Mission Calling. The obligation of the Committee is to see that we do not accept wives in the Mission who do not possess this capability. Therefore, not only the marriage, but also marriage to the specific person intended by the missionary, depends on the permission of the Committee. This permission will be given only after the Committee has formed a judgment about the qualifications of the intended. (Basel Mission Archives 1886)[13]

The marital alliances that evolved out of this policy fell into a distinctive pattern. As we have said, the men in the Basel organization had quite modest social origins. It is revealing to note, however, that they seldom married women from equally humble backgrounds. "Qualifications of the intended" included possession of an "acceptable" class background, which usually meant coming from a higher economic and prestige stratum than that from which the husband had come. The archival records indicate that the search for a bride often led to the daughter of a Pietist petit bourgeois or clergyman in the Württemberg region. In this way the committee sought to assure itself of wives who reinforced the religious uniformity, cultural compatibility, and respectability of the organization but who at the same time contributed directly to the social honor and upward social mobility of the missionaries.

A search of the records from the earliest period of the mission revealed that only four of the first twenty-five wives of Gold Coast missionaries came from the farm or craft backgrounds that characterized the vast majority of the husbands. The fathers of another three were clergymen, and the remaining eighteen brides came from the families of professionals, civil servants, and enterprise owners or managers. Comparing the origins of the husbands to those of their wives couple by couple, none of the women came from a background lower than her mate's, and fully fifteen of the twenty-five women came from clearly higher social origins than those of the men they married. The situation at the end of the century was essentially the same: of the twenty-five brides in the years just before World War I, fourteen were from bourgeois or petit bourgeois families (their fathers were factory owners, merchants, teachers, or civil servants); five came from the families of clergymen (pastors or missionaries), and six were daughters of farmers or craftsmen. Again compared couple by couple, fifteen of the twenty-five women came from higher and none from lower social categories than their husbands, who continued to be recruited from modest farm and village circumstances.[14]

Upward social mobility through education, ordination, and marriage was a fact of life, then, for most of the male Basel missionaries, but not for their wives. The men entered the seminary as members of the farmer, artisan, or laboring class, earned the educational credentials of a solidly middle-class professional, and formed marital alliances with families whose higher class locations further enhanced the missionaries' social capital. Comparison with the influential CMS is again instructive. In the 1840s an Anglican bishop described in this way the separation between leaders and followers in that organization:

> It has been the custom to think of missionaries as an inferior set of men, sent out, paid and governed by a superior set of men formed into a committee in London. Of course then you must have examiners and secretaries and an office to see that the inferior men are not too inferior; and you must have a set of cheap colleges in which the inferior men may get an inferior education and you must provide an inferior sort of ordination which will not enable them to compete in England with the superior men. (Qtd. in Roland Oliver 1965, 12n.)

Marriage was one means the CMS used to correct this "inferiority." For an interesting reason the CMS leadership ruled that male missionaries should not become engaged or married before they finished their training and achieved ordination. Because their seminary education was expected to elevate them in the social hierarchy, any mates they selected before they were ordained would, assuming typically class-endogamous choices, be from a station lower than the one into which they were moving. After ordination they could be paired with women from backgrounds "appropriate" to their new place in society. The CMS missionaries, like the Baselers, thus benefited first from their own direct social mobility and second from the indirect "betterment" imparted to them by the class and status origins of their wives. The men acquired cultural capital through these marriages, and the CMS found a way to counter any definition of itself as an organization staffed by those of less than solidly middle-class standing. The wives were able to marry into the respected Anglican clergy, but it is a matter of interpretation whether they were marrying at, above, or beneath their own stations. If the origins of the men they married serve as the point of reference, the women were downwardly mobile; if the achieved positions of those men are the focus, they were not downwardly mobile.

In an earlier essay Miller (1990) argued that, by serving in these ways as reliable channels of upward social mobility for men and their "families of procreation," missionary undertakings played a significant part in the transformation of social class relations in the nineteenth century. In the cases we have described, however, there was a pronounced inequality in the way missionary women and men participated in that process. If the men in the Württemberg region could not remain on the land or in their villages, their employment options were limited. By joining the Basel Mission, most of them gained substantial social capital by virtue of their seminary educations, their new professional identities as members of the clergy, and in many cases their marriages. The same can be said of the men attracted to the Church Missionary Society. It is also apparent in the evidence we have examined that the enhancement of male class identity was assigned a higher priority by missions than the protection or enhancement of female class identity.[15]

We expect that this pattern was general, not just in Europe but also in North America, and it is a commonality that goes far toward explaining why the men found their way into the missionary movement. It is clear that participation served their material (or class) interests at the same time that it satisfied their personal preferences and their very real religious convictions. But is there an equally persuasive explanation of the presence of women in the movement? To be sure, Basel Mission women were caught up in the same historical transformations and evangelical enthusiasms in their communities as the men, and there is no reason to doubt that their religious beliefs were as strong as the men's. But in society at large they had even fewer occupational options and opportunities to participate in public life than men did, and inside the missionary movement they more often than not occupied subordinate positions as lay teachers, nurses, or wives and helpmates of ordained male missionaries. Moreover, as we have seen, wives were more likely than their husbands to have married beneath their origins as a result of the choices they made or, as we suspect was more often the case, as a result of the alliances struck between missions and their families. Such observations are common in missions.[16] Women settled for less, and we must catalog the alternatives open to them in much more detail before we will fully understand the mixture of conviction, circumstance, choice, class interest, and coercion that shaped their decisions.

However varied the motives of individuals were, the Basel Mission's decision to include women in its overseas activities was clearly driven by necessity, and this forced a change in the conception of the place of women. No doubt this was true in many, if not most, other missions as well. Characterizing the inclusion of wives as "victories" for women, however, is problematic, if by that term we mean the winning of real concessions such as the carving out of regions of comparative independence from men. We have to look further for instances in which women's importance clearly enabled them to expand their options and exercise more agency on their own behalf. In the Basel organization illustrations are to be found in the experiences of two women, Wilhelmina Maurer and Catherine Mulgrave, both of whom were strong presences in the mission in Ghana. Maurer was the first single woman sent to Ghana from Basel and was assigned the task of organizing the education of African girls and women. Catherine Mulgrave was the first of a small number of African women who married white Basel missionaries.

A Single Woman in the Service of the Mission

From the beginning the women who worked alongside their missionary husbands in Ghana had a heavy load of responsibility. In addition to their household and childcare activities, they had major responsibility for the health care of the mission community, in itself a stressful and time-consuming activity. Added to all of this, the mission expected them to take charge of the education and religious instruction of African girls and women. It was increasingly difficult for them to stretch their energy to cover all of these duties. When their husbands became fully aware of their burden, they asked the leadership in Basel to send out single women to share the labor and, in particular, to focus on the education and religious instruction of native women. The committee hesitated to create this new category of female mission workers. An unsatisfactory earlier experience in the mission's settlements in India led them to believe that single women would soon be chosen as brides by the single missionaries in the field. To these unattached men, after all, single female coworkers represented opportunities to evade the mission's normally protracted marriage process, which required petitioning Basel for permission to marry and then waiting for the committee to find a "suitable helpmate" in Europe and send her out to Ghana. If expedient marriages to the new coworkers became the norm, then the quasi-independent status of those women would be lost, and the special tasks assigned to them would, once again, end up being carried out by missionary wives. Nevertheless, the committee suspended its misgivings and gave the arrangement another trial. As a result, for the first time in the emerging Christian community in Ghana, single European women would be present whose attachment to the Basel Mission was not dependent upon their marriage to a male missionary and whose work could be judged somewhat independently of that of the men.

Waltraud Haas (1994) has provided a rich account of the experiences of the first of these women, Wilhelmina Maurer, who went out to West Africa in 1857. Maurer's task was to establish a system of religious instruction and education for African women and girls, thus (in theory at least) relieving the missionary wives of this part of their workload. She was told that she would work under the general oversight of a married male missionary and that she would have a status below that of the missionaries' wives. Maurer was not qualified as a teacher and lacked the training that would prepare her for her complex responsibilities. After a few months Katherina Rüdi, who did have formal training as a schoolteacher, followed her to Ghana, and Maurer was told to accept Rüdi's leadership in matters of policy and organization.

The relationship between the two women quickly deteriorated when Maurer refused to take direction from Rüdi or to conform to the latter's commitment to a highly disciplined Pietistic educational regime. Maurer's approach to the women and girls she worked with was intimate and nurturing, which Haas suggests was effective because it was more in tune with African customs and less in conformity with the hierarchical Pietism of the Basel organization (1994, 35). Maurer and Rüdi clashed repeatedly, and each wrote frequently to the inspector in Basel, asking him to intervene against the other. Before a lasting resolution of this conflict was reached, however, Rüdi married a missionary and was assigned to another station. By doing this, she joined the missionary wives category, and Maurer seized the opportunity to consolidate her control of the nascent educational institute for girls, such as it was, that she and Rüdi had begun to create. Her "victory" was pyrrhic, however, because, although she managed to hold onto that control for over twenty-five years, no other female colleague was sent out from Basel to share her work until near the end of her tenure in Ghana. The large-scale educational system that she and Rüdi had been expected to launch received little institutional support from the mission and never came to full fruition in their lifetimes.

Maurer's experiences throughout this long period are a study in contradictions. On one hand, the contribution she could make to the Christian enclave was evident in the way African women and girls came to her and responded to her attention. This fact helped her to resist repeated attempts to control her, even in an organization that was well-known among missions for the unquestioning obedience it demanded of its members. On the other hand, as the Christian community grew, the significance of Maurer's solitary contribution became proportionally less impressive. Nor in the end did the missionary wives get the relief from their overload of work that had been a key reason for Maurer being sent to Africa. To be sure, Maurer successfully resisted all suggestions that she should be recalled to Basel, but Haas argues that her stubborn isolation in a limited zone of activity slowed rather than accelerated the evolution of a larger sphere of independence for women in the mission (1994, 34). It is as if her activities, which in the beginning were defined as substantial and important, were in the long run only tolerated and encapsulated—rendered "tokenistic," to use today's terminology—in a way that minimized their impact on other things that were going on in the mission.

The atmosphere surrounding Maurer's experience in the mission is captured by a remark made by one of her male supervisors, who wrote to Basel that, if all the single women sent out to Ghana could be like Maurer, there would be no need to worry that they would be quickly claimed by marriage. Haas captures the essential inequity in Maurer's experience when she points out that bitter animosities, factional struggles, and outright failures were common among the men in the mission, too, but were seldom grounds for abandoning their projects. For years the example of Maurer's "obstinacy" (should we call it strength?) was used as the pretext for scaling women's participation back to the single role of missionary wife. It is interesting that Maurer is remembered by women in Ghana today as the critical catalyst for the movement to educate females in that country (Haas 1994, 34).

Interracial Marriage

Catherine Mulgrave is a compelling figure in the history of the Basel Mission. According to information in the mission's records, she was born into a Christian (probably Catholic) family in Angola around the year 1827. In 1833, when she was about six years old, she was kidnapped by a slave trader and taken on board a ship bound for Cuba. The slave ship broke up in a storm off the coast of Jamaica, and most of the captives were killed. From the small band of survivors Catherine and another girl of about the same age were taken into the household and given the family name of Jamaica's governor, the earl of Mulgrave. This happened at about the same time that the governor was presiding over the abolition of slavery in the British West Indies. Under the sponsorship of Lady Mulgrave, Catherine was educated in a school run by Moravian missionaries, under whose tutelage she became a schoolteacher for the children of freed slaves. She entered the history of the Basel Mission in 1842, when she became one of some forty West Indian Christians who consented to be "repatriated" to Akropong on the Gold Coast to form the nucleus of the mission's convert community there. In that Christian settlement she was married to George Thompson, also a mission schoolteacher, who had been the first African to be educated in the Basel Mission seminary. To what degree this marriage was one of choice or a matter of calculation by the mission leadership is impossible to determine from the archival record, but, by establishing a prominent black Christian family, the Thompsons' union clearly served the mission's goals for the Gold Coast community.

For reasons that have been described elsewhere (see Miller 1991; 1994, 130ff.), the mission expelled George Thompson and allowed Catherine Mulgrave to divorce him. Her welfare and that of her children were matters of considerable concern because she and they remained valued members of the Christian community. A few years later, however, she became the center of concern of a different kind, when she married Johannes Zimmermann, a white missionary. Zimmermann, like Mulgrave, was an unusual personality, and together the two of them challenged mission policy in several ways. Their marriage, a fait accompli, caused consternation in Basel, first because of the direct affront to the marriage rules (they married without permission) and second for the sensation the committee feared it would cause in the Pietist community in Europe (it was an interracial marriage). As we have pointed out, policy in the mission at that time discouraged even casual social interaction between Africans and Europeans if it appeared "too familiar," and the mission's prohibition on interracial sexual contact and marriage was, in principle, absolute. Some members of the committee in Basel insisted on Zimmermann's immediate expulsion simply on the grounds that he did not petition for permission to marry or for approval of his intended mate. They had dismissed others before him, after all, for far less consequential transgressions, and it was written into the definition of the missionary's status that any willful breach of the rules was, if the committee cared to rule it so, tantamount to resignation from the mission community.

It was against all probability, therefore, that the committee decided not to dismiss the Zimmermanns. Instead, they accepted the marriage but with the strong stipulation that Johannes was no longer to consider himself a European citizen and that he must never expect to bring Catherine or their children to Europe. He was a talented, energetic, and respected missionary, and the usefulness of his work to the mission played a key role in this

Catherine Mulgrave-Zimmermann (1826–1891) and her husband Basel Missionary Johannes Zimmermann, together with their children (*l-r*): Augusta, Gottfried, Johannes, Johanna, Gottlieb, and Christoph. Photograph (1866) by Wilhelm Locher. (Basel Mission Archive QS-30.002.0237.03.)

relatively lenient decision. If no more than this could be said, this case could be described as a concession to Zimmermann's talent but not as a crack in the structure of patriarchy in the organization. In shaping the committee's decision, however, Catherine Mulgrave was just as important as the man she married. In one letter to the committee Johannes sought to win approval for his marriage by pointing out that Catherine, by then a key person in the mission's plan to establish a school for girls, had considered leaving the Basel Mission and joining a rival Methodist mission. By general consensus among the Gold Coast missionaries she was simply irreplaceable. It is interesting, too, that the committee members referred to the prospect of Catherine Mulgrave's loss when mission supporters at home asked them to justify the decision to allow Johannes to remain a missionary and Catherine to remain a teacher despite the shock of their unauthorized marriage.

In rationalizing its action, the committee reasoned that Johannes had been concerned not with his own gratification but with the good of the mission. By stepping forward to marry Catherine, he selflessly kept her talent at the disposal of the mission. After the first outrage had subsided there is an aura of "sacrifice" in the committee's description of his actions. The fact that Catherine was educated and was neither a recent convert nor a local woman swayed the committee members, and this says something important about the tangled nuances of race and class consciousness in the mission. Having been brought up as a Christian in the household of the British governor of the West Indies, she was considered to be more "cultured" than indigenous women of the West African region. She was not, in the committee's words, a "simple village girl," for which latter category, it was implied, no concession at all would have been made. A subtle form of European class prejudice thus intersected with matters of race and gender in this complex case.

We do not hesitate to describe what Mulgrave and Zimmermann did as a confrontation with patriarchal policy that, for them, produced a significant concession from the mission's circle of leaders. The importance of their case is amplified by the fact that the challenge to received "fatherly" wisdom was carried forward by a couple (and their supporters among the other missionaries), not by a woman alone. As compelling as it is, however, it is important not to overstate the long-term consequences of their actions. Despite their ability to construct reassuring after-the-fact rationalizations, the committee did not relish the compromise they had reached with the Zimmermanns, and they did not approve more permissive marriage rules for other missionaries. The committee members expressed private concerns about the precedent that had been set, fearing that other missionaries and, just as perilously, those outside the mission would see the dispensation given to them as a capitulation to personal initiative. In Pietist thinking about organizational governance that was a grave error.

In the years to come the resolve against interracial marriages hardened in Basel and in other missions. Horst Gründer argues that anthropologists contributed to this growing rigidity in racial attitudes when they lectured to mission leaders and seminary students, including those in Basel, about social evolution and the supposed relationship between race and levels of civilization (1982, 329ff.). This "scientific racism," Gründer believes, reinforced the biblical theory of the "curse of Ham" that many missions were already using to justify their approach to matters of race. In any event, in later years the Basel committee barely tolerated two missionary marriages to women of mixed race (one of whom, significantly, was a daughter of the Zimmermanns) but expelled outright two others involved in marriages to "simple village girls." Johannes and Catherine Zimmermann, however, finished their careers in the mission in good repute. Eventually, they were even able to break down the opposition to their marriage to the extent that the committee allowed their mixed-race children to come to Basel for their educations, and the couple retired to Germany when they had finished their work in the mission. After the death of Johannes in 1876 Catherine returned to the Gold Coast, where she died in 1891.

Like Juliane von Krüdener and Wilhelmina Maurer, this couple found points of opportunity in the prevailing regime of the mission and used their resources and not least their wiles to push back, for themselves if not so obviously for others, the confining definitions of marriage, race, and gender. For changes in gender regimes of greater reach and permanence, however, it is necessary to look beyond the Basel Mission.

Gender Relations in the Norwegian Missionary Society

The Norwegian Missionary Society was founded in Stavanger in 1842; at its founding it consisted of sixty-five previously independent local missionary associations, some of them established as early as the 1820s and 1830s. Inspiration for the Norwegian missionary movement came from abroad, mainly from Denmark, Germany, England, and, not least, Switzerland. Among the sources of learning and motivation was the Basel Mission, which from early on received monetary and other material support from more than four hundred Norwegian missionary friends and where the Norwegian J. W. Cappelen was a seminary student from 1824 (Molland 1979, 154–55). A common thread of interest in Pietism linked the two organizations. After 1843 the NMS had its own missionary school. In the nineteenth century it concentrated its overseas work in Madagascar (today the Malagasy Republic) and South Africa, and in the first quarter of the twentieth century China and Cameroon were added. By 1992 the NMS was represented in South Africa, Madagascar, Cameroon, Ethiopia, Mali, Japan, Hong Kong, Taiwan, Thailand, Brazil, France, and Croatia.

As in Basel, the NMS was initially designed as a male enterprise with an all-male membership and leadership and with an educational program reserved for male missionaries. In contrast to the leadership of the Basel Mission, however, which came from the economic, political, and religious elites of the Basel region, most of the 184 individual male founders of the NMS were either farmers or craftsmen. Only 10 were teachers, while 12 were theologians (Molland 1979, 158; see also Simensen 1986, 15). Although the positions of leader and secretary in the NMS were usually held by theologians, other leadership positions were occupied by middle-class individuals (Jørgensen 1992, 68). Much more than in Basel, the social background of the NMS-trained missionaries paralleled the background and culture of the founders, as the majority of the missionary school students in the period 1845 to 1897 came from rural families in which the father worked as a farmer, cotter, artisan, or petty trader (Simensen 1986,

27). Just as in Basel, however, the seminary training translated into social mobility for aspiring missionaries.

The "Affiliation" of Women

Norwegian women were soon to surpass the activity of men in the missionary movement, but from the beginning they were only loosely "affiliated" with the NMS per se. In practice this status meant that women could not vote or participate in any decision-making bodies within the NMS, even if they channeled most of their collective resources through that organization. Women were free, however, to participate at missionary meetings arranged by the NMS, and from the beginning the NMS had a positive attitude toward the missionary work done by women at home. Within a year of its founding the NMS made a public appeal to women in Norway to engage in work for the missionary cause by helping to clothe the missionaries themselves as well as "the Christian Negro" and the "heathen Negro disciples" (Nome 1943, 74). With the launching of this appeal to women, the NMS had not yet transgressed the ideals of gender relations that prescribed the domestic sphere as the proper domain for women in general and for women of the middle classes in particular. The ideal of domesticity that governed the lives of middle-class women (Cott 1977, 92; Prochaska 1980, 5; Vicinus 1985, 2), and therefore also the lives of the women in the NMS, who mostly represented middle-class backgrounds and values (Tjelle 1990), could be easily combined with participation in religious, voluntary social service.

After their beginning in the 1820s, 1830s, and 1840s the growth in independent local women's associations was explosive. Taken altogether, they came to constitute the first women's movement in Norway (Tjelle 1990, 104). In 1865, 300 of these associations were affiliated with the NMS. By 1882 there were 1,600 to 1,700 women's associations, double the number of men's associations. By the turn of the century between 3,000 and 4,000 women's associations were established around the country, with an approximate total of 90,000 members (108). These women's associations did not send any missionaries to the foreign field, and they were not united in a national organization. Their relationship was loose, based on solidarity to the missionary cause and common affiliation with the NMS. Their work consisted in the direct collection of money and in needlework sold at bazaars and raffles, the income of which was contributed to the NMS. The women's associations also adopted African girls and boys who were students at boarding schools established by the missionaries and shipped various supplies directly to mission stations in the field.

Not until 1884 did the women's associations achieve more formal relations with one another through the founding of the journal *Missionslæsning for Kvindeforeninger* (MLK, Missionary Readings for Women's Associations), which was the product of an initiative of the associations themselves, led by two prominent missionary women, Bolette Gjør and Johanne Borchgrevink. From then until 1925 this journal was published as a supplement to NMS's own journal, *Norsk Missionstidende* (MT), which was issued monthly and constituted the most important source of information for the organization. Moreover, an initiative shared by women at home and women in the missionary field abroad led to the establishment of the Missionary School for Women in Oslo in 1901. The NMS leadership endorsed the founding of this school, both because of the practical need for trained women missionaries in the field and to prevent the missionary women at home from establishing their own society and sending their own missionaries to the field. The competition from Catholic nuns and other mission organizations in winning women converts was also mentioned as a factor in the founding of the school for women (MLK no. 10, 1900, 73). The women educated at the school would still be evaluated by the NMS before they were hired and subsequently supported as missionaries in the field by the NMS itself. The NMS did not commit itself, however, to contributing financial support to the school.

As a clear limitation on the women's activity, and as an indication of the perhaps lesser importance attributed to the women's school in comparison to the men's, the NMS leadership made it a condition of their moral support that the women's associations must finance their school by collecting extra money and not by reducing their contributions to the NMS (Jørgensen 1992, 89; see also Høeg 1981, 3).[17] Accepting women as students at the main missionary school in Stavanger was not discussed, although in 1887 one man did suggest that the planned women's education ought to take place in connection with that school (MT no. 23, 1887, 464). Oslo was chosen as the site for the Missionary School for Women due to the already existing school for deaconesses in that city and the possibilities it created for cooperation, a factor that was thought to make the establishment of the mission school for women both easier and cheaper than the alternative of providing an education from scratch. That accepting women at the main school in Stavanger was not considered a serious alternative is indicative of the dominant perceptions of appropriate gender relations at the time. To share the same education at the same location would apparently have been unacceptable, but to give women and men different educations at widely separated institutions could more easily be approved. The varying degrees of importance given to the two schools, and by inference to the different roles women and men performed in the field, is reflected in the different lengths of study at the schools. For men at the missionary school in Stavanger, who were considered in need of a more thorough preparation than women, the length of study was five years. In Oslo, at the missionary school for women, only two years of study were required. The establishment of the women's journal and the missionary school for women served to strengthen bonds, however, not only among the local women's associations but also between the associations and the NMS.

Norwegian Missionary Women Abroad

Women had participated actively in the missionary field abroad prior to the founding of the missionary school for women. In the early years individual women went abroad only in the role of accompanying male missionaries, as when Jakobine Schreuder, the wife of missionary Schreuder, and Johanne Vedeler, teacher for the Schreuder family (and later Schreuder's second wife, when he became a widower), left Norway for South Africa in 1858 and 1866, respectively (Danbolt 1948). Many of the missionary wives, however, managed to do what was then called "indirect" missionary work in the form of sewing schools for women and girls. From the 1870s married missionary women such as Johanne Borchgrevink, who established a boarding school for girls in Madagascar, were able to occupy missionary roles independent of their husbands. At the same time, new opportunities for women were created when the NMS employed single women first as teachers and later as midwives and nurses in "direct" missionary work. Between 1870 and 1910, seventy unordained single women mission workers were sent abroad (MT no. 23, 1994, 5).

In contrast to the Basel Mission, which long had an uneasy attitude toward women, especially single women, in the field (as the career of Wilhelmina Maurer bears witness), the NMS quickly realized the potential benefits of having both wives and single women in the field. Norwegian women were needed to educate South African and Malagasy women in the "womanly skills" of good housekeeping and to "emancipate" these women by turning them into Christian housewives. Moreover, women converts were seen as essential to the establishing of a true Christian society, as they were to form "the pillars of the Christian family and society" (MT no. 19, 1887, 374). The policy of sending single women to the field originated not at the NMS home office but, rather, in repeated requests from male missionaries in the field. These women did not achieve ordained missionary status but were called "missionary wives" if they were married and "female workers in the mission field" if they were not. The NMS advertised a position for a "Bible Woman" in 1890, but this title apparently was not much used because it implied that women holding such positions were to preach, a practice that was not condoned by the NMS. Single women missionaries received only half the salary of male missionaries, and married women missionaries, who were not formally employed by the NMS, received no salary at all but were nevertheless expected to do their share of mission work.

During the 1880s the NMS received repeated requests from the field for an increase in the number of single women missionaries. In 1887 NMS regional assemblies voted to support these requests, and in 1888 the general assembly agreed to send more single women to the field. Meanwhile, in the field itself, in particular in Madagascar, the increasingly important contributions of single women mission workers toward the end of the nineteenth and beginning of the twentieth centuries were acknowledged by permitting them to participate in decision making at missionary conferences. At the 1903 conference in Madagascar it was suggested that women be given the right to speak and vote, with the proviso that they could only vote in matters concerning the women themselves. This proposal was approved by the NMS general assembly in Norway in 1904. The right to speak and vote in *all* matters at these conferences did not come until 1910, some six years after Norwegian women missionaries at home could vote at NMS assemblies. The national board at home added an exception to the rule, however, such that, if the matter to be decided by the missionary conference needed urgent implementation and could not await the board's approval, then women were not allowed to vote. Apparently, the NMS leadership considered it too risky to let women participate in decision making where there was not an opportunity to review and ratify the results. Women were to have a voice, but their decisions needed to be checked. Another gender difference to be observed is that, while male missionaries were *required* to participate at the missionary conferences, women missionaries could choose whether they wanted to participate or not.

In other areas, by contrast, women in the field were clearly ahead of women at home. Simple practical need led Hanna Pedersen Nygaard, in Madagascar from 1871 to 1898, to preach for both men and women at a time when such a role was strictly reserved for men in Norway. Her own attitude toward this crossing of gender boundaries (which, as we shall see, signaled changes to come at home) was clear:

> In the beginning, only some women came, but the crowd steadily increased, and in the end I had both men and women in my audience. This was somewhat critical, since according to our orthodox notions a woman should not speak in public, and even less when men are present. But what could I do? Should I have said to the men "go away, you can't listen?" Then my activity here would have ended . . . But fortunately

NMS Missionary Conference, Fandriana, Madagascar 1888. First group photograph of women and men at conference. (NMS Arkiv 1989/90, Stavager, Norway.)

> these Malagasys have never emphasized the words of [the apostle] Paul. They have received God's glorious gospel with [equal] pleasure if it was presented either by women or by men. (Nygaard 1923, 86)[18]

Nygaard was not alone in taking on a role intended for male missionaries, as women often preached in the schools, hospitals, and orphanages where they worked (Voll et al. 1985, 33). In practice they had crossed this crucial barrier well before it was officially acknowledged or approved to do so.[19]

The Right to Vote in Exchange for Organizational Loyalty

Developments at home and abroad did not follow the same patterns, as practical circumstances dictated the changing of gender relations in varying degrees in different areas. At home the NMS became increasingly dependent on the financial means provided by the loosely affiliated women's associations. At the turn of the century women were contributing fully two-thirds of the NMS's total income (Tjelle 1990, 81). This economic dependence created the conditions for increasing scrutiny of the demarcation between women's role as supporters and men's role as decision makers in the NMS. Substantial changes in the established gender regime were the result.

As early as 1892, the NMS faced severe economic problems and unbalanced budgets, despite the fact that the income from gifts steadily increased (Tjelle 1990, 173). At the same time, the NMS was competing with other missionary organizations, both abroad and at home, for the money collected by thrifty women. The independent status of the women's associations soon became a threat to the continuation of a secure income for the NMS. The prospect of losing two-thirds of its annual income was a dire one, and at the extreme there was even a possibility that the women could establish their own independent missionary society with their own missionaries to support. Such a development had already taken place in the United States, Canada, and England, and this was well-known to the NMS leadership (178). If not literally its survival, at least the scope of NMS's organizational activities was clearly at stake. As an indication of the organizational assessment of the importance of women's financial contributions, the following remark by a local NMS association is eloquent: "Eleven women's associations work for the [local] mission. One notices throughout the year, and especially towards its end, that here is the [main] artery of the missionary body, and if it is cut off or in other ways halted, it will be the deathblow for these funds" (NMS 55. Aarsberetning, 144; also qtd. in Tjelle 1990, 176). Women themselves also started to become dissatisfied with their lack of decision-making power within the NMS. As long as they were contributing such a large fraction of the NMS income, it would only seem fair that they had a formal voice in organizational matters.

All of these factors contributed to the changing of the institutional regime of the NMS by the gradual integration of the women's associations into its organizational structure. It does not seem, however, that directly articulated demands from the women themselves constituted the primary reason, certainly not the only one, for organizational change. Although participants at the various 1903 regional assembly meetings remarked that many individual women and women's associations expressed a desire for the right to vote in the NMS decision-making process, it was also noted that these women did not explicitly *demand* such a right. Indeed, at that time it was not considered proper behavior for women to put forward such demands, and the NMS leadership stated bluntly that the only decent thing to do would be for the men to give women their due influence without the demand being raised by the women themselves (*Cirkulære til gen-*

eralforsamlingen i Bergen 1904, 16). Moreover, in order to take the sting out of its proposal, the NMS leadership was careful to note that missionary women would not be given the right to vote just because the "spirit of the times" stemming from the growing feminist movement required a change in policy. But, even if the feminist movement was given little credit when the NMS leadership argued its case, the general secretary, Lars Dahle, commented that "even the feminist movement contains something justifiable that now has to come forward" (MT no. 15, 1904, 350). Thus, although officially it was not an argument in the case, the feminist movement probably contributed to the gradual shift among the NMS leadership toward giving women the right to vote. More officially, it was mainly the combination of financial problems, economic dependence on women's associations, and the clear discrepancy between the women's missionary zeal and their lack of organizational influence that led the NMS to reason that the women represented a large part of the solution to a persistent and serious problem and that it would therefore be unwise to jeopardize their support and goodwill. In response to this combination of influences, the patriarchal rules and practices of the NMS were altered, and the mission gradually became an enterprise more clearly shared by women and men. There was undoubtedly an element of co-optation at work in this process; nevertheless, the cumulative effects of the changes were profound.

In 1904 the NMS general assembly granted the right to vote in organizational matters to individual women members. In doing so, it assumed a pioneer role in Norwegian history because it was among the first institutions to extend its democratic principles to women. The majority in favor of this measure was quite large. From that time on women were also eligible to serve as elected representatives to both regional assemblies and the general (national) assembly. They had the right to be elected as members of local executive boards[20] but continued to be ineligible for seats on the national and regional executive boards, which were the most important administrative bodies in the organization.

The substance of the NMS decision is best assessed by placing it alongside other advances by Norwegian women. They did not achieve the vote in parliamentary elections until 1913. In that light the change in the NMS seems comparatively radical. Yet from 1889 women were eligible to serve as school board members, from 1900 they could be elected to poverty management boards, and women with a certain income or funds could vote in municipal elections from 1901. From 1903 women participated in elections to the Lutheran State Church's local congregational boards (Agerholt 1973). Viewed in the light of these earlier concessions, the achievement of the franchise in the NMS appears less striking. An issue in need of further analysis is how these sequential developments were causally linked. How was the NMS's 1904 grant of the franchise influenced by the women's achievements that preceded it, and to what extent did that 1904 decision provide arguments and force to the demand to grant equal voting rights with men in the election of the national parliament?

While these connections remain to be fully sorted out, what is clear is that the NMS was well ahead of the established Norwegian State Church, with which it necessarily had a close relationship (see Tjelle 1990, 166, 186). The fact that in the church women's right to vote was confined to local congregational boards preserved the ideal of domesticity in which women, as "caretakers of morality and religion," had a special role in safeguarding the family as a Christian unit (Vicinus 1985, 2). State church theologians objected to the NMS decision to allow women the right to speak and vote at the level of the national general assembly, and one prominent theologian, Sigurd Odland, withdrew his name from the NMS. Giving women such a visible public role was inconsistent with the ideal of the domestic sphere as the proper field for women's activities. In this region the missionary organization was clearly more progressive than its legitimating church institution, a fact at variance with the idea that missions generally represented the more conservative trends in religious thinking.

It is interesting to note that the NMS leadership produced a biblical interpretation sympathetic to women's participation in decision making to support these alterations in policy. This provides an intriguing illustration of the complex ways in which gender relations were negotiated within the mission, and it shows how organizational experience can have an effect on the use and interpretation of scriptural beliefs.[21] One of the prevailing arguments against women's inclusion in the organizational structure had been taken from the Bible, in which the apostle Paul counsels that women should not speak at church meetings (1 Corinthians 14, 34–35). A straightforward reading of this passage would imply the complete exclusion of women as representatives at the NMS general assembly. Yet, once the NMS leadership became intent on supporting women's right to speak and vote, it decided to offer an alternative interpretation of Paul (were they influenced by Hanna Nygaard's liberties with Paul's message?) that would allow for the changed practice. What Paul had meant, the NMS leadership now reasoned, was that women were not to participate as *preachers* in ecclesiastical services. Since Paul did not explicitly forbid women to hold *administrative* positions, however, the leadership concluded that women could participate in organizational management (*Cirkulære til generalforsamlingen i Bergen 1904,* 20–21). The NMS reliance on women's missionary efforts was such that the organization was willing to offer a new interpretation of a biblical text, and it made its decision to grant women the right to vote at the risk of considerable cost. Facing both internal disagreement and resistance from state church theologians, the NMS leadership stood firm in its decision to change its policy toward women's organizational participation.

Controversial Ties between Missionary Women and the Women's Movement

To return to a point made earlier, the full extent to which missionary women collectively demanded the right to vote or the right to be elected to decision-making bodies in the NMS is not clear. It is certain that both individual women and some women's associations actively and openly supported the development toward equal participation of women and men, and such equality could only be gained if individual women members, or the women's associations as collectives, were given the same standing in the organization as men. Crucially, however, some individual women were apparently not interested in obtaining the right to vote in organizational matters, and a few women even declared their outright opposition to the measure (see Referater fra kredsmøderne, MT no. 22, 1903). As early as 1853, Henriette Gislesen, a very prominent missionary woman, argued that women should not get together in associations outside the home and, instead, should work for the mission cause through "house- and family associations" (Gislesen 1853, 54). Moreover, Gislesen emphasized that "the concept 'association' refers to something that is independent, something that can exist in and for itself, [while] the concept 'woman' refers exactly to the contrary of independence, to something that according to God's holy order and will neither can nor shall exist for itself" (1853, 55). Fifty years later, in 1904, some missionary women still subscribed to conservative views on women's abilities and proper tasks.

Even if the women were divided on the right to vote in the NMS, however, it is premature to conclude that they were unconcerned about feminist issues. Indeed, many NMS women had strong ties to the feminist movement and argued vehemently for the right of women to make their own decisions. One such example is Bolette Gjør (1835–1909), who in effect became the leader of the women's missionary movement in Norway, served as the editor for *Missionary Readings for Women's Associations* from the start of that journal until her death, and worked to establish the Missionary School for Women. Gjør saw the women's missionary movement as a potential source of great power for women:

> In all one noticed more and more that the women's associations themselves expressed an eagerness to make the decisions over where to send their gifts . . . And among the women themselves the consciousness of

constituting a power in the mission was growing, [a power] which could make things happen when [the women] were joined together. (MLK, no. 2, 1905, 11)

While emphasizing the need for a close association between the women's missionary movement and the NMS, Gjør worked to unite the women's associations in their own national umbrella organization. She argued for giving women the opportunity to achieve full missionary status, and she wanted women attached to the missionary cause to join forces with non-missionary, more clearly feminist women. This last proposal was to become extremely controversial both in the women's associations and in the NMS and is illustrative of how negotiation and confrontation affected gender relations in the mission.

In 1904 the Norske Kvinners Nasjonalraad (NNCW, Norwegian National Council of Women) was established in order to promote cooperation between women's organizations in Norway and to represent Norwegian women in the global feminist organization the International Council of Women (ICW). Bolette Gjør became convinced that missionary women ought to become members of the NNCW, and she and other women started to work toward establishing a national organization that could represent missionary women within NNCW. This new national organization of women's missionary associations, called the Misjonsarbeidernes Ring (CMW, Circle of Missionary Workers) was established in 1907.

The Circle of Missionary Workers did not turn out to be a great success in organizational terms. Only a few of the several thousand women's missionary associations joined the organization, and from the outset it was met by opposition from the NMS. Apparently in an effort to maintain the close relationship with the NMS, Gjør had decided to inform the NMS leadership of her intentions to form the CMW. Much to her dislike, that leadership opposed the establishment of a separate organization and its inclusion in the NNCW (MT no. 24, 1906, 568). In defense of its position the NMS leadership argued that the feminist cause could under no circumstances be joined with the missionary cause, as the two were simply incompatible. Such a merger would not only threaten the women's commitment to the missionary cause but would also threaten the integrity of proper life within the mission, especially that of women.

The feminist cause was thus portrayed as a threat to the security of the NMS and, by inference, to the power monopoly men still exercised within the top NMS leadership. Even though NMS encouraged and made some concessions to the activities of women's missionary associations as financial contributors to the missionary cause, there was a limit to how far the leadership would stray from its venerable ideas about the appropriate nature of gender relations and, in particular, about the proper place and behavior of missionary women. As long as the women remained within the NMS, their actions could be subjected to organizational control. The decision to grant women the right to vote in organizational matters and to participate in local decision-making bodies in the NMS expanded the roles of women and changed the structure of gender relations within the organization, but, by reserving the seats in the national and regional boards to men, the NMS kept patriarchy, albeit in a modified version, in control. When women expressed interests that exceeded the prescribed limits of female behavior set by the leadership, they saw their efforts once again discouraged. Despite the degree of freedom they had attained within the NMS, they nevertheless had to endure restrictions on their activity outside the mission.

In a brave act of independence Bolette Gjør decided to overlook the "advice" and warnings given by the NMS leadership and went ahead with her plans to form the Circle of Missionary Workers and to make that organization a member of the broader NNCW. After all, the women's associations were not formally a part of the NMS organizational apparatus and were thus in principle free to make their own decisions. A struggle over control of the women's associations was initiated, however, when the NMS leadership in effect censored Gjør by forbidding her to write about the CMW in *Missionary Readings for Women's Associations,* the women's own journal, of which she was editor.[22] This left Gjør without the opportunity to explain or defend her own position and left the CMW without the potential legitimacy it could have received through the journal. Moreover, in a further attempt to enforce organizational control, the NMS made sure to inform all the women's associations of its position in the matter. Gjør was outspoken in her criticism of this treatment of the women's associations, but her loyalty to the NMS continued, as did her dependence on the goodwill of the leadership in publishing the women's journal. She did not try to publish the journal through other channels. She did, however, write about the CMW cause in other journals and newspapers that were not NMS controlled.

This confrontation over the Circle of Missionary Workers created tension not only within the NMS but also among the numerous women's associations themselves. In 1907, 233 women signed a warning against membership in the CMW. The connection between the missionary and feminist movements was therefore a controversial one both for women and men associated with the NMS. It is interesting to speculate whether the women's support of the CMW would have been stronger if the NMS leadership had abstained from interference in the matter and from coming out so strongly against it. In the end this controversy shows quite plainly that there was an interaction between the missionary and feminist causes in nineteenth- and early-twentieth-century Norway. If the range of opinions among the women on the missionary side is properly acknowledged, the interaction was by no means always an antagonistic one. Although Bolette Gjør ultimately was unsuccessful in her pursuit of a joint organizational effort of missionary and feminist women, the mere fact that the proposal was discussed over a period of several years indicates that it probably had direct effects on both the NMS and women's own perceptions of proper gender relations.

Conclusion

To return to where we began, Protestant missions have not been simply patriarchal or patriarchal in simple ways. Women were always indispensable to the missionary movement, participating in the overall enterprise in complicated ways as necessity and their own resourcefulness dictated. In every mission of which we are aware there were women who pushed back the limitations that were imposed upon them and who were able to capitalize on the small concessions that were made to their striving for independence. Juliane von Krüdener, for example, participated prominently in the creation of the Basel Mission and for a time joined its inner council of decision makers. Wilhelmina Maurer, whatever her limitations, created a significant zone of autonomy for herself in her work among school-age girls in Ghana, and she sustained her project for many years. Catherine Mulgrave commanded the mission's support during and following the breakup of her first difficult marriage and then kept her respected place in the Ghanaian Christian community, despite having defied mission policy in her second, unapproved marriage to a European.

To be sure, these are scattered points of concession involving particular women, and they do not describe a continuous arc of social change toward gender equity in the Basel Mission. To the contrary, Juliane von Krüdener's energy and resources were not enough to protect her when it was feared that her presence jeopardized the mission's relationship with powerful political interests in the community. Her experience compels one to ask *how often* and, above all, *why* women have held then lost positions of influence in religious organizations. The latter question is not even posed when unbroken male hegemony is simply taken for granted. The interracial marriage of Catherine Mulgrave and Johannes Zimmermann represented a personal victory for that couple, but in the decades that followed the policy of racial separation became more, not less, rigid for other missionaries. Wilhelmina Maurer protected her independence, it is true, but she was given few resources and enjoyed little support from other European members of the mission community in Ghana. Her enterprise did not survive long after her departure from the scene.

The extended historical perspective in Waltraud Haas's work (1994) offers testimony of the slow pace of change in the Basel Mission between Wilhelmina Maurer's time and the present. Women today talk about the anachronistic governance structure of the mission and look for redefined relationships and renegotiated egalitarian structures that will finally produce a permanent change in organizational governance. It is interesting to speculate that at present there actually might be more ambivalence about such changes among women in the Presbyterian community in Ghana, the Christian community that traces its origin to the arrival of the first Basel missionaries in 1828, than in Switzerland. The uncertainty of today's African church women is suggested by the "women's column" in the June 1992 issue of the *Christian Messenger,* the authoritative newsletter of the Presbyterian Church of Ghana. In that column Margaret Tenadu argued for the independence of women and for the importance of their jobs and roles in advising the nation on matters of morality, tradition, and the family. In the same piece, however, she restricted the legitimate role of women to *just* those private spheres and, within them, to activities that in no way challenge the positions of men. Men, in her words, are "the bread winners and heads of the house," but they have "little time at home, thus . . . little role to play in the home." She goes on: "We have to be ideal women whose relationships with our husbands, relatives and neighbors be mutual and peaceful so that our working husbands may have peace of mind at their working places for an increased productivity." If Tenadu's position is representative of the Presbyterian Church of Ghana (we have not confirmed that it is), then the "uplifting" institutionalized gender arrangements brought by the nineteenth-century mission and passed along to the present generation of Christian women in Ghana might prove more resistant to change than the original European templates upon which they were based. What further complicates this issue is that from the beginning indigenous gender arrangements have surrounded, interacted with, and therefore modified the customs that European missionaries have tried to implant. That comparative researchers must be alert to these intertwined evolutions before drawing conclusions about the institutionalization of Western practices abroad is a caveat well worth noting.

In the Norwegian Missionary Society not only individual women but the women's missionary associations as collectivities were granted substantial concessions that expanded their participation in the main organization. A signal of accommodations to come was given when the NMS revised a long-standing interpretation of a scriptural belief by stating that the apostle Paul had not meant to exclude women from administrative positions. The 1904 decisions extending the right to vote and serve as representatives at regional and general assembly meetings provided the women's associations with a significant new tool for shaping and influencing organizational politics. These changes might have been prudent moves of co-optation (triggered by men's awareness of the organization's dependence on the economic support of women) as much as they were responses to demands from the women themselves. Whichever motive predominated, however, the decisions acknowledged the indispensability of women and gave them an active voice in organizational matters. The change illustrates that victory is seldom complete, however, as seats on national and regional boards continued to be reserved for male representatives. The right to participate in one area expanded, but restrictions that preserved male hegemony were reinforced in other areas.

The same juxtaposition of constraint and freedom is apparent in the founding of the Missionary School for Women in 1900. At that time the women's associations had only a loose affiliation with the NMS and thus were technically autonomous. Accordingly, the male leadership acknowledged and supported the women's right to establish their own school. Nevertheless, they prevailed upon the women not to decrease their contributions to the NMS in order to finance the operation of the school. In one sense success was achieved by the women, in that the NMS did not block the creation of the school, but the cost of that success was the agreement to redouble their fund-raising efforts so that the male-dominated institution would not see its resources diminished.

The complex and often contested nature of gender relations is also illustrated by the mixed success of NMS women in forming an alliance with other organized Norwegian women, some of whom were clearly feminist in their philosophies. Although she tried to be open and accommodating, Bolette Gjør was denied the support of the NMS leadership when she tried to focus the interest of missionary women on activities outside the narrow boundaries of the missionary movement itself. A likely explanation is that participation in mission work could easily be defined as an extension of the ideal of domesticity, in which women assumed the primary responsibility to protect and strengthen the bonds between home and family, morality and religion. The limitations implicit in this domestic ideal were inconsistent with a more active, public role of women beyond the missionary movement. Because the proposed missionary-feminist alliance languished in the face of NMS opposition, we might conclude that patriarchy was effectively maintained in this instance. At the same time, the cluster of missionary women who worked for the alliance effectively raised the cost of maintaining patriarchal rule by demonstrating that they were not always willing to accept the restrictions on their activities imposed by the NMS.

Ambiguity is the best word to pull this summary together. Most of the cases of compromise and change that we have described can be read in two ways. From one perspective we must remind ourselves that these two organizations are over 150 years old, and yet fundamental issues of gender equity continue to be posed by their members. That fact alone is a measure of the resilience of control structures that have been deeply rooted in Western ecclesiastical history. Indeed, nothing in our discussion is meant to minimize the very real power imbalances that have existed. To the contrary, we regard the persistence of gender inequality *in the face of the indispensability and resources of women* as the single greatest puzzle in political economy that mission scholarship still needs to solve.

Seen from a different perspective, however, it must be stressed that control by men has always been challenged in the Basel Mission and the Norwegian Missionary Society, to greater apparent effect in the latter than in the former organization. Patriarchy is never invulnerable, and hegemony is never complete. If *patriarchal hegemony* accurately describes the larger nineteenth-century societies in which the Basel Mission and the Norwegian Missionary Society operated, our case studies show that different forms of gender regimes, with different degrees of resistance to structural change, can be found within this same broad social-hegemonic context. In Basel individual women and men posed significant challenges to the patriarchal gender regime of the mission and of the Swiss and German cultures in which it was grounded, but the episodes we analyzed did not in their time directly change the shape of the internal regime and had little if any significant impact outside the organization. The Norwegian case illustrates a situation in which women's collective action challenged both the mission and the general society and actually transformed the patriarchal gender regime of the mission, if not so obviously the patriarchal hegemony of Norwegian society.

Two key differences that we noted at the beginning help to account for these disparate outcomes in the two organizations. The first has to do with the class origins of the founders. In Basel there was a vast social separation between the "urban aristocrat" founders and the much humbler rank-and-file members. That separation—which the leaders embraced, rationalized in religious terms, and were determined to preserve—no doubt imparted a stubborn resistance on their part to democratic leveling in any form. By contrast, the relative social equality of leaders and followers in the NMS took some of the social and ideological threat out of proposals for internal democratization, including, quite probably, changes aimed at the fuller participation of women.

The second difference concerns the fact that the Basel Mission was created where it was (in neutral Switzerland) and organized as it was (as a nondenominational undertaking) in order to avoid the complications of state interference and control by a single established church (for a fuller discussion of this point, see Miller 1994, chap. 1). Although it was by no means impermeable, there was a membrane of isolation around the mission that limited the internal impact of external politics at the same time that it prevented the comparatively minor organizational changes that we have described from spilling beyond the boundaries of the mission and its circle of direct supporters. The NMS, by contrast, was the missionary arm of an established national religion, and the dynamics that evolved inside the mission both reflected and had consequences for the politics of the state church and, beyond that, for the secular political structures to which the church in turn was attached. The larger organizational changes affecting women's status and position in the NMS were probably accommodated in part as a result of the increasingly egalitarian social climate that developed in Norway in the last quarter of the nineteenth century.

As research on women in missions continues, we believe that there will be few cases in which women have simply assented or been compelled to assent, without comment or resistance, to the gender regimes in which they have found themselves. Such unquestioned biblical patriarchy, like a Weberian ideal type, defines one end of a continuum of possibilities, but the constellation that defines that pole is not often found in concrete cases. The empirical challenge we face, then, is twofold. First, we need to place specific regimes accurately on that continuum by recording how their internal realities both approach and depart from the patriarchal extreme. Then, we must catalog the ways in which those regimes are simultaneously reproduced and eroded from within. We conclude our discussion on a theoretical note by calling attention to a factor that will always complicate these efforts.

When those who exercise control make concessions to necessity (however reluctantly), they inevitably alter the terms of their own hegemony (however subtly). Yet what invariably clouds this picture is the way in which hierarchical dominance is reinforced by ideological dominance. Historically, in the missionary movement it has been men and not women who have set the moral agenda and therefore have defined what is properly regarded as "scriptural" and thus "morally necessary." The establishment of patriarchy as a Christian imperative has determined from the beginning what is to be taken as the norm (and therefore protected) in Christian organizations and what is to be seen as a threat (and therefore opposed). It has also been men for the most part who have written the official record. This control of the institutional memory has quite simply allowed men in turn to say what has happened and what has not, that is, to control the definition of what is historically "factual." In an extreme case, for example, no word at all of an internal change may enter the formal record if leaders believe that acknowledgment or dissemination of that knowledge will be troublesome. Similarly, challenges that have been raised by women and changes that have been accepted in one place (say, in a mission station in Ghana) may not be revealed to those working in another (in a mission station in India). This tactic of isolating change is especially effective when most of the communication among the subparts of the organization is channeled through the center. When the record is under such strict control, moreover, leaders may allow no hint of internal challenge or flux to reach audiences outside the organization, including potential recruits who are thinking of becoming the next generation of insiders. Finally, and even more consequentially, if what is on the record defines precedent and precedent in turn conditions the future course of change, then record keepers, by encouraging open discussion or stifling it by closing the files, can determine whether a given alteration in practice, made for reasons of expediency, becomes an isolated incident with few long-term implications or one in a series of sequential changes that accumulate in importance.

In other words, control of the historical record coupled with control of the moral agenda can be used to reinforce both the perception of unbroken patriarchal dominance and the justifications that have been offered for radically imbalanced gender regimes. If only from hubris, however, that same control of the record and mastery of the agenda encourages exaggeration of the imbalance in power. There is inevitably some disparity between the rhetoric of seamless male hegemony, on one hand, and the cracks and emergency sutures that characterize the reality of contested gender regimes, on the other. In many ways the interactions between women and men in various missions recapitulate the dialectic in the experiences of women and men throughout biblical and Christian history. In recent years feminist theologians, biblical historians, and archaeologists seem to be converging on the conclusion that long periods of resolute male dominance have always alternated with shorter periods of challenge and even relative equality between men and women (Brown and Parker 1989; Achtheimer et al. 1993; Murphy 1993).

As the record of the missionary movement is opened to the critical scrutiny of scholars with a variety of substantive interests, previous certainties begin to give way to new questions. On the comparatively microscopic scale of mission history this should motivate social scientists working in this area to factor questions about gender directly, not tangentially, into their investigations and to proceed from the premise that gender relationships are not given but, rather, are situational and therefore contingent. The mutations that appear from one period to the next in an organization and the differences that are evident from one mission to another will depend on changing historical circumstances, on the specific organizational and broader institutional context, and, not least, on the particular cast of characters active in a place and time.

NOTES

This research has been supported by National Science Foundation grants SES-830892, SES-8520752, and SBR-9320808. The discussions and opinions expressed are those of the authors and do not represent the views of the NSF.

1. We assume, with Judith Stacey and Barrie Thorne (1985, 306), that "gender organization and relations [are significant] in all institutions . . . in shaping men's as well as women's lives." Gender is more than a collection of culturally prescribed "sex roles." It represents a relatively independent axis of social organization, although one that is complicated by race, class, and sexuality. Statements about biological differences and universalistic assumptions about human nature are transhistorical and essentializing, we believe, and therefore are insufficient to account for the ways in which gender relations develop and vary. An investigation of gender relations that is historically and situationally informed is essential.

2. Our ideas about hegemony and the capacity of members to alter and evade it are heavily influenced by, but not identical to, those of Antonio Gramsci (1971). In our discussion we take the term *patriarchal hegemony* to mean the social ascendancy of men in civil society, such that men constitute the dominant group, while women belong to subordinated groups (see Gramsci 1971, 12–13; Williams 1960).

3. See Nyhagen Predelli (1998) for more extensive historical documentation and sociological discussion of women's experience in the NMS. See also Tjelle 1990.

4. Deniz Kandiyoti has suggested the term *patriarchal bargain* to describe a process in which "women strategize within a set of concrete constraints" (1988, 274). This term, and an analogous term such as *negotiated patriarchy,* can be taken to imply that exchanges take place on relatively balanced terms, with essential agreement on the consequent outcomes. These terms do not fit in situations characterized by radically imbalanced power, nor are they useful for understanding situations described by constant fluidity and change, in which reality emerges over time and in which active or passive contestation is combined with developments that are neither planned, intended, nor anticipated.

5. See also Prochaska (1980, 230) on "nineteenth-century definitions of female emancipation."

6. Others who argue against a close connection between women's and missionary movements include Hunter (1984, 1989), Mitchison (1977), and Welter (1980). Offering evidence in favor of a close connection is Montgomery (1910), who many years ago described a link between women's access to educational institutions and the development of the missionary movement. Nancy Cott (1977, 154), however, has suggested that women's religious voluntary associations "had an

ambiguous effect on women's autonomy and status" and that to label women's religious associations as either pro-feminist or anti-feminist might be equally inaccurate (1977, 156).

7. Publicly expressed motivations cannot be taken at face value as a guide to the reasons that lie behind individual decisions to join the mission cause. Mission societies often accept as members only those whose stated aspirations conform to accepted reasons for joining, and calling attention to anything other than pious commitment to a religious cause is likely to be grounds for nonadmission. On this point, see Miller 1994, 41–64.

8. Most serious mission histories stress that missions were committed to raising the status of women in non-Christian cultures, which meant opposing what was seen as their subjugation and safeguarding what were regarded as their rights. In addition to the sources we have discussed elsewhere in this essay, see the work of Paul (1984) and Klein (1994) on Presbyterians; Stanley (1992) on British Baptists; Strayer (1978) on Anglicans of the Church Missionary Society; Ingham (1956) and Warren (1965) on various British missions; and Yesudas (1980) on the London Missionary Society.

9. Württemberg Pietism, called after the region in which it found its strongest expression, was influential in the evangelical and reformed churches of southern Germany and Switzerland, respectively, in the late eighteenth and early nineteenth centuries. Shared Pietist beliefs included a strong commitment to missionary evangelism, and the Basel organization played a visible and important part in the overseas missionary movement that accompanied the colonial expansionism of nineteenth-century Europe.

10. This worry was a reflection of the precarious position that Basel, and its somewhat fractious ruling elites, occupied in the complicated politics and military realities of the period of the Napoleonic Wars; see Miller 1994, chap. 1.

11. This was a common pattern in nineteenth-century mission funding, as the discussion of the NMS will confirm. For an account of the Basel Mission's *Hilfsvereine* (support groups), see Tschudi-Barbatti 1991. Many of the patterns of female participation in the missions prefigure the ones recorded by Arlene Daniels (1988) in her account of elite women's participation in volunteer efforts in the United States.

12. A broad distinction can be drawn between missions that equated Christian salvation with godly community life, on the one hand, and those that relied on widespread broadcasting of the Gospel without regard for the creation of permanent communities, on the other. For a more complete discussion of the practical correlates of this distinction, see Miller 1993.

13. All translations from the German are our own.

14. We compared these observations on 25 early and 25 late Ghana missionaries with the marriage records of 100 early- and 100 late for missionaries from the mission's other overseas postings (including those to China, India, Persia, and Russia). This comparison showed that bride selection for the Gold Coast missionaries was not atypical. In the larger samplings three out of four brides came from professional, clerical, bureaucratic, or bourgeois families. Measured another way,

between a fourth and a third were from the families of clergymen. Only a small minority came from the modest farm and craft backgrounds that supplied most of the men.

There were a small number of men who wanted to be missionaries who came from much higher social origins than the typical Württemberg villager. One such case reveals the circumstances that could lead the committee to alter its normally unbending rules and, at the same time, illuminates the point at which class consciousness interfered with gender expectations. A missionary named Charles Strömberg engaged in a prolonged dispute with the committee over his repeated requests for permission to marry. Strömberg was unlike the typical Basel missionary in two important ways: he was Swedish, not German or Swiss, and his family was of the privileged social stratum of professional military officers. This background set Strömberg apart and gave him a certain marginality—he would have called it superiority—in the circle of Württemberg Pietists, who made up the majority of Basel missionaries. His years in the Mission House did little to erase the difference in his mind.

After the committee posted Strömberg to West Africa, his marriage requests challenged official policy in three ways. He insisted on marrying a person of his own nationality, of his own choosing, and of his own social class. Contrary to his wishes, point for point, the committee wanted him to marry not a Swede but a German or Swiss woman selected by them from the same broad middle-class categories that provided the brides of most of his fellow missionaries. In Strömberg's view of things this represented a downward step socially. He reminded the committee that his social standing was the same as their own, and when they accused him of arrogance he replied that it was not arrogance simply to want to associate and be conjugally linked with members of his own social stratum. It is revealing that the committee agreed with him on this point. Concern for the class privilege of "one of their own" struck a responsive chord, and, in a manner that was quite outside the norm for such decisions, they factored this concern into their treatment of his marriage request from that point forward. In the months that followed six prospective brides, including, significantly, both Germans and Swedes but all from higher-than-usual social class backgrounds, were considered by the committee but passed over for one reason or another. Ironically, before this bride search came to a successful conclusion, Strömberg confessed to a drunken attempt to have sexual intercourse with a young African servant woman, and the committee ordered him expelled from the mission. While in neither of these episodes (mate selection and behavior in the field) was his behavior typical of Basel missionaries, it suggests that for him class was a barrier to a marital alliance "beneath his station" but not a barrier to the sexual exploitation of women he encountered in his work.

15. This is a common observation in research on social class and mobility and is also reflected in patterns of interracial marriage.

16. As Ann White (1988, 26) points out, mission women, especially the unmarried, have typically occupied a de facto "assistant" status, which has been consistent with their lower pay and the relative devaluation of their work compared to that of their male colleagues.

17. The Missionary School for Women became formally affiliated with the NMS in 1910 and was closed in 1979.

18. This and all subsequent translations from the Norwegian are our own.

19. In 1910 the NMS general secretary Lars Dahle in effect approved of this practice by stating that "our [mission] society will not tolerate any preaching by women, *unless the situation is such that it is covered by the rule that 'necessity knows no law,'* and strict control of this practice will be enforced in our mission fields" (MT no. 16, 1910, 383; emph. added).

20. The women's associations as organizational collectives became fully integrated in the NMS structure in 1927. It was not until 1939, when women finally became eligible for seats on national and regional executive boards, that individual women and men enjoyed equal rights.

21. See Miller 1994, chap. 3, for a detailed example of how scriptural beliefs can affect organizational practices.

22. The fact that Gjør was denied the opportunity to write about the case in "her own journal" led to an exchange between the editors of the journal *Norsk Kirkeblad* and the NMS general secretary, Lars Dahle, in which the NMS was criticized for its "patriarchal" practices (Norsk Kirkeblad nos. 12–13, 1907; no. 19, 1907). Dahle replied that the journal for women's associations was the property of the NMS and not to be considered "Gjørs' own journal."

REFERENCES

Achtheimer, Elisabeth, Mary Jo Winn Leith, Sidnie Ann White, and Valerie Abrahamson. 1993. Women. In *The Oxford Companion to the Bible,* ed. Bruce M. Metzger and Michael D. Coogan, 806–18. New York: Oxford University Press.

Agerholt, Anna Caspari. 1973. *Den norske kvinnebevegelsens historie.* Oslo: Gyldendal Norsk Forlag.

Basel Mission Archive. 1886. *Verordnungen über die persönliche Stellung der Missionare.* Series Q-9:21, 7:13.

Beaver, R. Pierce. 1980. *American Protestant Women in World Mission: A History of the First Feminist Movement in North America.* Rev. ed. Grand Rapids, Mich.: William B. Eerdmans.

Bowie, Fiona. 1993. Reclaiming Women's Presence. Introduction to *Women and Missions: Past and Present. Anthropological and Historical Perceptions,* ed. Fiona Bowie, Deborah Kirkwood, and Shirley Ardener, 1–19. Oxford: Berg.

Brouwer, Ruth. 1990. *New Women for God: Canadian Presbyterian Women and India Missions, 1876–1914.* Toronto: University of Toronto Press.

Brown, Joann Carlson, and Rebecca Parker. 1989. For God So Loved the World? In *Christianity, Patriarchy, and Abuse,* ed. Joann Carlson Brown and Carole R. Bohn, 1–30. New York: Pilgrim Press.

Connell, R. W. 1987. *Gender and Power: Society, the Person, and Sexual Politics.* Stanford: Stanford University Press.

Cott, Nancy F. 1977. *The Bonds of Womanhood: "Woman's Sphere" in New England, 1780–1835.* New Haven: Yale University Press.

Danbolt, Erling. 1948. *Det norske misjonsselskaps misjonærer, 1842–1948.* Stavanger: Det norske misjonsselskap.

Daniels, Arlene Kaplan. 1988. *Invisible Careers: Women Civic Leaders from the Volunteer World.* Chicago: University of Chicago Press.

Gagan, Rosemary Ruth. 1992. *A Sensitive Independence: Canadian Methodist Women Missionaries in Canada and the Orient, 1881–1925.* Montreal: McGill-Queen's University Press.

Garrett, Shirley S. 1982. Sisters All: Feminism and the American Women's Missionary Movement. In *Missionary Ideologies in the Imperialist Era: 1880–1920,* ed. Torben Christensen and William R. Hutchison, 221–30. Aarhus: Aros.

[Gislesen, Henriette]. 1853. *Den kvindelige virksomhed for misjonen. Et avskedsord til søstre.* Christiania [Oslo]: F. Chr. Abelsted.

Gramsci, Antonio. 1971. *Selections from the Prison Notebooks.* Ed. and trans. Quintin Hoare and Geoffrey Nowell Smith. New York: International Publishers.

Grimshaw, Patricia. 1983. Christian Woman, Pious Wife, Faithful Mother, Devoted Missionary: Conflicts in Roles of American Missionary Women in Nineteenth Century Hawaii. *Feminist Studies* 9, no. 3: 489–521.

———. 1989. *Paths of Duty: American Missionary Wives in Nineteenth-Century Hawaii.* Honolulu: University of Hawaii Press.

Gründer, Horst. 1982. *Christliche Mission und Deutscher Imperialismus, 1884–1914.* Paderborn: Ferdinand Schöningh.

Haas, Waltraud. 1994. *Erlitten und Erstritten: Der Befreiungsweg von Frauen in der Basler Mission, 1816–1966.* Basel: Basileia Verlag.

Hageman, Alice L. 1974. Women and Missions: The Cost of Liberation. In *Sexist Religion and Women in the Church,* ed. Alice L. Hageman. New York: Association Press.

Hill, Patricia R. 1985. *The World Their Household: The American Woman's Foreign Mission Movement and Cultural Transformation, 1870–1920.* Ann Arbor: University of Michigan Press.

Høeg, Johanne. 1981. *Misjonsskolen for kvinner, Oslo, 1900–1979.* Stavanger: Informasjonstjenesten NMS.

Hunter, Jane. 1984. *The Gospel of Gentility: American Women Missionaries in Turn-of-the-Century China.* New Haven: Yale University Press.

———. 1989. The Home and the World: The Missionary Message of U.S. Domesticity. In *Women's Work for Women: Missionaries and Social Change in Asia,* ed. Leslie A. Flemming, 159–66. Boulder: Westview Press.

Hyam, Ronald. 1990. *Empire and Sexuality: The British Experience.* Manchester: Manchester University Press.

Ingham, Kenneth. 1956. *Reformers in India, 1793–1833: An Account of the Work of Christian Missionaries on Behalf of Social Reform.* Cambridge: Cambridge University Press.

Jørgensen, Torstein. 1992. De første hundre år. In *I Tro og Tjeneste: Det Norske Misjonsselskap 1842–1992,* ed. Torstein Jørgensen, 11–145. Stavanger: Misjonshøgskolen.

Kandiyoti, Deniz. 1988. Bargaining with Patriarchy. *Gender and Society* 2 (September): 274–90.

Klein, Laura. 1994. "Timid Women Do Not Make Good Missionaries in Alaska": Gender and Mission in Southeastern Alaska. In *The Message in the Missionary: Local Interpretations of Religious Ideology and Missionary Personality,* ed. Elizabeth Brusco and Laura Klein, 23–42. Studies in Third World Societies, no. 50. Williamsburg, Va.: Department of Anthropology, College of William and Mary.

Miller, Jon. 1990. Class Collaboration for the Sake of Religion: Elite Control and Social Mobility in a Nineteenth-Century Colonial Mission. *Journal for the Scientific Study of Religion* 29 (March): 35–51.

———. 1991. Institutionalized Contradictions: Trouble in a Colonial Mission. *Organization Studies* 12, no. 3: 337–64.

———. 1993. Missions, Social Change, and Resistance to Authority: Notes toward an Understanding of the Relative Autonomy of Religion. *Journal for the Scientific Study of Religion* 32 (March): 29–50.

———. 1994. *The Social Control of Religious Zeal: A Study of Organizational Contradictions.* Rose Monograph Series of the American Sociological Association. New Brunswick, N.J.: Rutgers University Press.

Mitchison, Wendy. 1977. Canadian Women and Church Missionary Societies in the Nineteenth Century: A Step towards Independence. *Atlantis: A Women's Studies Journal* 2, no. 2: 57–75.

Molland, Einar. 1979. *Norges Kirkehistorie i det 19. århundre.* Bind 1. Oslo: Gyldendal Norsk Forlag.

Montgomery, Helen Barrett. 1910. *Western Women in Eastern Lands: An Outline Study of Fifty Years of Woman's Work in Foreign Missions.* New York: Macmillan.

Murphy, Cullen. 1993. Women and the Bible. *Atlantic Monthly* 272, no. 2: 39–64.

Nyhagen Predelli, Line. 1998. Contested Patriarchy and Missionary Feminism: The Norwegian Missionary Society in Nineteenth Century Norway and Madagasascar. Ph.D. diss., Department of Sociology, University of Southern California.

Nome, John. 1943. *Det Norske Misjonsselskaps Historie i Norsk Kirkeliv.* Bind 1. Stavanger: Dreyers Grafiske Anstalt.

Norwegian Missionary Society Archive. 1904. *Cirkulære til generalforsamlingen i Bergen 1904* (Minutes of a General Conference in Bergen in 1904).

Nygaard, Hanna. 1923. *En missionærhustrus erindringer.* Stavanger: Det Norske Misjonsselskaps Boktrykeri.

Oliver, Roland. 1965. *The Missionary Factor in East Africa,* 2d ed. London: Longmans.

Paul, Glendora B. 1984. Presbyterian Missionaries and the Women of India during the Nineteenth Century. *Journal of Presbyterian History* 62, no. 3: 230–36.

Piggin, Stuart. 1974. The Social Background, Motivation, and Training of British Protestant Missionaries to India, 1789–1858. Ph.D. diss., Kings College, University of London.

Prochaska, F. K. 1980. *Women and Philanthropy in Nineteenth-Century England.* New York: Oxford University Press.

Simensen, Jarle, ed. 1986. *Norwegian Missions in African History,* vol. 1: *South Africa, 1845–1906.* Oslo: Norwegian University Press.

Stacey, Judith, and Barrie Thorne. 1985. The Missing Feminist Revolution in Sociology. *Social Problems* 32, no. 4: 301–16.

Stanley, Brian. 1992. *The History of the Baptist Missionary Society, 1792–1992.* Edinburgh: T and T Clark.

Strayer, Robert W. 1978. *The Making of Mission Communities in East Africa: Anglicans and Africans in Colonial Kenya, 1875–1935.* Albany: State University of New York Press.

Tenadu, Margaret. 1992. The Role of Christian Women in Nation Building. *Christian Messenger,* June 1992, 6.

Tjelle, Kristin Fjelde. 1990. Kvinder Hjælper Kvinder: Misjonskvinneforeningsbevegelsen i Norge, 1860–1910. Master's thesis, Department of History, University of Oslo.

Tschudi-Barbatti, Beatrice. 1991. Die Halbbatzen-Kollekte: Ein Kapitel aus der Finanzgeschichte der Basler Mission. Lizentiatsarbeit, Philosophische Fakultät I, Universität Zürich.

Vicinus, Martha. 1985. *Independent Women: Work and Community for Single Women, 1850–1920.* Chicago and London: University of Chicago Press.

Voll, Hilde Margrete, Gunvor Lande, and Sissel Hodne Steen. 1985. *Skjulte Lys: Misjon og Kvinner.* Oslo: Luther Forlag.

Warren, Max. 1965. *The Missionary Movement from Britain in Modern History.* London: SCM Press Ltd.

Welter, Barbara. 1980. "She Hath Done What She Could": Protestant Women's Missionary Careers in Nineteenth Century America. In *Women in American Religion.* ed. Janet Wilson James, 111–25. Philadelphia: University of Pennsylvania Press.

White, Ann. 1988. Counting the Cost of Faith: America's Early Female Missionaries. *Church History* 57 (March): 19–30.

Williams, Cecil Peter. 1976. The Recruitment and Training of Overseas Missionaries in England between 1850 and 1900: With Special Reference to the Records of the Church Missionary Society, the Wesleyan Methodist Missionary Society, the London Missionary Society, and the China Inland Mission. Master's thesis, University of Bristol.

Williams, Gwyn A. 1960. The Concept of "Egemonia" in the Thought of Antonio Gramsci: Some Notes on Interpretation. *Journal of the History of Ideas* 21:586–99.

Williams, Peter. 1993. The Missing Link: The Recruitment of Women Missionaries in Some English Evangelical Missionary Societies in the Nineteenth Century. In *Women and Missions: Past and Present,* ed. Fiona Bowie, Deborah Kirkwood, and Shirley Ardener, 43–69. Oxford: Berg.

Yesudas, R. N. 1980. *The History of the London Missionary Society in Travancore, 1806–1908.* Trivandrum: Kerala Historical Society.

Altruism and Domesticity: Images of Missionizing Women among the Church Missionary Society in Nineteenth-Century East Africa

T. O. Beidelman

In the nineteenth century a few British women found that overseas missionary work provided opportunities for independence and leadership exceeding those afforded them at home. Yet women never described entering mission work as a way to find more freedom. Instead, they described this as volunteering for God's work or as joyfully accompanying husbands whose enthusiasm they shared. Of course, all missionaries describe missionizing in idealistic, altruistic terms. Yet women and men also saw evangelizing abroad as more challenging and adventurous than life at home. Perhaps at that time, some women were keener to volunteer than men because they considered their lives in Britain more restricted than did men. There are, however, no grounds to assume that women volunteers comprehended what life on mission stations would be like. Consequently, none would fully anticipate the possibilities for greater freedom and autonomy that such life offered. No missionary recruiting propaganda suggested this. Yet mission life abroad often provided new autonomy for women, an autonomy denied them at home. Once missionary women found this new independence, they struggled to maintain these benefits whenever missionary men challenged them.

I here argue that evangelical Protestantism provided especially promising conditions for missionary women's independence due to its commitment to contradictory or ambivalent beliefs. Women were valued for evangelistic qualities as model wives, mothers, and homemakers. Yet some missions encouraged situations that denied married women missionaries these very domestic attributes they claimed to promote. Furthermore, some missions increasingly employed single women who worked outside the domestic sphere, conflicting with traditional homemaking qualities that these same missions extolled. This is because women were credited with their own inspiration by the Holy Spirit, inspiration making them equal to men as evangelists. Such contradictory practices were complicated by evangelical notions about altruism, asceticism, and suffering, which undermined domestic and gender relations that missions hoped to promote.

This essay considers these issues in terms of a small group of mission stations in what was once German East Africa (later Tanganyika and now Tanzania), those of the Church Missionary Society (CMS) in Ukaguru.[1] I limit my consideration mainly to the period from 1876, when the Church Missionary Society arrived in Ukaguru (located about 150 miles inland in what today is east-central Tanzania), to 1914, when mission work was temporarily halted by World War I. After that war mission work underwent radical change due to declining funding and recruitment and to new demands set by secular colonial institutions. This postwar period also marks a decline in archival information. After the war few missionaries (at least in Ukaguru) wrote long, informative reports to provide a picture of everyday life.

The Church Missionary Society and Its Ukaguru Mission

The Church Missionary Society (henceforth CMS) is an evangelical branch of the Church of England. It was founded in 1799 by John Venn and Thomas Scott. From the first it placed more stress on the Holy Spirit and right motivation than on formal clerical training and ritual. Laymen and clergy were equally valued workers for Christ. The direction of the CMS was never monopolized by clergy, and CMS emphasis on religious enthusiasm and spontaneous preaching rather than formal training led to sending out doctors, engineers, and craftsmen as well as clerics. Eventually, this included women. The CMS sent missionaries to West Africa and later to India, Canada, the Pacific, the Far East, and East Africa as well as areas occupied by the underclasses in Britain's cities.

The CMS considered emphasis on ritual, vestments, and other formalism wrong and signs of harmful leanings toward Roman Catholicism, a brand of Christianity toward which they showed deep hostility, especially during the time covered by this essay. Formal theology was underplayed in favor of Bible reading, preaching, prayer, hymn singing, and revival. The CMS prided itself on fostering family values and thought its married clergy superior to celibate priests as models for aspiring converts to emulate. Since the Holy Spirit could visit anyone, women were considered as qualified as men to receive and express God's message (P. Williams 1993, 46). Even so, during the earliest days of CMS work, conditions in Africa and elsewhere were considered too dangerous to allow missionary men to bring their wives with them, and it was thought morally unseemly to allow unmarried women to work abroad alongside missionary men or among immoral natives and supposedly dissolute white colonialists. Yet by the 1850s the CMS liberalized its views on missionary wives, and by the 1880s, shortly after the Ukaguru mission was founded, unmarried missionary women were sent abroad (Kirkwood 1993, 34–35; P. Williams 1993, 54). Today over half of all CMS personnel are women (P. Williams 1993, 39).[2]

The CMS reached Ukaguru, the land of the Kaguru people, in 1876.[3] This makes it one of the oldest inland mission stations in East Africa. Ukaguru lies 150 miles inland and is reached after passing over rough terrain, so that before World War I a caravan trip to the area from the coast took ten days to two weeks and was especially arduous in the rains. The lower altitudes of Ukaguru are subjected to unhealthy flooding and disease during the rains; higher areas are rugged and difficult to traverse but were thought salubrious to Europeans and consequently favored by missionaries. These conditions isolated CMS from most other Europeans who later arrived to govern and set up plantations in the unhealthy lowlands.

Located amid warlike neighbors and along well-used caravan routes, the area was subject to raiding and pilfering, which endangered both Kaguru and missionaries during the twenty years between establishing the first CMS station and German colonial government in the 1890s. The early CMS stations in Ukaguru were founded as stopovers between the coast and the great and successful CMS mission in Buganda. The Ukaguru mission was the only CMS African mission not located in territory controlled by Britain. Consequently, the CMS Home Committee in Britain was never enthusiastic about its prospects and was loathe to invest heavily in funds or personnel. These factors impeded mission development.

The sanctity of missionizing, as well as contradictory views about mission methods and goals, validated activities by women that many British at the time would otherwise have considered threatening or wrong. Missionary women faced pressure to conform to stereotypes as wives and mothers subordinate to men, but the colonial and religious aspects of missionizing modified what was thought to be proper feminine conduct.[4] Crow characterizes religion as providing Victorian women with a respectable outlet for "moral insobriety" (1971, 57). The high value placed on the family in Victorian and Edwardian times, with their associated stereotypes of women as succoring and self-sacrificing homemakers, propelled women into exotic regions as needed helpmates (Christ 1980).[5]

The CMS glorified women's domestic qualities as wives, mothers, and homemakers and encouraged women as missionaries to provide models for native women to emulate and inspire secular colonial women and their men as well. Yet women missionaries "demonstrated that there was another career open to women besides marriage" (Warren 1970, 69). Although traditional Anglican Christianity encouraged male domination of women, evangelicals such as the CMS granted women a wide range of missionizing powers. For them personal religious fervor and calling were more important qualifications than clerical or theological authority, and in this sense spiritual justification for missionizing transcended gender.[6]

The Evangelical Spirit

Students of mission sociology consider the particular forms of spirituality and theology endorsed by a particular mission, since these often have implications for the definitions of the kinds of persons fit for such work and how they should be organized. In the case of the CMS those personal attributes legitimizing qualification to evangelize were not closely tied to gender, education, or age. The CMS was committed to evangelical validation in terms of animation with the Holy Spirit. The CMS saw this as a commitment to an original, democratic form of Christianity uncorrupted by hierarchy, which they considered a major defect of the Roman Catholic Church and even of "high" Anglicans. Some high Anglicans told me that the "low" CMS are "little better than unruly Methodists." The validity of animation by the Holy Spirit could be realized from within by intense and unflagging conviction. It was recognized by others in a person's unremitting zeal and energy and by a demeanor of gravitas, which the CMS termed "seriousness." Such qualities clearly did not depend on theological training or rank, though obviously knowledge of Scripture was important. This emphasis upon spirit and seriousness had two significant influences on CMS recruitment and organization. This meant that many persons not trained in theology and certainly not clerics could evangelize, including women but also artisans and others (after all, Jesus was trained as a carpenter). This meant that missionaries could work alone or under weak supervision. Individual missionaries could set up stations, plot their own itineraries, and need not be closely bound to supervising clerics.

The CMS represents the evangelical, or low, branch of the Anglican Church. Its members were (and are) both lay and clergy, the essential qualification being spiritual commitment to evangelism rather than formal theological training. This low branch stresses conversion or being "born again," a change of heart and a new way of life, paying less attention to sacraments and theologizing, than do high church Anglicans, much less Roman Catholics whom the CMS disliked. Born-again Christians with intense zeal but modest formal religious training were accepted for mission work. Women qualified equally with men as suitable to transmit the Holy Spirit evangelically. One woman missionary met her husband at a revival service (Watt n.d., 16); she credited her ability to missionize to being "born-again":

> Some people think any person with a fair show of piety, or a form of godliness, and a reasonable aptitude for acquiring a foreign language, is properly endowed for the foreign Mission field. But how can men and women deliver the message of the regeneratory Gospel of the Grace of God if they have never been regenerated themselves? (22)

As nonclergy, women were denied authority to conduct formal rites of the church (see Best 1974, 38).[7] While this relegated women to a secondary ritual position, it did the same for male lay missionaries, including doctors and teachers. Since the CMS set great value on preaching, prayer services, Bible reading, revival, and the fellowship of meetings, lay men and women could conduct nearly every side of everyday mission evangelism as well as nursing, teaching, record keeping, and chores of maintaining housing and communications.[8] This may have been especially important in isolated missions like Ukaguru. Stations in Ukaguru were small and thinly staffed, often run by one missionary. Even where stations held both sexes, it was difficult for much to be done without mutual consideration, since work was heavy and diffuse and staff too few to allow persistent disagreements or authoritarian imposition of rules by men. The usual solution to differences was for each to work at his or her own outpost. Under such circumstances it mattered relatively little what a putative local head tried to enforce, since the relative isolation of stations allowed each person to pursue what she or he wanted. This policy continued up to World War I; then a more formal organization was maintained wherein new stations were rarely established, at least in Ukaguru (cf. Strayer 1973; Hewitt 1971, 435), so that dissidents were unable to find new ground.

CMS missionaries associated their work with sacrifice and atonement. Yet views of missionary work as an adventurous and sacrificial act or even as penance are not exclusive to evangelicals. What distinguished the early CMS was their extreme earnestness and intense rejection of "guilty leisure" (Cust 1886, 1; cf. Houghton 1957, 229, 243), their belief that comfort, art, and ordinary happiness endangered spiritual well-being. Mission life was to provide "evidence of the victory of the spiritual over the natural" (CMS Archives, General Instructions to Missionaries, 4 February 1886). Bradley notes: "What gave the Evangelicals' view particular potency and influence was the noble and altruistic purpose which it gave to colonialism and imperialism" (1976, 88). To the CMS theirs were services to "new lands and child races" (Elliott-Binns 1936, 375). There was a parallel between these and services of CMS missionizing at home, where middle-class evangelicals sought to uplift slum people nearly as different from themselves as were the peoples of Asia and Africa (see Heasman 1962; Burn 1965, 269–70; Lyons 1975, 103).[9]

Evangelicals denied themselves material pleasures; they nurtured a sense of moral superiority and self-satisfaction that made them nearly impervious to criticism from outside their ranks. This contributed to their ability to allow women freedoms otherwise suspect, if not downright unrespectable, in the eyes of others. One of the chief CMS propagandists characterized them thus:

> The Missionary is undoubtedly the highest type of human excellence in the Nineteenth Century. He has the enterprise of the Merchant without the narrow desire of gain, the dauntlessness of the soldier without the occasion for shedding blood, the zeal of the Geographical Explorer, but for higher motives than the advancement of Human Knowledge. (Cust 1895, 104; see also Cust 1885)

Nonmissionaries sometimes interpret evangelical otherworldliness differently:

> To them Christianity was not a solution of all problems of life so much as a means of escape from them, and many definitely believed, as the explanation of the powerlessness of the Gospel to transform society, that God had handed the world to the devil. (Cell 1976, 284; cf. Kitson Clark 1962, 149–205)

A former leading CMS missionary concedes that this was sometimes the case (Warren 1971, 51).

Certainly, CMS actually prized the prospect of martyrdom. From their arrival in East Africa CMS women suffered. The Reverend Krapf (the European discoverer of Kilimanjaro) buried his wife and daughter in July 1844, shortly after arriving as the first CMS worker on the East African coast. (Krapf was a German Pietist who agreed to work for the CMS.) It was judged that "the victories of the Church are gained by stepping over the graves of its members" and "Our God bids us build a cemetery before we build a church. The resurrection of East Africa must be affected [*sic*] by our destruction" (Elliott-Binns 1936, 382; CMS Archives, Instructions of the Committee to Out-going Missionaries, 23 July 1896).[10] Cust remarked on the death of a CMS woman:

> Some are selected to live and work: to others is conceded the peculiar grace to die nobly, and set a glorious example. Deaths are required as

well as lives to complete the picture of the new life. (Qtd. in Stock 1899, 1:181)

CMS writings refer to mission work as warfare against evil and ignorance, and this bellicose imagery may have reinforced an expectation of suffering and casualties (cf. Houghton 1957, 233). Missionaries were praised "who have not preferred the ties of blood or the claims of family to the work" (Cust 1892, 16017). When her infant son died during her trek inland to Ukaguru, Rachel Stuart Watt's determination seemed only further resolved (n.d., 21).

As a result of Krapf's losing his wife and daughter, the CMS Home Committee ordered that for these first years, until proper stations were built and roads improved, male missionaries to East Africa must leave their families behind if married or, if single, temporarily forgo marriage. At first marriage was not allowed until after a year's service; later, recruits had to remain single for three to five years. Even then, dependents remained in Britain. One CMS writer advocated ten years of celibacy to measure altruism and character building, though financial reasons also figured. The CMS supported widows and children of those who died in the field. (The CMS is reported to have had more comprehensive welfare services for members and their kin than some of their mission competitors [C. Williams 1980, 302–3].) Overseas housing and equipment for married couples would be more expensive than for men roughing it alone (Stock 1899, 3:355–56; Cust 1891, 12; 1892, 14–15; CMS Archives, Lang to Baxter, 21 April 1886).

Some CMS argued that mission wives were needed to prevent male missionaries from sinning with native women.[11] It was pointed out that the immoral life of other, secular Europeans set a bad example to Africans; this was a failing caused by the absence of European women, whose moral presence would supposedly uplift not only their husbands but other men as well (see Hooper 1911, 79). In practice such wide moral influence was unlikely, since CMS tended to avoid contact with other Europeans whose morals were judged below their strict standards.[12] These conflicting judgments about the physical vulnerability and frailty of women and their crucial roles as stalwart moral supporters to men colored CMS writings for forty years following the death of Krapf's wife and daughter, barring posting to Ukaguru until the 1880s yet perennially fueling demands to admit them.

Those arguing for a more liberal view regarding sending out women to dangerous areas were quick to point out that God would provide divine protection to any and all laboring in his cause. Whatever happened, it would be God's will and consequently further some divine purpose. During this period zealous, evangelical women pressed to be sent to East Africa, welcoming the danger as a test of faith or a path to martyrdom. Both men and women argued that God would protect them until their appointed time. In this spirit Rachel Stuart Watt writes of being threatened by Maasai (Baraguyu?) warriors in Ukaguru:

> I realized in a moment our defenceless position, and the probability of the immediate slaughter of my child, myself, and the whole caravan in the absence of my husband; and lifting up my heart to God I peremptorily commanded the terror-stricken porters to fall into line. Acting as if under the influence of some external power the men of the entire caravan fell into order at the words of command. Such a formidable phalanx was thus presented to the on-coming warriors that, under the providence of God, they at once slunk off into the forest and disappeared. (n.d., 93)

The missionaries remained convinced that God would protect them or, if not, that God's hand lay behind any misfortune, which would be a trial from which good would come. Such views, mixtures of self-confidence, fatalism, and resignation, contributed to CMS willingness to post women before other European colonials did so.

The First British Women at the Ukaguru Mission

In a few years all this would drastically change, and the CMS in Ukaguru would change from a mission with no women to one in which women outnumbered men. This eventually became the norm for the CMS as a whole as well.

While women were forbidden going to Ukaguru during the first years of CMS work, this presented the mission with a dilemma. The CMS claimed superiority over Roman Catholic competitors in part because Catholic priests were unmarried and therefore could not provide proper models of Christian families for Africans to emulate. (Obviously, this was contradictory to CMS endorsement of celibacy among their pioneer men.) The CMS Parent Committee in London emphasized the crucial value of mission married life:

> The Committee would only add that they attach much value to the exhibition before the eyes of the Natives of Christianity in its concrete form—not only of personal Christian life but of Christian life in the family—they will therefore be glad when the time comes that you are

> able to let them know that you are prepared to receive your wife—if not your children. (CMS Archives, Instructions to the Rev. J. Lamb, Mrs. J. C. Clark and Mr. W. N. Robertson, 29 March 1876; see also Instructions Delivered to Missionaries at Meetings of Committee, 5 July 1898; Houghton 1957, 343)

> Bear in mind Dear Friend that the initial ideas of Christianity will probably penetrate into the minds of the heathen by examples of its life giving power. The domestic happiness of your Home will be a powerful means of touching the affectionate hearts of the people. Awaken an inspiration first in the women after a higher kind of life and the men must follow. Win the women through the children. (CMS Archives, White to Last, 30 June 1881)

A new wife was seen as an essential helpmate to the struggling missionary bachelor:

> To do such work out here with no nurse, no reliable worker or assistant of any kind is beyond the physical capabilities of any man. And as there are so few hardships, I have written to a lady at home and asked her if she will come out as my wife. (CMS Archives, Pruen to Lang, 24 February 1887)[13]

Yet the arrival of white women at mission stations had effects unanticipated by those who formulated mission policy. Women's presence did not always improve evangelizing. Married missionaries often led lives more insulated from African affairs outside the station than did single ones (cf. Rotberg 196, 53). Marriage disrupted the close ties and physical proximity that many earlier missionaries sought with Africans, since most CMS men demanded that their wives be afforded privacy from native observations, especially from pagan men who drank, danced, and wore little clothing. Before marriage some lonely mission men mingled with Africans even in their leisure. Others remained alone and depressed in their houses, behavior that was often demoralizing to the missionaries and (though missionaries did not realize this) associated by Kaguru with antisocial, witchlike attitudes. With the arrival of missionary wives, missionary men were now less likely to spend their leisure, nonevangelizing hours with Africans, but at least, if they did now spend time apart, Kaguru could understand it, though no doubt many missionaries would have been shocked to realize that Kaguru would have assumed that this domestic seclusion was to afford missionaries opportunity for copulation. Kaguru did not and still do not see much sense in husbands and wives wanting to spend long hours alone together except for sexual relations. Men should properly spend time with other men and women with other women.

A wife legitimized a missionary man's need for free, "personal" time. The CMS were suspicious of leisure and urged members to spend all their waking hours in "the work." Yet a spouse legitimized some withdrawal into a private, Europeanized world away from Africans because the concerns of domestic life were themselves viewed as an essential feature of Christian conduct. To give time and attention to a spouse was not selfish and for CMS couples, time alone together for prayer, for sharing thoughts and feelings, was considered part of the essential, spiritual character of marriage, a conception of domestic privacy very different from that of Kaguru.

Even relations between male missionaries changed sharply after marriage. Unmarried missionary men resided together in one house, but once a man married the remaining bachelors could not associate freely with the new couple. These difficulties are illustrated by the Reverend Roscoe's complaints about the proximity of a single male missionary whose personal habits affronted Roscoe's wife (e.g., the offender strolled about outside his house in his bathrobe, shaving, brushing his teeth, and performing other morning and evening hygienic rites for all to see [CMS Archives, Roscoe to Lang, 7 November 1888; see also, CMS Proceedings 1883–84, 49; cf. Burn 1965, 37]). Marriage legitimized privatized space not previously dividing male missionaries from one another and sharply separating them from Kaguru.

In contrast to males, who should not share domestic space, single missionary women often resided with a mission couple, since women were not expected to cultivate assertive habits offensive or intrusive to others in the way single men might. Single women were expected to fit into the routine of men in any household, as boarders as well as wives and daughters. In such households the two bedrooms, each with an adjoining toilet, lay at opposite ends of a common sitting room. The kitchen was on the wife's side of the house, and the office where the extra woman worked was on the other. Such proximity posed a danger that a single woman would become a servant to the wife who assumed a role as head of housekeeping activities. Ideally, a single woman was to be a full-time missionary, but she could be turned from mission work into domestic service if her sister missionary were ill or tired (CMS Archives, Rees to Baylis, 18 April 1903; Waite to Baylis, 16 April 1895).[14]

The first woman missionaries to Ukaguru arrived in quick succession. J. T. Last's wife, Annie Jackson, arrived in Ukaguru in November 1880, becoming the first European woman in Ukaguru and probably the first

European woman to reside in Tanganyika. (Krapf's wife had died at Mombasa, on the Kenya coast [CMS Proceedings 1880–81, 38.) Henry Cole married H. Millington in 1881; Charles Stokes married Ellen Sharrett, a UMCA missionary, in 1883, against objections by both missions. By early 1883 there were three missionary wives, one at each station: Mrs. Last at Mamboya, Mrs. Cole at Kisokwe, and Mrs. Stokes at Mpwapwa.

Misfortune followed these women's arrival. Mrs. Last died in March, Mrs. Cole in July, and Mrs. Stokes the following spring, shortly after bearing a daughter, apparently the first European child born in Tanganyika.[15] The following year Stokes "married" a pagan African (an African ritual was used). The mission severed official ties with him although it still employed him to run caravans (see Luck 1972, 63–64; see also CMS Archives, Lang to Baxter, 26 March 1886).[16] Cole was sent home to study theology; Dr. E. J. Baxter, who had not yet married, went to England to wed. This left Last alone, but he soon was joined by the Reverend John Roscoe and his wife at Mamboya in central Ukaguru. Some months later Last was caught sleeping with African women and expelled from the mission, although he refused to leave East Africa. Last's exposure appears due to Roscoe's repeated inquiries into what Africans could tell him about Last's goings and comings. Roscoe appears to have been a zealous and disapproving investigator into the morals of all about him, both Europeans and Africans.

Despite earlier debate about dangers for women in the field, these deaths caused no setback for women going to Ukaguru. Missionary wives and even single women served regularly in the area, if not continuously, at least most of the time. Yet no more missionary women died. Often women missionaries outnumbered men in the area. As early as 1894, there were two married couples working in Mamboya, central Ukaguru, as well as the first two unmarried women who resided together south of there. Some women ran stations without the help of any men. Indeed, it is doubtful that the mission could have survived without these women. During one particularly difficult period, when the lone clergyman was sick for over a year, the various mission stations and services were entirely run by women (CMS Proceedings 1894–95, 86; CMS Archives, Bishop Tucker to Baylis, 9 September 1896; Spriggs to Baylis, 31 October 1910).[17]

Victorian Background to CMS Views of Women

The CMS view of women as missionaries was largely based on broader Victorian attitudes, which elevated women's moral and intellectual status at the price of suppressing their sexuality. At the same time, women's roles as wives and mothers remained rooted in the very sexuality that was suppressed. CMS consequently expressed these stereotypes of women in mixed and at times contradictory ways that sometimes allowed women to assume considerable independence in the field.

In 1876, when the CMS began its work in Ukaguru, its views regarding women appear typical of those held by most middle-class Victorians. As homemakers, women provided a moral haven for their toiling husbands. They served as models of probity, goodness, and nurturance to be emulated by others. One CMS article advocating the presence of mission women in the field argued that, "as a stream cannot rise above its source, so can no nation arise above its mothers" (Ball 1895, 4); the writer assumed that mission women, not men, were the proper evangelists of native women. If women had any proper calling to serve outside the home, it was to teach, help, and nurse children, other women, or the infirm. The CMS initially pictured missionary women as such beings to be emulated by other women, not only native women but coworkers and other Europeans. Furthermore, women's presence would prevent missionary men from "going native," as Last and Stokes had done, from losing sight of British values which were thought inextricably bound to family life.

Despite their roles as sensitive, nurturant, caring wives and mothers, Victorian women were seen as passionless and sexless. Cott remarks that Victorian evangelical women gained standing as moral and intellectual beings, finer and purer than men, at the price of being suppressed sexually (1971; see also Wohl 1978, 16; Holcombe 1973, 7).[18] This desexualized character probably accounts for the ease with which unmarried women were sent abroad. Missionary women were eventually even allowed to work alone in a wilderness surrounded by native men and occasionally by unmarried European men, both missionary and secular. While CMS writers mention the danger that missionary men might be sexually tempted (blamed on the licentiousness of native women and the morally debilitating African climate), no writer even implied that missionary women were in any way sexually compromised or tempted by their prolonged proximity to African men, who went about unclothed in a manner improper for men in Britain. At times it was argued that mission women should be spared undue exposure to what were viewed as the grosser sides of native or colonial European life, but this was to honor their sensitivity and purity, rather than suggest that they would be sensually stirred or corrupted. Even missionary wives and mothers, as portrayed in the CMS literature, are sexless creatures more motivated as missionary workers than as wives of missionary husbands.

While the CMS described missionary women contributing to a model of an ideal Christian family, this soon became a model seriously flawed according to local African (Kaguru) standards. Children born to such couples were sent home to Britain for rearing and education as soon as they left infancy. The CMS in Britain maintained a home and boarding school for mission children. Not surprisingly, many of these children grew up to become missionaries as well (Hewitt 1971, 460–61). Consequently, it was never likely for Kaguru to see a missionary family involved in childcare. The other major womanly task valued by Africans was the production and preparation of food. Yet most women missionaries relied on native servants to fetch water and firewood and to prepare, cook, and serve food.

Before a mission woman was sent to the field in Africa, she was (as was a man) interviewed by members of the CMS Home Committee to determine her moral and emotional character as well as her physical health. The mission would refuse to pay the passage and upkeep of an undesirable spouse, though I found no record of such steps ever being necessary.

CMS workers in Africa had to petition the Home Committee for permission to marry and bring a wife to the field. If a woman already in the field married someone outside the mission, she had to refund part of the costs that the mission had spent for her training and boat passage (CMS Archives, Baxter to Lang 18 June 1888). In any case marriage in the field was such a complicated process that no one could undertake it without extensive planning and great expense. During this era a mission couple had to undergo a civil as well as a religious service before they could live together. Before these rites could be held, the couple had to reside for a month in a "European community" (for those in Ukaguru, this usually meant Zanzibar), where banns could be published. If the woman journeyed to Africa to marry, the two had to take up residence in Zanzibar, where a British official lived or else the man had to meet the woman en route, perhaps in Aden or South Africa, so that other Europeans could witness their residence. This was frightfully expensive (CMS Archives, Baxter to Wright, 26 November 1879; Baylis to Beverley, 4 December 1898). It also meant that one or both missionaries were gone from work in Ukaguru for several months: it took weeks to get to and from Zanzibar, and another month or more was spent in Zanzibar itself. Finally, British officials and Anglican clergymen were busy and scarce so that finding two such men available, along with suitable witnesses, at the required time in these remote outposts could also be time-consuming. With all these rules and obstructions it was likely that, when a CMS couple did get married, they were well matched for their arduous work and had given much time to considering their decision:

> the marriage of one missionary to another is always a happy thing because one is sure not only of unity of purpose, so deep a bond, but

> also that each will have carefully and prayerfully sought God's guidance before taking so important a step. (CMS Archives, Manley to Barling, 22 June 1921)

The CMS initially proclaimed itself superior to its Roman Catholic rival because it had married missionaries who could serve as models of Christian family life to Africans. It then set up so many regulations that CMS families were hard to find in Ukaguru. Furthermore, those families that did exist hardly fit either Victorian or Kaguru stereotypes anyway.

Middle-Class Background of the CMS

The CMS has been repeatedly described as a middle-class and lower-upper-class body, though after the 1880s (the time I am concerned with here) it increasingly recruited from a wider social range that included those at the lower fringes of the middle class (P. Williams 1993, 54–57; cf. Strayer 1978, 5–6). Some evangelicals found that by entering mission work they could eventually raise their social standing, though this was probably not their primary motive for religious service. CMS missionary work was both rooted in the middle class and also epitomized class standing to such a degree that mission work itself added an aura of class standing to all who served, at least in the eyes of some. Mission work sometimes facilitated class mobility. More important to my present argument, middle-class characteristics supported ideas and values that empowered women as overseas missionaries.

In most ways CMS women's work in Ukaguru was grounded in what middle-class women had learned at home. For women of that class working for money was considered degrading, but labor itself was virtuous, since idleness was ungodly. Those women who found work at home insufficient for their needs to prove themselves took on charitable deeds. While soliciting funds figured in such activities, securing money for oneself was never a motive (Hewitt 1971, 457).[19] Many CMS women who were sent to East Africa had earlier worked among the urban poor, sick, aged, and orphaned.[20] Women were seen as empathizing or at least sympathizing with the unfortunate more than men could do because they were considered more sensitive and impressionable. For such middle-class women the urban poor were a different "tribe" from themselves. Most middle-class British women had lower-class servants who provided them with stereotypes of benighted beings comparable to Africans. Consequently, such work began to teach these women habits of supervision and a sense of superior noblesse oblige that would be repeated in their later treatment of Africans (Thorne, in this volume). Most evangelical social work among the British poor was in the hands of middle-class women (Heasman 1962, 23). Such women became altruistic beings thought to have special, unmercenary, moral qualities ideal for mission work.

There were, however, more practical middle-class traits generally not emphasized in CMS writings, though this may be because these were taken for granted. These were middle-class women's expertise in supervising the running of households employing some servants. Most middle-class Victorian married women employed at least one or two full- or part-time household servants and supervised them, showing and teaching them their skills, duties, and schedules. Such women were also expected to administer household records and accounts (see Branca 1975, 25, 47, 54–55; Scott and Tilley 1975, 145–78, esp. 160; Calder 1977, 20).

The leading trainer of CMS women noted that the main skills she cultivated in mission candidates were "domestic science and personal relations" (CMS Archives, Instructions to Missions, 5 July 1898; see also Baylis to Beverley, 4 December 1896; Instructions Delivered to Missions at Meeting of Committee, 5 July 1898; White to Last 30 June 1881). Consequently, middle-class CMS women arrived in Ukaguru with considerable ability in management and instruction of subordinates as well as many clerical (secretarial, not religious) skills. Africans, much like lower-class servants and the poor in Britain, were treated as perpetual, surrogate children in constant need of teaching, supervision, and correction. CMS women soon filled valuable roles as supervisors of African evangelists, nurses, teachers, and servants as well as becoming record keepers. CMS archives and publications suggest that many reports were prepared and sometimes written by these women. Some of the most useful and informative descriptions of missionary life in the field were provided by women.

Middle-class charity itself conveyed a profound sense of moral entitlement upon CMS women. The fact that one deigned to serve others socially inferior to oneself and without monetary reward conveyed a deep sense of impregnable moral rectitude. That sense of moral superiority guaranteed that such women could assume a freedom of movement and activity that would have been challenged in women of lower class or pursuing noncharitable tasks, a Major Barbara syndrome. This served CMS women richly in Ukaguru and contributed greatly to their newfound independence.

CMS Attitudes toward Women's Freedom and Independence

Initially, some CMS stereotypes about women's domesticity and fragility tended to restrict women's spatial movements in the field. Yet CMS leaders never seemed to rate women as second-class workers. Early on the

CMS Central Committee (on which women sometimes served) recognized that women were vital to successful evangelism. As the Ukaguru mission grew, women missionaries' roles in its work grew correspondingly and in ways that saw an ever-increasing and widening of women's freedom, both regarding movement over the Kaguru countryside and in autonomy regarding what they did.

All the CMS women first to arrive in Ukaguru were married to missionary men. Their movements were considerably restricted, both by their protective and solicitous husbands and by instructions from the Home Committee. At that time the CMS was uncertain about how safe the Kaguru countryside might be or how friendly local Africans were. According to early accounts, the countryside still harbored leopards, elephants, and even an occasional lion. Maasai (Baraguyu) warriors and Kamba hunters, all heavily armed, traveled amid local Kaguru and repeatedly fought with them. Arab and Nyamwezi caravans containing many rowdy and rough porters and armed guards geared for slaving and ivory hunting trekked through the countryside and often threatened local villagers for food and supplies.

Given early Ukaguru's wild state, it is understandable that CMS men feared to let their wives go far. At first it was felt that women should go everywhere accompanied by another missionary or some trusted African employees, usually armed. Furthermore, the very garb of Victorian women made hiking about Ukaguru extremely difficult, since the land is very rugged. Women in their cumbersome long skirts were often carried about in hammock-like contraptions slung between African porters.[21] These difficulties of getting about were exacerbated by the fact that at first the CMS preferred establishing stations on mountainsides rather than in valleys because they thought elevated areas healthier and more defensible (CMS Archives, Waites to Baylis, 16 April 1895; Baxter to Lang, 17 February 1886).

Later, even after CMS women gained more freedom to wander among Kaguru, mission men discouraged women from contact with German colonial administrators and certainly from German troops. Germans were considered unprincipled and unfit for proper contact with English ladies. This made some sense in the case of ordinary enlisted men, but German officers and administrators came from the nobility or at least the middle class and behaved very properly (CMS Archives, Executive Conference, 12–13 December 1902; Baylis to Briggs, 9 May 1905).

Soon the CMS Home Committee encouraged more freedom of movement by women missionaries, yet they still sought to limit women to working among Kaguru women and children, not Kaguru men:

> A woman Missionary will not (except in those rare cases where National custom and the sanctions of the local governing body allow) herself undertake Missionary work among men or lads: but while addressing herself to the great sphere open to her among her own sex, she will pray for the rich blessings of God to rest upon the parallel labours of her Missionary brethren among the Men. (CMS Archives, Doulton to Spriggs, 15 November 1909)[22]

At first it was felt that out of a sense of decorum CMS women should not mingle with African men. Yet it must have been obvious that all women missionaries in Ukaguru would inevitably encounter a wide range of African men constantly—villagers, servants, mission staff, porters, and traders in supplies. The Home Committee's argument gradually switched to claiming that women were ineffectual in evangelizing men, presumably because African men would be more impressed by European men.

> [The] Executive Committee feel that poor success [occurs] among women because lady missionaries [are] assigned work outside [the] women's sphere—thus women were instructing male Africans, interviewing male applicants, women preach[ing] to men, women employ[ing] male rather than female servants—supervisory council condemns all this. (CMS Archives, Executive Committee Report, Annual Report, received 12 January 1909; see also Doulton to Spriggs, 15 November 1909)

It may be that attempts to establish a separate domain for women evangelists encouraged CMS women's sense of independence, since this set up a sphere free of male supervision and interference.[23]

Missionary women were expected to visit native women in their villages, teach childcare, termed "mothercraft" (Hodgson 1928), homemaking, sewing, nutrition, simple reading, and to provide religious instruction to those women who sought conversion, especially those whose husbands had already taken this step. The CMS also required all their employees to attend special religious classes, and this included classes taught by women for the women so employed. Missionary women were assumed to be especially adept at dealing with children, an art none of the mission literature ever credits to men. Missionary women were expected to hold weekly meetings with local women and children from outlying areas and daily meetings with loyal Africans living closer to the station. These classes combined religious learning with practical instructions, so that African women could become useful aids to their converted husbands. Women preached Christian doctrines, led prayers, and taught and sang hymns. The mission also sometimes held Sunday prayer services for women apart from the services for men (CMS Archives, Annual Report from Berega, Rees 1911; Report of the Usagara-Ugogo Mission for 1909; Pickthall to Baylis, 10 November 1909; Hodgson 1928, 40–42; Pruen to Lang, 24 February 1897; Executive Conference received 12 January 1909; Edwards to Long, received 22 November 1882; Annual Report, received 12 January 1909; Doulton to Spriggs, 15 November 1909; Stock 1902, 47; CMS Proceedings 1880–81, 37).[24]

Missionary men felt uncomfortable about prolonged contact with native women. In this sense they were almost as restricted as early mission women and were relieved when women finally arrived and eliminated the problem. Before any women missionaries came out to Ukaguru, missionary men were proud to provide sanctuary to runaway slaves from caravans passing through the area, yet these same missionaries were perplexed about how they should deal with such slave women (Pruen 1891, 254–55; cf. Oliver 1952, 83–85; CMS Archives, Baxter to Wright, 13 June 1878; 10 July 1878; 18 April 1879).[25] Missionary men were even uneasy about dealing with local African women employed as servants, yet such women were essential, since Kaguru men did not customarily fetch water, collect firewood, or cook. (This has changed with decades of colonial contact, though, even as late as when I lived in the area, male servants wanted to employ women out of their own wages for some female-associated tasks, such as washing clothing and fetching water.) Missionary men had to employ a married couple or else a male servant employed his kinswomen to do female-associated tasks.

Though some missionaries at first felt uncomfortable about keeping servants, it soon became obvious that without servants the missionaries would spend most of their time sunk in the everyday drudgery of household tasks such as fetching firewood and water, cleaning, processing food, cooking, and hauling goods. African servants became an integral part of CMS station life in Ukaguru, and such servants always necessarily included some women. It was admitted, even by the Home Committee, that once women missionaries were in the field African women could be more safely employed (CMS Archives, Baxter to Lang, 18 June 1886). Despite this, Kaguru preferred to keep their women at home to cultivate and tend children. Though the CMS never seemed to recognize this fact, employment of women by the mission posed as many problems for Kaguru as it did for the missionaries.

The period when the Ukaguru mission was being expanded and stabilized coincided with a time when the CMS was revising its attitudes about employing single women in Africa. By the 1890s the CMS showed a growing willingness to allow single women in the field and even granted such women considerable independence in their work (P. Williams 1993, 63; cf. Cust 1885; see also Stock 1909). It should be remembered, too, that by this time about 20 percent of CMS women missionaries were self-supporting financially and therefore could reasonably demand more voice in how they might be employed (P. Williams 1993, 58). Cust, one of the most important CMS publicists for recruiting missionaries, was one of the first advocates to encourage both married and unmarried women into the African field. In one of his recruiting tracts he sketches a picture of a woman missionary's reception by heathens that would have appealed to the ego and romantic ardor of someone who may have felt unfulfilled and unappreciated in Britain:

> To the village-women the appearance of a Female Evangelist must be, as it were, the vision of an Angel from Heaven: to their untutored eyes she appears taller in stature, fairer in face, fairer in speech, than anything mortal that they had dreamed of before: bold and fearless, without immodesty: pure in word and action, and yet with features unveiled: wise, yet still a woman loving and tender. Suddenly their eyes . . . their ears, and their hearts seem to realize, faintly and confusedly, the Beauty and Holiness, when they begin to hold converse only too brief, with the wondrous desire to save souls. [She] has come across the Sea from some unknown country to comfort and help them. Short as her stay, she has as it were, with a magic wand, let loose a new fountain of hopes, of fears, and desires. (1895, 105–6)

The CMS considered itself enlightened and progressive in its treatment of women, though there seems little to distinguish the society from many other evangelical protestant groups on this score. The CMS was concerned that its women not be exploited and that their talents be properly used. The Home Committee feared that missionary men and their wives would sometimes unfairly dominate single women. That domination often involved restrictions in such women's range and scope of activities:

> You know that we have rather questioned the wisdom of arranging the house accommodations so that one single lady is placed in any centre with a married couple because we feel that in that way the work of the single lady is made practically to depend on the health of the wife. (CMS Archives, Baylis to Colsey, 10 January 1900; see also Waites to Baylis, 16 April 1895; Instructions to Missionaries, 5 July 1898)

In all these gradual changes of policy the CMS advocated increasing freedom of movement and independence by women workers, especially single women or women whose husbands were ill or traveling.

The CMS leadership in London once singled out the Ukaguru mission as being prone to exploit women workers:

> We often feel that there is some need to protect the women missionaries from the assumption which may creep into a Mission that the function of the ladies is to be a sort of assistant worker under the Superintending Missionary, much as ladies working in a Parish at home are under the Clergy. We feel that in all the circumstances of our Missionary work that ought not to be assumed as the normal position, though when circumstances require it may be the right one. It is, however, very unfortunate if the time comes that some ordained man claims the authority and control over the work of quite senior lady missionaries just because he is a Clergy man and they are ladies. We feel that each lady has the same general claim to recognition as a Missionary of full rank as has any of the men. There seems a tendency in your Mission for every man to become either Superintending Missionary or the Principal of a central Institution, and for every lady, on the other hand, to remain in subordinate work. We think that must be likely to lead to difficulties, and for my own part I sometimes think it would be a good thing to secure as soon as possible a more independent status for some at least of the ladies. It would be a different thing if there were junior male Missionaries doing the same thing: but I do not think there is much work planned on those lines in East Africa. (CMS Archives, Baylis to Colsey, 10 January 1900)

This warning reflects a struggle for influence between senior, strong-minded, veteran women missionaries and a man who was newly arrived and not experienced running a mission or working with Kaguru but claiming rank as a clergyman. Such conflict was not a constant problem at the Ukaguru mission, though even in the 1950s and 1960s, when I did fieldwork in Ukaguru, occasional conflicts of this sort still occurred. That such a cautionary letter was written from the Home Committee to an arrogant male missionary powerfully reflects the influence women could exert back to the Home Committee. Women workers became essential to CMS survival, and the Home Committee became increasingly concerned to keep women satisfied with how they were treated. When this letter was written, some CMS women had run mission stations single-handedly, and women back in Britain continued to show interest in entering mission service even while men's recruitment was beginning to slacken. All CMS missionaries, women and men alike, savored the opportunity and challenge of running their own shows (cf. Strayer 1973, 229–48). One of the reasons women continued to volunteer even after men lost enthusiasm may be because at this time such work still offered women challenges, fulfillment, and independence not so easily available to them as to men back in Britain.

By the turn of the century CMS women were only occasionally limited in what they did and where they might go. When this did occur, this was more on account of an occasional case of ingrained sexual bias on the part of some individual male missionary and not due to mission policy. By 1900 that policy strongly advocated radical sexual equality between men and women missionaries. Where this was not achieved, this was condemned and lamented by those in charge back in London. While male monopoly on religious offices put all Anglican women missionaries at a disadvantage, evangelical missions, such as the CMS, which downplayed clerical roles and stressed instead the Holy Spirit, advanced women more than other Christian groups. Femininity was seen as an essential aspect of women's qualifications as workers, even though it was denied at times, especially in terms of sexuality and child rearing.[26]

By then the mission's tendency sometimes to write and speak about separation between the sexes was more an empty slogan than a prevailing practice, though it did encourage access to over half the population (women and children) to women alone. There were, however, too few missionaries at any station for sexual compartmentalization ever to be practicable, and where it was ignored, it was on the side of allowing women wider access to the entire population. Women missionaries ordered and worked with Africans of both sexes; they had to in order to run a station or even a section of one. Local Africans found this easy to accept, since most did not think now of missionary women as primarily women but, rather, first and foremost as Europeans.[27]

CMS Women's Work as Evangelists

The CMS never envisioned women as any less committed to evangelical work than men, and some of their attitudes toward women appear more egalitarian than those of many other British at this time. This may relate to the strong CMS emphasis upon individual, spiritually inspired work rather than clerical ritual activities and upon their assumption that laity are as important as clerics in doing mission work and in making policies. Women as well as men could be animated by the Holy Spirit and inspired through revival meetings or intensive prayers and self-searching. Lay people as well as clerics were always on the various committees in Britain, and some were women. These views undermined male monopoly of CMS affairs, at least in practice in the field if not in higher policy-making.

> it is of the utmost importance that you endeavour to take your fair share of the distinctly missionary work of your station, not merely for your own soul to profit, but in order to supply an object lesson to the wives of native workers and Native Christians generally. They [the Committee] have recently had occasion to deplore the lack of such evangelistic enterprise on the part of many of the wives of Native workers in the field. This, they believe, can best be corrected by the whole-hearted devotion and consecrated lives of their European missionaries. (CMS Archives, Instructions to Missions, 5 July 1898; see also Baylis to Beverley, 4 December 1895; Instructions delivered to Missions at Meeting of Committee, 5 July 1898; White to Last, 30 June 1881)

For these tasks women received little formal training until after World War I, but most missionary men received little more. For evangelicals such as the CMS seriousness and a born-again religious experience made up for deficiencies in formal theological training. Two establishments in England, The Willows and The Olives, as well as a hostel, provided basic practical and religious training for CMS women (see Stock 1907, 28; Beidelman 1982a, 154–55).[28] Yet no training in African languages or culture was ever provided to either men or women before any workers went to the field. As a result, the first years abroad for all missionaries, women and men, were difficult and bewildering as newcomers struggled to absorb enough about local languages and customs to interact with Africans, even on the simplest level of securing basic needs and wants, let alone evangelizing.

This lack of training about African culture was due to a general missionary disparagement of African cultures. African customs did not merit serious study, and only J. T. Last ever undertook anything resembling serious ethnographic study of Africans and Ukaguru, and in his case the CMS could point to how that interest had led Last into "going African" and sleeping with African women. African languages were thought to be skills that one could pick up in the field, not to be taught in schools as one taught French or Latin. In any case African customs were to be changed, not learned, and African languages, including Chikaguru, were soon reduced to irrelevancy by the colonial government's promotion of Swahili. Mission interest in local languages gave way to a concern for Swahili as a lingua franca that could serve for all of East Africa, regardless of which tribal area one might be assigned to evangelize. When missionary men and women were newly arrived and consequently ignorant of local practices, they invariably found themselves dependent on old-timers for learning and advice. Often this meant that male newcomers had to depend on women veterans for help and wisdom.

While the first women missionaries received little formal training about missionizing, many had gained considerable practical experience that would serve them well in East Africa and elsewhere. (Warren fondly describes CMS missionaries getting "their education the hard way" [1970, 62].) Many came from mission families and were familiar with rudimentary aspects of the work through talking to kin at home, though that can hardly have prepared them for the shocks of life in a tropical wilderness. Many had been involved in mission work at home, especially in the cities. Indeed, most evangelical social work in Britain was in the hands of middle-class women (Heasman 1962, 23). While London's and Manchester's poor were hardly pagan Africans, they presented a picture alien and hostile to these CMS women's ordinary middle-class experiences and surroundings. In such work in Africa as in the slums of Britain, missionary women proselytized, organized, led subordinates, and ministered care.

Conclusion

During the period between the 1880s and World War I, CMS women were increasingly important in running the Ukaguru mission. These stations could not have managed without women teaching, nursing, supervising African staff and servants, and keeping accounts and records. At times some stations were run entirely by women. These women's roles were far removed from the stereotypes of mission women as mainly supportive wives; in any case the CMS in Ukaguru never seemed to picture women as "relatively invisible" in the way described by Kirkwood (1993, 28). Certainly, CMS women had found responsibilities and opportunities far beyond those afforded in the home. Long after many middle-class women in Britain had begun to lose servants and been forced to assume household chores themselves, mission women in East Africa continued to employ servants. Not even the burdens of motherhood interfered for long with their evangelistic work, since most mission couples sent their children home for an education not available in East Africa. The price women missionaries paid for these new tasks and freedom was a loss of some of the roles of homemaking and motherhood (cf. Bowie 1973, 9). While it may be true that many women welcomed these new freedoms, some married women saw these denials of wifely and motherly responsibilities as another proof of sacrifice on their part. But CMS women were supposed to find altruism and denial of "natural" urges to be a gift to God and a way to build character, so long as such rigors advanced "the work." Women missionaries' roles were increasingly validated as sacrifice and evangelistic service rather than by serving as models of domestic Christian virtue and nurturance. This steady transformation in women's roles was clearly rooted in the CMS commitment to evangelism inspired by the Holy Spirit rather than by theological training. It appears that evangelical missions such as the CMS, while conservative regarding many economic and political issues, were radical in their commitment to equality toward women as Christian workers. The Holy Spirit was very demanding, but it was an equal opportunity employer.

NOTES

1. Earlier I published extensively on this mission regarding its history and its recent affairs (1974, 1981, 1982a–b). My book (1982a) contains an extensive bibliography on the CMS.

I am grateful to the National Science Foundation, the Wenner-Gren Foundation, and New York and Duke Universities for funds and time to complete this work. I thank Karen Blu, Gillian Feeley-Harnik, Mary Huber, Patricia Lamb, Nancy Lutkehaus, John Middleton, Rodney Needham, and Annette Weiner, for reading various drafts. This essay remained unpublished for over twenty years due to the thinness of the data. My revision is due to a 1989 Ida Bean Visiting Lectureship in history at the University of Iowa, for which I am grateful, and to Mary Huber and Nancy Lutkehaus, who invited me to give a condensed version of this at a session of the American Anthropological Association meetings in 1993.

The material for this essay derives almost entirely from the CMS Archives and from early CMS publications, which, at the time of my research, were located in London but have subsequently been moved to Birmingham. These sources fail to provide many details on the social background of missionaries that would enhance my arguments. I have tried to tease out what I could from them. The CMS themselves did not seem to regard the mission to Ukaguru as typical, and yet much of what I report probably pertains to CMS stations elsewhere, though perhaps not in such accentuated forms.

The CMS Archives contain reports, instructions, diaries, and correspondence. They are cited by author (if known) and title or, if letters, by the last names of the sender and recipient and the date sent. These early sources provide no explicit information about how local Kaguru viewed missionary women. I know, however, how conservative Kaguru viewed colonial women in the 1950s and 1960s, when I did fieldwork in Ukaguru. There is little reason to doubt that Kaguru responses would have been even more critical and perplexed at this earlier period of contact. In these terms I can make a few cautious remarks about how Kaguru were likely to have viewed what missionaries said and did.

2. The CMS leader Max Warren goes too far in claiming that the transfor-

mations in emancipation achieved by women missionaries may be the most remarkable of all those in the Victorian age (1970, 69). Compare his observations with Bradley (1976, 91) and Bolt (1971, 140). Strayer reports that by 1913 women missionaries far outnumbered men in the CMS stations in Kenya (1978, 5–6). CMS attitudes resemble those exhibited by many nineteenth-century Protestant groups elsewhere, although Welter suggests that British missions were in advance of Americans in conceding opportunities to women workers, especially those who were unmarried (1980, 111–25). Strobel remarks how missions brought new options to women (1987, 376).

3. Ukaguru is occupied by the Kaguru, a Bantu language–speaking people today numbering over one hundred thousand (Beidelman 1971). I earlier published general historical studies of Ukaguru (1962, 1978).

4. Cominos notes that religion afforded the one area in which work outside the home did not detract from a Victorian middle-class woman's status (1973, 163). Where a woman missionary such as Mary Slessor worked beyond the ordinary reach of mission and secular colonial authorities, she secured power and authority comparable to men's (Burns 1981; Livingstone 1916). CMS women in Ukaguru did not equal Mary Slessor, but they were often stationed alone in Ukaguru and did hold considerable power. Similarly, American black missionaries found their work abroad a compensatory avenue to power and prestige (W. Williams 1982, 92–96).

5. The historical study of women missionaries during the Victorian and Edwardian eras has received far less attention than it deserves. The most distinguished exceptions to this are Hunter's useful study of American women missionaries in China (1984) and Langmore's excellent study of missionaries in Papua New Guinea (1989). Valuable but less searching studies of American women missionaries in Hawaii are among the few others to address such issues (Grimshaw 1983; Welter 1980).

6. Given these richly contradictory factors, it is surprising how little attention has been given to examining careers of mission women and the ways they were judged, even though other areas of nineteenth-century women's activities have attracted much attention from scholars. For surveys and discussion of recent research on women of this period, see Kanner 1973, 1980; L'Esp'rance 1972; Vicinus 1980. During this period Britain experienced a surplus of women who could not or did not want to marry (Kanner 1973, 182–85). It is not clear to what extent missionizing alleviated these redundant middle-class women's plight (Vicinus 1980, xvi). The CMS sent its first woman missionary to Africa (Sierra Leone) in 1820 (Stock 1907, 7).

7. Women workers are not unusual in Christianity; for example, they appear in early Christianity and more recently in early English Methodism.

8. Strayer argues that CMS women in neighboring Kenya were treated as "second-class missionaries." Though they outnumbered missionary men by 1913, there they were unrepresented on local decision-making bodies and affected policies only indirectly. Strayer maintains that even when women missionaries lodged complaints they were ignored or castigated. My impression for CMS in Ukaguru is

somewhat different. This policy of freely setting up new stations continued up to World War I; then a more formal organization was maintained wherein new stations were rarely established, at least in Ukaguru (Strayer 1978, 6; cf. Strayer 1973; Hewitt 1971, 435).

9. The moral upliftment did not usually involve any sustained policies for material betterment or class mobility (Pelling 1969).

10. Best (1974, 54–55) comments on the ease with which evangelicals confronted death. Burn illustrates how Victorian missionaries saw such deaths as moral lessons (1965, 44–45).

11. This fear was sustained in two cases in which a recently widowed missionary slept with Africans and another "married" one. In both cases the missionary was dismissed (CMS Archives, Roscoe to Wigram, 1 June 1885; Baxter to Lang, 29 January 1886; Baxter to Lang, 27 February 1886; Lang to Baxter, 21 April 1886; see Beidelman 1981, 91–92). Some CMS missionaries thought this demonstrated an urgent need for women in the field.

12. This avoidance was still the trend when I was in Ukaguru in the 1950s and 1960s. Nonmissionary colonial Europeans often drank and smoked heavily, enjoyed dancing, and often swore colorfully. The CMS condemned all of this (cf. Strobel 1987, 385).

13. Pruen's argument is self-contradictory; nevertheless, his plea was granted, and his wife was among the first CMS women to survive a tour in Ukaguru.

14. It may be that missionaries projected Victorian views of the wife's sister upon female missionaries. A wife's sister was sexually unavailable, even after the wife's demise, yet she was expected to provide frequent aid to her sister's household, especially if she herself were unmarried (see Burn 1965, 37). Regarding the tensions between women domiciled in the same house, see CMS Archives, Baylis to Colsey, 10 January 1900; Waites to Baylis, 16 April 1895; Instructions to Missionaries, 5 July 1898. No reports are available about what Kaguru made of such arrangements. Kaguru custom finds it unthinkable that an adult male would be domiciled with two women with one hearth, even if he were married to both. Kaguru must have considered such arrangements among missionaries shameless.

15. Death in childbed was very common among all classes of Victorians, so there was no reason that the mission had to credit such a death to being in Africa; see Branca 1975, 86–96.

16. A more recent biography of Stokes adds nothing (Harman 1986).

17. Even much later a woman missionary nurse describes herself as the sole medical worker in all of Ukaguru, running a clinic with two African nurses (Hobbs 1927).

18. In a fascinating essay discussing the impact of British colonialism on Nigerian women, van Allen points out that missionary emphasis on the primary role of women as homemakers undermined the traditional power and security of many African women (1972, 112).

19. Some idea of the formidable skills required to manage a Victorian middle-class household may be gained by reading Beeton (1861, 1, 21–23).

20. Women were especially valued as nurses. Anderson believes association of

medical work with women lowered its esteem among missions (1956, 10; see also Pope 1977, 299, 319, 321).

21. Some Kaguru still recall this mode of travel by missionaries and remark on how weird they consider it to be. Such hammocks had been originally fashioned by Kaguru to transport corpses to graves.

22. Similar pleas were used to validate women's mission work in Muslim areas where purdah was practiced. In Ukaguru, when women missionaries were absent, few African women attended services (CMS Archives, Annual Letter from Deekes to Baylis, 19 November 1909).

23. Wright found this true among the Moravian missionaries of East Africa (1971, 11).

24. Even today, while Kaguru men and women jointly attend church services, they rarely sit intermingled.

25. Local Kaguru would have expected women captured from slave caravans to become wives or concubines to those lucky enough to acquire them. Since single African women without kin had no kind of social security during these times, these women themselves would have expected to be given some such kind of status as a guarantee of their benefactors' goodwill. It is certainly clear from what little we have reported in the archives that such women did all they could to ingratiate themselves with their male saviors.

26. For useful comments on relations between European women's subordination to their own men but their superiority over a colonially subordinated ethnic group, see Balhatchet 1980, 8–9, 114–15.

27. In contrast, American Protestant missions in Hawaii required all women missionaries to be married so that the demands of childrearing usurped most of these women's original plans to evangelize (Grimshaw 1983).

28. Only in 1917 did the CMS assume formal responsibility for training women missionaries; previously training centers such as The Willows and The Olives were run by others (Hewitt 1971, 556–667).

REFERENCES

Anderson, H. G. 1956. *The New Phase in Medical Strategy.* London: Church Missionary Society.

Balhatchet, Kenneth. 1980. *Race, Sex and Class under the Raj.* New York: St. Martin's Press.

Ball, A. E. 1895. The Need and the Scope of Women's Work. *Church Missionary Intelligencer* 20:40–43.

Beeton, Isabella. 1861. *The Book of Household Management.* London: Beeton.

Beidelman, T. O. 1962. A History of Ukaguru, Kilosa District: 1857–1916. *Tanganyika Notes and Records* 58–59:11–39.

———. 1983 [1971]. *The Kaguru.* Prospect Heights, Ill.: Waveland Press.

———. 1974. Social Theory and the Study of Christian Missions. *Africa* 44:235–49.

———. 1978. Chiefship in Ukaguru. *The International Journal of African Historical Studies* 11:227–46.

———. 1981. Contradictions between the Sacred and the Secular Life. *Comparative Studies in Society and History* 23:73–95.

———. 1982a. *Colonial Evangelism: A Socio-Cultural Study of an East African Mission at the Grassroots.* Bloomington: Indiana University Press.

———. 1982b. The Organization and Maintenance of Caravans by the Church Missionary Society in Tanzania in the Nineteenth Century. *The International Journal of African Historical Studies* 15:601–23.

Best, Geoffrey. 1974. Evangelicalism and the Victorians. In *The Victorian Crisis of Faith,* ed. Anthony Symondson, 37–56. London: Society for the Promotion of Christian Knowledge.

Bolt, Christine. 1971. *Victorian Attitudes to Race.* London: Routledge and Kegan Paul.

Bowie, Fiona. 1993. Reclaiming Women's Presence. Introduction to *Women and Missions: Past and Present. Anthropological and Historical Perceptions,* ed. Fiona Bowie, Deborah Kirkwood, and Shirley Ardener, 1–19. Oxford: Berg.

Bradley, Ian. 1976. *The Call to Seriousness: The Evangelical Impact on the Victorians.* New York: Macmillan.

Branca, Patricia. 1975. *Silent Sisterhood: Middle Class Women in the Victorian Home.* London: Croom Helm.

Burn, W. L. 1965. *The Age of Equipose.* New York: Norton.

Burns, James. 1981. *The Expendable Mary Slessor.* New York: Seabury Press.

Calder, Jeanni. 1977. *The Victorian Home.* London: Batsford.

Cell, J. W., ed. 1976. By Kenya Possessed:The Correspondence between Norman Leys and J. H. Oldham. Chicago: University of Chicago Press.

Christ, Carol. 1980. Victorian Masculinity and the Angel in the House. In *A Widening Sphere,* ed. Martha Vicinus, 146–62. Bloomington: Indiana University Press.

Church Missionary Society (CMS). 1880–95. *Proceedings of the Church Missionary Society.* London: CMS.

———. Archives. Birmingham, England.

Cominos, Peter T. 1973. Innocent Femina Sensualis in Unconscious Conflict, In *Suffer and Be Still,* ed. Martha Vicinus, 155–72. Bloomington: Indiana University Press.

Cott, Nancy. 1971. Passionlessness: An Interpretation of Victorian Sexual Ideology, 1789–1850. *Signs* 4:219–36.

Crow, Duncan. 1971. *The Victorian Woman.* London: Allen and Unwin.

Cust, R. 1885. The Female Evangelist. *Church Missionary Intelligencer* 10:687–710.

———. 1886. *A Cry for Missions and a Missionary Spirit.* Hertford: S. Austen.

———. 1891. *Africa Rediviva, or, the Occupation of Africa by Christian Missionaries of Europe and North America.* London: Elliot Stock.

———. 1892. *The Hero Missionary and the Heroic Missionary Society.* Hertford: S. Austen.

———. 1895. Dr. Cust on Missions and Missionaries. *Church Missionary Intelligencer* 10:103–10.

Elliott-Binns, L. E. 1936. *Religion in the Victorian Era.* London: Lutterworth.

Grimshaw, Patricia. 1983. Christian Woman, Pious Wife, Faithful Mother, Devoted Missionary: Conflicts in Roles of American Missionary Women in Nineteenth-Century Hawaii. *Feminist Studies* 9:489–521.

Harman, Nicholas. 1986. *Bwana Stokesi and His African Conquests.* London: Jonathan Cape.

Heasman, Kathleen. 1962. *Evangelicals in Action.* London: Geoffrey Bles.

Hewitt, Gordon. 1971. *The Problem of Success: A History of the Church Missionary Society, 1910–1941,* vol. 1. London: SCM Press.

Hobbs, Violet H. 1927. Medical Work in Ukaguru, Tanganyika Territory. *Mission Hospital* 31:313–16.

Hodgson, E. G. 1928. Settling at Kongwa. *Westward Ho!* 38:40–42.

Holcombe, Lee. 1973. *Victorian Ladies at Work.* Hamden: Archon.

Hooper, W. 1911. Missionary Policy. *Church Missionary Review* 61:72–82.

Houghton, Walter E. 1957. *The Victorian Frame of Mind.* New Haven: Yale University Press.

Hunter, Jane. 1984. *The Gospel of Gentility: American Women Missionaries in Turn-of-the-Century China.* New Haven: Yale University Press.

Kanner, S. Barbara. 1973. The Women of England in a Century of Social Change, 1815–1914: A Select Bibliography, Part 1. In *Suffer and Be Still,* ed. Martha Vicinus, 173–206. Bloomington: Indiana University Press.

———. 1980. The Women of England in a Century of Social Change, 1815–1914: A Select Bibliography, Part 2. In *A Widening Sphere,* ed. Martha Vicinus, 199–270. Bloomington: Indiana University Press.

Kirkwood, Deborah. 1993. Protestant Missionary Women: Wives and Spinsters. In *Women and Missions: Past and Present. Anthropological and Historical Perspectives,* ed. Fiona Bowie, Deborah Kirkwood, and Shirley Ardener, 23–41. Providence, R.I.: Berg.

Kitson Clark, D. 1962. *The Making of Victorian England.* Cambridge: Harvard University Press.

Langmore, Diane. 1989. *Missionary Lives: Papua, 1874–1914.* Center for Pacific Islands Studies, Pacific Islands Monograph Series, no. 6. Honolulu: University of Hawaii Press.

L'Esp'rance, Jeanne. 1972. Women's History: Work in Progress in the United Kingdom. *Women's Studies* 3:179–92.

Livingstone, W. P. 1916. *Mary Slessor of Calabar,* 7th ed. London: Macmillan.

Luck, Anne. 1972. *Charles Stokes in Africa.* Nairobi: East African Publishing House.

Lyons, Charles H. 1975. *To Wash an Aethiop White: British Ideas about Black Educatability, 1530–1960.* New York: Teachers College Press, Columbia University.

Oliver, Roland. 1952. *The Missionary Factor in East Africa.* London: Longmans.

Pelling, Gary. 1969. Religion and the Nineteenth Century British Working Class. *Past and Present* 17:128–35.

Pope, Barbara C. 1977. Angels in the Devil's Workshop: Leisured and Charitable Women in Nineteenth Century England and France. In *Becoming Visible: Women in European History,* ed. Renate Bridenthal and Claudia Koonz, 1st ed., 296–324. Boston: Houghton Mifflin.

Pruen, S. 1891. *The Arab and the African.* London: Sesley.

Rotberg, Robert. 1965. *Christian Missionaries and the Creation of Northern Rhodesia.* Princeton: Princeton University Press.

Scott, Joan W., and Louise A. Tilley. 1975. Women's Work and the Family in Nineteenth-Century Europe. In *The Family in History,* ed. Charles E. Rosenberg, 145–78. Philadelphia: University of Pennsylvania Press.

Stock, Eugene. 1899. *The History of the Church Missionary Society,* vols. 1, 3. London: CMS.

———. 1902. *Church Missionary Society Centenary Volume.* London: CMS.

———. 1907. *A Historical Survey of Women's Work in the C.M.S.* London: CMS.

Strayer, Robert. 1973. The Dynamics of Mission Expansion: A Case Study from Kenya, 1875–1915. *The International Journal of African Historical Studies* 6:229–48.

———. 1978. *The Making of Mission Communities in East Africa: Anglicans and Africans in Colonial Kenya.* London: Heinemann.

Strobel, Margaret. 1987. Gender and Race in the Nineteenth- and Twentieth-Century British Empire. In *Becoming Visible: Women in European History,* ed. Renate Bridenthal et al., 2d ed., 375–96. Boston: Houghton Mifflin.

Van Allen, Judith. 1972. "Sitting on a Man": Colonialism and the Lost Political Institutions of Igbo Women. *Canadian Journal of African Studies* 6:165–91.

Vicinus, Martha. 1980. Introduction to *A Widening Sphere,* ed. M. Vicinus, ix–xix. Bloomington: Indiana University Press.

Warren, Max. 1970. The Church Militant Abroad: Victorian Missionaries. In *The Victorian Crisis of Faith,* ed. Anthony Symondson, 57–70. London: Society for the Promotion of Christian Knowledge.

———. 1971. *Social History and Christian Mission.* London: SCM Press.

Watt, Mrs. Stuart [Rachel]. N.d. *In the Heart of Savagedom.* London: Marshall.

Welter, Barbara. 1980. "She Hath Done What She Could": Protestant Women's Missionary Careers in Nineteenth Century America. In *Women in American Religion,* ed. Janet Wilson James, 111–25. Philadelphia: University of Pennsylvania Press.

Williams, C. P. 1980. "Not Quite Gentlemen": An Examination of "Middling Class" Protestant Missionaries from Britain, c. 1850–1900. *Journal of Ecclesiastical History* 31:301–15.

Williams, P. 1993. "The Missing Link": The Recruitment of Women Missionaries in Some English Evangelical Missionary Societies in the Nineteenth Century. In *Women and Missions: Past and Present—Anthropological and Historical Perspectives,* ed. Fiona Bowie, Deborah Kirkwood, and Shirley Ardener, 43–69. Providence, R.I.: Berg.

Williams, Walter. 1982. *Black Americans and the Evangelization of Africa, 1877–1900.* Madison: University of Wisconsin Press.

Wohl, A. S. 1978. Introduction to *The Victorian Family,* ed. A. S. Wohl, 9–19. New York: St. Martin's Press.

Wright, Marcia. 1971. *German Missions in Tanganyika, 1891–1941.* Oxford: Clarendon Press.

Why Can't a Woman Be More like a Man? Bureaucratic Contradictions in the Dutch Missionary Society

Rita Smith Kipp

The Dutch Missionary Society (Nederlands Zendelinggenootschap, NZG) was the first and long the premiere missionary organization in the Dutch East Indies.[1] As a nondenominational body founded in 1797 in Rotterdam on the model of the London Missionary Society, it was not officially linked to any particular church. By the end of the nineteenth century several other sending organizations had emerged in Holland, some of them more orthodox and evangelical in orientation than the NZG, whose support then came mostly from the Hervormd rather than the Gereformeerd Church. That is, the NZG was increasingly associated with the more liberal stream in Dutch Protestantism.

The theologically liberal NZG was, however, socially conservative in its deployment of women. It was unusually slow to commission women as independent professional missionaries compared to counterparts in other countries. For example, the feminization of the American missionary ranks began to occur when a handful of single women entered missionary work before the Civil War. Many more followed them in the latter half of the nineteenth century and the first two decades of the twentieth. The British and Swiss experiences were similar.[2] In contrast, the NZG commissioned its first professional woman missionary for independent evangelistic work only in 1935, and then only under pressure from a new, and explicitly feminist, missionary support group, the Women's Missionary Bond (Vrouwen-Zendingsbond, VZB).

I will view the NZG through the lens of one particular local installation, or "field," that carried the misnomer *Deli Zending* for most of its history. *Deli* was the name by which Hollanders referred to the entire East Coast region of Sumatra, a region famous for its plantations and infamous for its labor conditions and general rowdiness. The field did not in fact target the entire Deli region but really only one ethnic group there, the Karo Batak. Like other installations of the NZG, the Karo Zending, as it finally came to be known, gradually included more and more women nurses and teachers as a result of its expansion into social services such as health care and education. The eight women who worked in the Karo field between 1914 and 1942, most of them coming and going over rather brief periods, generated a disproportionate share of the personnel problems that found their way into the letters, minutes, and reports from this period.

My attention here falls on the two women on whom the archival materials were unusually rich. The conflicts surrounding these two revolved around questions of competence and, from today's retrospective vantage, appear as sites of feminist struggle. I will examine these troublesome sites in the light of theories about bureaucracy in order to explore two contradictions. The first of these contradictions applies generally to bureaucracies everywhere, while the second is specific to missions and other bureaucracies pointed toward religious goals.

First, the bureaucratic ideal of hiring and evaluating personnel according to objective standards clashed with an intransigent gender inequality in Dutch society at large. Although the women who worked in this mission field were hired to act like men in professional respects, they came to their positions without the formal and informal training their male colleagues had had. Their prior experiences—in families, schools, and other institutions as well as in interpersonal relations—had not prepared them for the behaviors required in their new roles. Even so, male colleagues probably underestimated the competence of these women (and one of these women clearly underestimated her *own* competence) because of persistent gender stereotypes. In this sense some of the problems of hiring women and judging their performance were external to the bureaucratic structure of the missionary organization.

Second, the formal rationality of bureaucracy is associated culturally with maleness, while the substantive rationality of the missionary endeavor, I will argue, is culturally associated with females. Pursuing this second contradiction, I will show that the problems of these two women were due not merely to the mission's external, gendered environment but also to the limitations of bureaucratic forms themselves. These limitations inhibited women's effective deployment as missionaries, to be sure, but may also have undermined the ultimate purpose of the mission—converting the Karo to Christianity. The growing hierarchy, impersonalization, and formality that characterized the mission to the Karo undercut the religious ends and values that the missionaries embraced as their reason for being, ends and values that, in the gender logic of Western societies, were feminine.

The Bureaucratic Conundrum

Bureaucratic organizations and the bureaucratic management of information were key elements of colonial domination (e.g., Fields 1985, 36–41). The (provisional) success of colonialism depended not merely on technological or military advantages but also on organizational forms by which "an extraordinarily small number of officials, scattered sparsely across vast territories and populations" (Dauber 1995, 82) ruled through surveillance, record keeping and filing, report writing, map making, and other bureaucratic arts. Furthermore, bureaucratic structures and ideals were a significant part of the legacy colonialism left to the new nations carved out in reaction against it. Examining colonial bureaucracies, therefore, uncovers both the mechanics of colonial superordination and the models that colonial subjects appropriated when constructing later their own governments, schools, churches, and businesses.

Colonial missions were also bureaucracies. Challenged to stretch their limited funds and personnel to reach the non-Christian masses and to deal with other colonial bureaucracies such as the government and businesses, they were under continual pressure to operate efficiently and to maintain a presence with which other colonial players had to reckon. Missions were thus one of the important places where subject peoples learned about bureaucratic forms while participating in schools and churches, and in the women's groups, youth groups, and other clubs that spun out of these (e.g., Barker 1995). Especially, indigenous peoples experienced bureaucratic cultures firsthand when they became employees of missions.

T. O. Beidelman, in an important programmatic essay on colonial missions and social theory, was the first to suggest that colonial missions be examined "as variants of a far broader type, that of the complex bureaucratic organization." Beidelman cited Max Weber, inevitably the starting point in theories of bureaucracy, and saw that the study of colonial missions might "provide provocative new perspectives into some of the problems of the relation between 'rational' social organizations and 'non-rational' cultural values" (1974, 236). Weber's vast explorations of religion never included detailed attention to Christian missions, but the conundrum of the rational and nonrational was central in *The Protestant Ethic and the Spirit of Capitalism* (1958). There he argued that the "rational" pursuit of profit among early European capitalists was fueled by their nagging worries about salvation. In that famous essay Weber showed, furthermore, the relativity of rationality, suggesting that the endless pursuit of profit appears anything but rational outside the capitalistic value system. As Beidelman argued in 1974 and later showed ethnographically (1981, 1982), colonial missions raise conundrums about rationality because they sprang from values, goals, and assumptions that defy rational accounting, yet, like other colonial bodies, their success and continuity depended on overcoming material and managerial problems.[3]

The interplay of the rational and nonrational is by no means unique to religious groups or organizations but is, rather, a recurrent dilemma in all bureaucracies (Weber 1947). Bureaucratic authority rests on "rational legal" bases, or what Weber termed "formal rationality." Action exhibits formal rationality to the extent that it approaches maximum efficiency in the pursuit of specified goals.

> Following Weber, the modern bureaucracy is usually described as an organization having the following traits: a complex rational division of labor, with fixed duties and jurisdictions; stable, rule-governed authority channels and universally applied performance guidelines; a horizontal division of graded authority, or hierarchy, entailing supervision from above; a complex system of written record-keeping, based on scientific procedures that standardize communications and increase control; objective recruitment based on impersonal standards of expertise; predictable, standardized management procedures following general rules; and a tendency to require total loyalty from its members toward the way of life the organization requires. (Ferguson 1984, 7)

Because bureaucracies are technically efficient, Weber thought, they have competitive advantages over organizations in which authority rests in traditional roles or on charisma, and he foresaw creeping bureaucratization as a pervasive if not inevitable modern trend.

Efficiency, however, is merely a means to human projects, not an ultimate end in itself, and Weber termed the culturally specific, ultimate ends to which we aspire "substantive rationality." Ironically, our substantive desires—for community, love, or simply for pleasure—often elude us exactly because of the depersonalization, formality, and relentless work demanded of us in bureaucracies (Brubaker 1984, 36–37). Weber thus did not regard the quest for efficiency as rational in an absolute sense of the term (e.g., 1958, 193–94 n. 9) but only so with regard to specific assumptions of value. In fact, individuals' personal goals and values, and sometimes the very purpose of a bureaucracy itself, may be undermined by its expansion and formal rationalization. One sociologist terms this the vicious cycle of bureaucracies: the more they succeed at achieving the goals to which they are pointed, the more their growth threatens the achievement of those goals (Crozier 1964).

The irony of bureaucratic elaboration is especially acute in religious organizations, the ultimate aims of which are not financial profit but spiritual fruit. Although a colonial plantation or mine might have exhausted and dehumanized the people working in it, including those who wielded power at the top as well as those who labored physically at the bottom, this was a peripheral consequence of the *organization*'s purpose, which was to increase profits. But, if missionaries' administration of schools and hospitals left them little time for spreading the Gospel (not to mention time for the prayer and study they thought necessary for their own spiritual lives), the very reason of the mission's existence was negated. Although the substantive-rational goals of missions and missionaries may be especially vulnerable to bureaucratic erosion, missionaries find bureaucratic forms nonetheless irresistible.

The specific bureaucratic contradictions I explore here concern gender. They draw my attention as scholars are beginning to assess the impact of legislation, corporate policies, and personal commitments over the last twenty-five years to remedy gender discrimination in the workplace. One recent collection of essays, for example, reflecting "a sense of disillusionment with the pace of change," asked, "why, after a quarter of a century of reforms, power in organizations continues to be monopolized by men" (Roper 1994, 87). A new sobriety has dawned about the complexity of gender, and about its deep roots, not just in the family but also in institutions throughout society (e.g., Cockburn 1994; Kwolek-Folland 1994). The difficulties of women at work that I uncover in this historical instance, seemingly long ago and far way, thus look disconcertingly familiar to us in many respects.

Male Bureaucracies and Female Missions

A number of contemporary writers have suggested that bureaucracies are not culturally transcendent, existing in some abstract realm of pure efficiency, but are implicitly *male* institutions (e.g., Hennig and Jardin 1976; Kanter 1977). "While the rational-legal or bureaucratic form presents itself as gender-neutral it actually constitutes a particular kind of masculinity based on the exclusion of the personal, the sexual and the feminine" (Pringle 1994, 118). This observation has spawned a liberal feminist how-to literature for ambitious women who wish to succeed in these foreign settings (e.g., Harragan 1977; Haslett et al. 1992; Kennedy 1980).[4] The very market for these popular how-to books indexes the fact that a gender hierarchy subverts our avowedly neutral bureaucratic standards. Bureaucracies work on the presumption that placement and advancement are based on ability and expertise, measured "objectively" whenever possible through certification or standard examinations (Weber 1947, 340). Weber understood these opportunities based on merit to exert a leveling effect with regard to employees' class backgrounds (1954, 350). Liberal feminist discourse pushes the idea of leveling to include gender, recognizing the gap between ideals that insist people should be judged impartially in terms of their technical competence ("equal opportunity") and the hard realities of recruitment and promotion for women in the modern corporate world ("the glass ceiling") (e.g., Kanter 1977; Carone et al. 1977).

Radical critiques of bureaucracy, both from postmodern as well as feminist perspectives, suggest that bureaucracy is a historically contingent form and, furthermore, oppressive of men as well as women (Clegg 1989, 1990; Savage and Witz 1992). Kathy Ferguson (1984) draws her critical perspective from Michel Foucault, who regarded "the increasing organization of everything" as the central issue of our time (Dreyfus and Rabinow 1982). Radical feminist discourse challenges not simply the roadblocks in women's careers but also the very concept of *career* and the taken-for-granted relationship between public and private life on which it is predicated as well as the most basic premises that undergird bureaucratic operations, especially their assumptions of hierarchy and rationality. From this radical perspective rationality is illusory, and the best organizations are those in which power is openly reciprocal and dispersed rather than centralized and hierarchical.

The stories of two women who worked in the Karo Mission will illustrate the liberal feminist insight that women's feminine attributes often shroud their competence, leading colleagues to underestimate and undervalue their work. Women entered this mission's employment disadvantaged by their previous socialization and their restricted professional experiences. But the struggles of these two women point also toward the more radical insight that bureaucracies institutionalize values associated with males. The NZG, like other modern bureaucracies of the time, was overwhelmingly male in its composition and in its workaday ethos. Male missionaries faulted female colleagues for being too loving, too personal and egalitarian with their underlings, and not authoritative enough for the responsibilities they were assigned. That this small bureaucracy proved itself the enemy of feminine virtues is especially ironic, since these virtues are also synonymous with some deeply held Christian ideals, namely humility and love. When professional women in the mission displayed reticence, diffidence, and nurturance, their male colleagues decried their lack of intelligence and initiative.

If bureaucracies are gendered as male, the ethos of missions, I would argue, is female (see also Lutkehaus, in this volume). Missions have been historically a women's cause (Hill 1985; Hunter 1984; Thorne, in this volume). Women's donations raised an "astonishing proportion" of the funds that financed American missionary activity (Hyatt 1976, 67). The same was true in Holland, where local women's clubs formed a strong and reliable financial support for missionary work. The NZG Women's Auxiliary Society of Rotterdam aimed modestly to collect "only one, two, three or more stuivers" weekly from its members, "for the most part from the lower classes," women who were too poor to pay the regular membership fees of the NZG (Rauws 1922).[5] From thousands of these tiny but regular donations, the proverbial "widow's mites," and from an annual bazaar the Rotterdam women's group contributed between 1,200 and 3,000 guilders annually to the NZG treasury. Such groups often provisioned missionary wives to teach sewing classes in the Indies and later, when there were mission hospitals, provided these with linens.

C. J. Hoekendijk (1914), an evangelical Hervormd missionary with the Nederlands Zendelings Vereeniging, noted that women, primarily, read the missionary newsletters, told their children stories about missionaries, and prayed for and lent moral support to missionaries. They were really the backbone of the mission effort in the home country, this leader admitted. In the Dutch Missionary Society women were similarly the supportive background but were virtually invisible as NZG members, never occupying leadership positions.[6] The auxiliary women's clubs that supported the Dutch Missionary Society financially and spiritually had little official contact and communication with it well into the twentieth century (Rauws 1922).

It is surely no coincidence that the nineteenth century, which church historians have termed the Century of Missions, was also known in its closing decades as the Woman's Century (Montgomery 1911, 1). In the United States all the significant social movements of this period had women's organizations—reformist, charitable, or political—at their centers. Women's enthusiasm for missions fits under this general feminine impulse of the period to uplift, help, and reform. Perhaps more pertinent to understanding why missions' support came from women is simply women's preponderance in the churches. By the nineteenth century congregations in Britain and the United States were overwhelmingly feminine (See Douglas 1977, 97–99), so much so that H. G. Wells is said to have predicted that by the end of the twentieth century all educated men will have discarded Christianity but women will be as much attracted to it as ever (McCabe 1905, 92). It seemed quite natural to everyone at the time that women were engaged by the idea of missions, because women were more religious than men. Joseph McCabe, former priest and indefatigable proponent of rationalism, argued in *The Religion of Woman* that "the religious sense or religious instinct is stronger and more imperious in women" (1905, 59). He ventured that men's engagement with material concerns and the world of work conduced to their having "less spiritual texture" than women, but he went on to attribute the gender difference to "a radical difference in nerve structure" that made women more emotional and imaginative, key elements for a greater religious capacity.

Missions piqued the sympathies of Western women across all classes, but especially middle-class women (Hill 1985) because, I suspect, the image of the missionary symbolized a virtue that was not only Christian but traditionally feminine: the sacrifice of self in service to others. Male missionaries in the Dutch Missionary Society often used the biblical quotation "the love of Christ compels us" to express their irrepressible calling into missionary work. This ideal that, imitating Christ, Christians should sacrifice themselves to serve and redeem others and that a love for Christ expressed itself as a love for others resonated with women's own relationally forged identities and with a social and familial order that demanded of women relentless ministering to the physical and psychological needs of others, often at the expense of meeting their own needs. Women's own domestic servitude was, like missionary lives, valorized as Christian *service* based on sacrificial love. Unlike their sisters in Britain and the United States, Dutch women could not be recruited as foreign missionaries throughout the nineteenth century, but the "romance" of the missionary hero enthralled them (cf. Hill 1985 on American women), and missionary club work and contributions made women vicarious participants in the missionary's noble adventure.

Toward the end of the nineteenth century and into the twentieth a decidedly feminist element also began to characterize women's (and some men's) support of missionary efforts. Christianity was lauded as the road to women's emancipation in primitive, backward societies (Hyatt 1976, 66–67), and this assumption propelled a movement of British and American women into the ranks of professional missionaries, women who saw their unique calling as evangelization by and for women (Hunter 1984, xv; Hill 1985). Rhetoric about women's *emancipatie* entered Dutch discourse about missions somewhat later than this, beginning with articles and letters in missionary periodicals in the early decades of the twentieth century but continuing well into the 1920s and 1930s, even as the American women's missionary movement had begun to decline.

"In Christ There Is Neither Male nor Female": Gender in the NZG

Long before the NZG employed women, it was a thoroughly gendered bureaucracy and one in which heterosexuality for males was quite literally compulsory. As a matter of policy, the NZG sent no man into his assignment unmarried or at least unengaged. Each student in the missionary program had to find a suitable spouse before he received his assignment, but he was not allowed to become engaged until his last year of the program nor to marry while still a student. Typically, new missionaries married in their early twenties, just after graduating from the training program and just before going to the Indies.

The primary duty of a missionary wife was that of homemaker. Above all, her role was to enable her husband's work and, secondarily, to exemplify high standards of housekeeping for the natives (Neurdenburg 1879). Missionary wives often had several children, but, as they returned to Holland for education as early as age six, childcare responsibilities diminished rapidly as a woman's childbearing years ended. Many missionary wives entered gradually into the work of the mission through their life course, taking on teaching or administrative duties. The extent to which missionary wives participated was optional, however, and in any case, never did they receive remuneration for it, nor were they regarded as missionaries. In 1918, for example, one missionary recently assigned to a new position as head of a teachers training school requested that the NZG board cover his wife's travel costs as well, since she was going to play a large role in the school. "The wife of a missionary never receives a separate allowance for her part in the work," the board reminded him, denying the request (*Extract Acten* 1918, 57).

When mission supporters in Holland began to justify the incorporation of women as working missionaries, they noted the consonance of mission service with women's nature. In a speech before the annual gathering of the NZG in 1904, J. H. Meerwaldt, a Dutch missionary in service with the Rheinish Mission among the Toba Batak, began by repeating his talk's title:

> "The woman in the service of Christian love in the mission field" is the subject to which I would ask your attention momentarily.
>
> Mission work is love work! Where one speaks of love, that is to say, where it manifests itself in action, it behooves us to make room for women. (Meerwaldt 1905, 436)

Women missionaries would have greater freedom to interact with native women than male missionaries had, he argued. Missions thus needed women to reach the female half of any mission field.[7] The NZG board published his essay the following year. Comparing British and American missions with those from the Netherlands, he continued: "In our fatherland and its colonies people have now also in the last decade begun to advise about the necessity of sending out unmarried women in the service of missions among the heathens and Mohammadans." In fact, as early as 1894, conventions of missionaries in Amsterdam and Batavia had agreed that the sending out of "missionary sisters" was a good idea, but nothing had come of it. Meerwaldt envisioned these women serving as evangelists and as pastor-like helpers in the Christian congregations, especially among the women. The native Christian women were "understandably less developed and less capable" Christians than their male counterparts, because they often began "passively" as Christians when their husbands had converted, rather than from their own initiative. He supposed that their household and child-tending duties often prevented them from following church sermons and lessons as faithfully as men (Meerwaldt 1905).

In the same year that Meerwaldt's speech appeared in print, Hoekendijk published a similar essay in a missionary newspaper called *De Opwekker.* He began: "Although we are absolutely not feminists, we can still not wholly agree with that trite saying that for centuries has reigned as the law of society: 'The woman's place is in the church, the kitchen, and the nursery.' No, the woman, just as the man, belongs in society at work at those things which she, through her characteristic way of working, can honorably perform." Native women lived in cloistered, separate spheres from males, he pointed out, so males, especially Western males, failed totally to understand them. Only a "female heart" could properly empathize with and reach women of the Indies. "Thus, if we believe that in Christ there is neither male nor female, and that women's hearts are for the most part closed to the missionary," he reasoned, "then the sending out of missionary sisters is not just *desirable* but *necessary* unless we are to be liars with regard to our own principles" (Hoekendijk 1905).

Hoekendijk firmly rejected the possibility that women might replace or compete with men in mission fields. They should work in separate spheres from those of the male missionaries. He did not suppose that missionary sisters would do a great deal of direct evangelization themselves. They could establish girls' schools, talk with women in the hospital, especially obstetric patients, and lead and train a cadre of native Christian women, who would then evangelize their unconverted sisters. In a later publication Hoekendijk repeated this idea. The European woman would "remain the general, she must lead, she's the one who doles out the sheets, but she must also take care that native deaconesses come forth" (1914). In missionary hospitals a nurse deaconess would be "a white officer among a brown corps." Over and again he stressed that a woman missionary was not to take the place of or usurp her male peers. She must not pioneer new fields but be added as a helper in a field already established by a man, and she would simply "fill in the gaps in his work." She should not give separate religious services for women, and "in no circumstances does she have to administer the sacraments." In other words, missionary sisters should not be sent out as "half-men" and must guard, too, that, in developing and leading the native women, they do not try to turn them into half-men either, "but she should remain totally a woman and try to develop only what is genuinely feminine in her sisters."

Both Meerwaldt and Hoekendijk anticipated certain problems that might arise in using women missionaries and certain objections that some people might raise. When missionary societies in Holland had first begun to discuss the idea of sending women missionaries, in the 1890s, someone had objected that, since there were many unmarried men and few marriageable women in the Indies, the chances were great that unmarried workers would soon marry and leave missionary service. The costs of their passage to the Indies would then be money wasted. Answering this objection, Meerwaldt suggested that, while the NZG could not take away a woman's freedom to marry if she wished, it could well stipulate that, if she married, her husband must compensate the NZG for her travel costs.

These writers clearly felt that God "called" women to serve him even as he did men and that women could respond to that call as did men. Meerwaldt, for example, imagined missionary women as "sisters who, having given themselves unconditionally to the Lord Jesus Christ, and thus, driven by the love of Christ, will apply themselves wholly and without ulterior motives to the wonderful task of showing lost sinners the way to their Savior and Helper." Yet both writers also assumed that such women might at any time marry and that, if they did, they would naturally quit their mission positions. The call of marriage, for women, apparently usurped any other calling. Whereas male missionaries were supposed to make their family lives conform to their calling (by marrying women who would agree to the sacrifices of the missionary life, especially to the cruel necessity of separating from their young children), women missionaries were expected to abandon their missionary calling if they married.[8] This presumed a hierarchy of callings in a woman's life. Taking care of a husband and children was woman's first priority, coming ahead even of work directly in God's service. An American writer around the turn of the century phrased it this way:

> Deaconesses must be either maidens or widows. This is necessary in the nature of the case. A married woman can have no regular calling in the exclusive service of the church. Men are not hindered by marriage in the duties of their office, but if a woman wishes to serve the Lord without restraint, in an ecclesiastical office, she must, under all circumstances, be free from the bonds of wedlock, so long as she holds the office. (Thoburn 1893)

Meerwaldt worried, too, about jealousy from the missionary wife, who saw someone coming to do the work that her own family obligations had always prevented her from doing. Perhaps she would resent a woman who became a colleague in her husband's work in a way that she had never done. Always in missionary work, Meerwaldt argued, human weaknesses such as this emerge but do not justify failing to pursue our goals. Hoekendijk anticipated problems of authority at times, too, when the missionary sister would not consult the male missionary sufficiently about the work: "Aside from the character of such a sister, the cause of this might also lie in her having a higher intellectual position than the missionary to whom she is subordinated, and also, for example, having reached a greater knowledge of the language." Hoekendijk felt that such clashes of judgment and authority presented few real administrative problems: if the missionary and the sister continually disagreed, the sister simply would be transferred.

Both Meerwaldt and Hoekendijk considered the problem of where and how such women would live in the Indies, and both decided against the idea that they board with the family of the male missionary. They should be sent by twos, and the two women set up an independent household. Some months later, Mrs. A. Vermeer, a missionary wife writing from the Indies, responded in the *De Opwekker* to Hoekendijk's article.[9] First, she resented his suspicion that missionary wives would be jealous of women missionaries and would not want to see them come to the field. Missionary wives, of all people, saw the great need for women workers. It was the issue of housing, however, that really prompted this missionary wife to write. Specifically, she contested Hoekendijk's assumption that single women could easily set up housekeeping in the Indies. This underestimated the volume of housekeeping, and implicitly undervalued the work that she and other missionary wives contributed to the mission effort:

> Given that two come out together and those two live in the same place so that it is possible for them to set up their own household, does Brother Hoekendijk indeed realize that setting up one's own household in the Indies is not as simple as it appears? If she (or they) take in interns, then their freedom is over, and the missionary sister will not be able to come and go freely, something that is very necessary in the interest of the work. If she lets the housekeeping go, then she must repatriate within a short time, for the body will not be taken care of well enough and eventually will not be able to withstand the so called "murderous Indies climate." (Vermeer 1905)

Vermeer felt that the best solution was to send single women one at a time and for them to live with the missionary family. She suspected that Hoekendijk, although he had not said so explicitly, did not like such arrangements because he feared that the natives in this polygynous land would perceive the sister as the missionary's second wife. As Vermeer had foreseen, the difficulty of housekeeping often did arise for those single professional women who worked in the Indies. In 1912, when European nurses had been working at Mojowarno (East Java) for several years, the *Extract Acten* recorded this item:

> Br. Kruyt thinks it very desirable that the sisters' house at Mojowarno is better provided in the needs of housekeeping. When the Sisters come home tired from the hospital, it is desirable that they find everything done there and not have to look after the housekeeping themselves. It will be necessary to send out a woman who can be charged exclusively with the housekeeping. Decided to take this into earnest consideration. (226)

Both Meerwaldt and Hoekendijk also raised the issue of where missionary societies would recruit women missionaries and how they should be trained. Should these women be trained as missionaries? Meerwaldt perceived "many difficulties" with that idea, but the only difficulty he actually listed was that of expense. Raising the risk of sending out persons who were not suited, Hoekendijk felt, nonetheless, that special training was not necessary for missionary sisters: "Naturally, she must learn the native language, be familiar with the morals and customs, know something of medicine and obstetrics, and also be able to teach from the abundance of what she already knows, but the primary thing for her will always remain the tact with which she leads." Hoekendijk felt sisters could learn the local language and customs from the missionary in the field.[10] Although women doctors and nurses soon found a place in Dutch mission hospitals, the nonmedical missionary sister, as Meerwaldt and Hoekendijk had described her, did not emerge in the NZG until the 1930s.

The Vrouwen-Zendingsbond (VZB) formed in 1927 to finance the training of candidate missionary wives as well as women who felt called into evangelistic "work among women by women" (Jongeling 1985; Rauws 1922). It aimed to cooperate closely with the established missionary societies, conceding their exclusive authority to send missionaries into the field. Joining these new voices in the VZB were missionary wives stationed in the Indies as well as many of the local conferences of missionaries, who begged the board to send women missionaries to help with evangelistic work directed at women (*Extract Acten* 1929).

After several years during which the VZB and the NZG leadership disagreed about which of two candidates to send, Christina Slotemaker de Bruine was finally chosen and commissioned in 1935 (Jongeling 1985,

25–27) but not before a painful discussion about what kind of ritual was appropriate for the event. Missionaries were usually ordained into service with a solemn "laying on of hands," but this woman was not being given the rights to administer sacraments and act as clergy as male missionaries did. "Should this missionary be ordained in the usual way, or just be sent off in the way of a female doctor or a deaconess? Decided: that one does not have to speak of ordaining in this case because this missionary is being sent out for a special purpose, not for regular fieldwork as a missionary-teacher" (*Extract Acten* 1934, 222). In this decision the board was following a precedent that had been established thirty years earlier, when Dr. A. M. Pijsel, who had recently completed her training in medicine, applied to work in the Indies as medical missionary. The board accepted her application but made her placement contingent on the agreement of the male colleagues with whom she would work. She was sent to fill a three-year replacement position at a mission hospital in Java in 1904. At that time sixteen members of the board had voted against the symbolic laying on of hands, outweighing four votes in favor.

The Bureaucratization of the Dutch Missionary Society

NZG installations in the nineteenth century were generally very small. In their pioneering years, certainly, fields consisted of no more than three missionaries who often lived with their families in widely scattered posts and who operated relatively independently of one another. While the missionaries conferred among themselves and the senior person in the field always attempted to exercise what authority he could over his juniors, each missionary took his assignments and his counsel directly from the NZG board, and especially from the director, an explicitly metaphorical father (*Maandberichten* 1891). This relatively "flat" paternalistic structure characterized the NZG throughout the nineteenth century.

Starting around 1900, the NZG entered an advanced phase of bureaucratic elaboration (Van Randwijck 1981). The driving force behind these changes was a new leader at its head, J. W. Gunning, who worked on two fronts to modernize the century-old organization and streamline the Protestant missionary movement in the Netherlands. Externally, he was a tireless lobbyist, fund raiser, and advocate for ecumenical cooperation among Protestants, urging the numerous small sending organizations in Holland at that time to pool their financial and human resources and coordinate their efforts. The NZG was eventually encompassed within a larger grouping, the Cooperating Mission Corporations (Samenwerkende Zendingscorporaties), of which it was the leading member. Internally, Gunning divided the director's roles, parceling directorial functions to men at the top ranks of the NZG. Correspondence, which until that point had consisted of long, rambling, highly personal letters between missionaries in the field and the director, was depersonalized. The board instructed missionaries to write letters concerning only one topic (to facilitate filing), and their letters were answered by the correspondence committee of the board. Missionaries often did not know which of the two or three cosigners of their letters had in fact written it. At the level of each field Gunning instituted a new governance structure, transforming the local unit into a "conference" that interacted cooperatively with the board, further mitigating the personalistic, dyadic interaction of each missionary and the fatherly director that had been the pattern for the previous century.

The mission to the Karo was begun in 1890 with money donated by planters and other businessmen in Sumatra's East Coast who felt their investments threatened by Muslim agitators in neighboring Aceh (Kipp 1990). In its first decade the field never had more than three missionaries at any one time. By the mid-twentieth century the Karo field was thus one part of an expanding, newly differentiated, hierarchical, and impersonal bureaucracy, and the incorporation of women was not simply coincidental but in fact necessary to that process. As in the expansion of some secular bureaucracies in Western history, women were incorporated as menial laborers, freeing men for the conceptual and managerial tasks (Kwolek-Folland 1994). As paternalistic and nepotistic systems were made "rational," women were incorporated beneath men, who filled middle-level positions, paralleling the newly impersonal subordination of those males under their superiors (Savage and Witz 1992). The presence of women, then, amplified the emerging hierarchy of the missionary organization.

The incorporation of male nonmissionary specialists, however, such as doctors and school administrators, was similar. Regardless of the presence of numerous lay professionals, a field remained a *missionary* enterprise, with evangelization its ultimate aim. For the missionaries the medical and educational spheres were logically subordinate to the religious goal of evangelization because the provision of social services was undertaken as a way of spreading the Gospel. A hierarchy of authority thus followed from this hierarchy of goals. The control of each field rested in the missionaries' hands. Although membership in the conferences gradually included all European personnel who worked in a field, male or female, missionary or other kind of professionals, within conferences there was an implicit hierarchy of those who were *real* missionaries and those who were not, a status marked ritually with laying on of hands. As in any bureaucracy, technical competence is the basis of authority, and in a mission bureaucracy the highest credentials were thus missionary credentials. Nor were these credentials merely symbolic. NZG missionaries underwent a six-year training program that included the study of language and culture of the Indies as well as practical fields such as medicine, in addition to religious studies. None of the lay specialists who were hired to work for the NZG could thus match the missionaries' credentials in "technical competence" as missionaries, but women, already disadvantaged by the gender hierarchy, were further disadvantaged by this rationalized scale of values.

While the board upheld its own democratic guidelines in favor of women, it had problems persuading male members to follow them. When the local conference of missionaries in Java decided that Dr. Pijsel's temporary status precluded her membership in the conference, the board responded that, on the contrary, Dr. Pijsel should have "the same rights as other members" (*Extract Acten* 1904, 41). The regulations about conference membership had expanded by the mid-1930s, however, to include some nonmissionary specialists with both voice and vote, as long as they worked independently and without an immediate supervisor (NZG Archives, Samenwerkende Zendings-Corporaties: Reglement op de Conferenties, January 1936). Because most nurses worked either under doctors or under missionaries, this eliminated most women employed in mission installations. Male specialists, such as doctors and school administrators, who did not occupy positions that made them directly subservient to other European males, did not as often face this impediment to participating in conference decision making.

In 1922 the missionaries in the Karo field asked if missionary wives might attend the conference meetings. The board responded that they might attend on some occasions as guests. In 1937 the conference again raised the question with the board, and again the board demurred, pointing out that, while it valued the work of missionary wives, who worked as far as their family commitments allowed, it would not advise that they participate as regular members of the conference. The discussions would go more smoothly, the board thought, if only those directly involved and responsible for decisions were there. Despite this advice, the Karo conference admitted missionary wives as members in 1938 (*Extract Acten* 1919, 1922, 1938; NZG Archives, Board to Deli Conference, 27 October 1937).

The majority of the women professionals who worked for the NZG were nurses. An unpublished document on the history of the Karo field covering the period from 1889 to 1956 (Neumann 1966) lists fifteen women among a total of fifty-eight mostly European personnel. Six of these women worked in the early 1950s, after Indonesian independence and the founding of an autonomous Karo church. Of the nine women who worked during the colonial period the earliest was a missionary wife who assumed leadership of the field for almost one year upon the sudden death of her husband in 1894 (see Kipp 1990). In the twenty years after her departure no women were employed in this field. The first two professional women, two nurses, arrived to work in the Karo Mission in 1914, and six others came and went in the ensuing decades between the World Wars. One of these women was hired to manage a student hostel. In contrast to their male colleagues, who were invariably married, all these missionary "sisters" were unmarried, and none were trained professionally as missionaries.

The presence of these eight women, mostly nurses, between 1914 and 1942 suggests the expanding scope of the field during these years, when two hospitals, a leprosarium, a nurses' training program, an infants' orphanage, a trade school, and other kinds of schools were run under the missionaries' purview, financed in large part by subsidies from the colonial government. A similar process of expansion was occurring elsewhere in the Indies in other NZG fields as the Dutch deepened and extended their hold over the colony. The missionaries were sometimes ambivalent about the extent to which the need to administer these mushrooming social services took them away from their teaching, preaching, and personal ministry, but they were also afraid that the colonial government would set up "neutral" (secular) schools and hospitals if they neglected to do so or that the Catholics would enter with schools and hospitals, winning with these the competition for hearts and souls. Hiring nurses, whose small salaries could be met with government monies, was the best way to make scarce financial resources stretch to fit the missionaries' expansionary ambitions.

Here I will recount the stories of two women as illustration of professional women's experiences in the NZG. While both these women were criticized for exhibiting traits that were too feminine, one of them managed to overcome this handicap, very likely because, as a nurse, she was expected to act nurturantly. She grew into greater and greater managerial responsibilities as she, like the women described by Lutkehaus (in this volume), was given the space to develop these "male" abilities. The other woman, who was hired as an administrator, found it harder to negotiate the pulls between being a woman and being a bureaucrat. Interestingly, the distant board of directors was consistently supportive of each of these women when male colleagues were critical of their performance, yet the board protected above all the bureaucratic *structure* it managed, in particular its own authority, the control of information, and the authority of the local conferences, dominated by missionary professionals.

Pieternela Wynekes

Pieternela Wynekes was thirty-five years old when she applied to become a missionary nurse in 1913. "She is among the silent in the land," one of her recommendations read, "those who say little but do all the more." She

Pieternela Wynekes

was one of the first two professional women to work in the Karo field, starting in 1914. She arrived along with Taliena Smit, who, because of her "strong personality," was judged by Gunning to be more capable of independent work and was assigned to oversee a leprosarium. Wynekes, whose character was "softer," was to work at a small hospital under the supervision of missionary J. H. Neumann, who was posted at the same locale.

Three months after her arrival Neumann expressed fear that Wynekes was "not suitable" for the work, mainly in that she showed "too little independence" (NZG Archives, Neumann to Board, 5 June 1915). Wynekes admitted, in one of her first letters to Gunning, that she, too, was a little disappointed in her assignment. She had not anticipated how difficult walking between villages would be in this hilly region nor how difficult it would be to learn the language. Above all, she feared that Neumann had unrealistic expectations of her. She had never studied pharmacy in Holland, yet Neumann expected her to mix medicines and fill prescriptions. Unlike Neumann, she had not had two years of training in medicine and had not learned to examine patients or diagnose illnesses. She had had no obstetric training. She had learned only to care for patients' immediate physical needs and "to follow what the doctors told us and write a good report." She was unprepared to relieve Neumann of the totality of his medical work, which is what he had wanted. Mrs. Neumann, never one to mince words, had told her: "At night my husband is still called out to deliver a woman who lives an hour away. My husband needs someone who can stand in for him . . . We are not any better off now that you are here" (NZG Archives, Wynekes to Gunning, 3 August 1915).

A new hospital building was opened at Wynekes's post some months after she arrived. She and Neumann worked closely together in it, but she did not trust herself to handle serious cases. Once when Neumann was out of town for several days, a man who was deathly ill was brought to the hospital, and she was terrified until Neumann returned to take charge. She admired Neumann tremendously, but after six months his assessment of her was still negative, especially of her diffident character.

> She has a certain timidity about her that makes her unsuitable to be independent with natives and Europeans. She does not dare to talk, and she makes herself a laughingstock with her shy mannerisms. She does not have enough nerve, enough force, to be in a leadership position, although she does what is asked of her. (NZG Archives, Neumann to Gunning, 27 September 1915)

After she turned her ankle and was unable to work for three weeks, he concluded: "Truly they did this girl (*meisje*) wrong when they sent her to the Karo Batak Mission." She would be better off at a big hospital where she could work constantly under supervision, Neumann wrote Gunning. The board, however, defended Wynekes to Neumann and counseled her to have patience with herself (NZG Archives, Gunning to Wynekes, 13 October 1915; Gunning to Neumann, 9 February 1916).

As Wynekes began to learn the language and to adjust to her surroundings, she did become bolder, taking over management of the hospital and of a clinic set up weekly near a market. On market day, she saw fifty to sixty outpatients, but people were not as receptive to the idea of going into a hospital, which they viewed as a last resort, a place from which no one expected to emerge alive. In October 1915, for example, she had only five patients in the hospital and counted it a victory that she had treated and released three of these. Traffic in outpatients continued to grow, however, to twenty-five on a daily basis and up to one hundred on market days. She hired some indigenous helpers, a girl to do the hospital housekeeping and a man to help her with the patients.

Her letters to the board were filled with stories from her work, for which she apologized. "I am not sure what to write about except my patients, for that is always what is on a sister's mind." She had set up a ward to isolate patients with infectious illnesses and was pleased to have successfully treated a case of typhus. She was beginning to thrive in her new level of responsibility, although Neumann, who had sensed that she was lonely living alone, requested in 1917 that she be transferred, "for her own good." When she made it clear to him that she wanted to stay, Neumann revoked his request for her transfer and, later that year, praised her work in a letter to Gunning. After three years he reported that she had assumed most of the medical work, had gained a great deal of practical experience, and had set up a well-established routine (NZG Archives, Neumann to Gunning, 14 July 1917; 29 September 1917).

In 1916 Wynekes and Smit requested of the board ("although we are only sisters") to be allowed to read the published extracts of the minutes of the NZG board, which were sent to missionaries in the fields. Correspondence from the fields was often recorded in these extracts. "I do not find it pleasant always to write letters but not to know what is being said about them," she wrote. Gunning responded that he would send her the society periodicals, but not the extracts. "Only recently has the Board been sending these to the missionaries," Gunning explained to her. "There are matters dealt with in there that you would rather not know about" (NZG Archives, Gunning to Wynekes, 9 February 1916).

In the next year she requested a raise from the board, saying that her salary of 100 guilders a month was hardly enough to meet her expenses, which she enumerated. Despite the fact that she did not get the raise and that she admitted to the board that, indeed, she did suffer from a profound loneliness, she decided to stay. Her doubts had abated further by the time she anticipated the end of her first five-year contract. In March 1920 she wrote to the board that she still loved the work. The woman who had once shrunk from the responsibility for making decisions about people's lives had grown to relish the exhilaration of effecting cures, to judge from what she described in letters to the board. Two of her vignettes were about women patients, and this too marked a triumph. In the beginning the hospital's patients had been almost exclusively male, but by 1920 many women and children were coming as well. She received a furlough to Holland that year, too, and upon her return was granted the raise she had requested two years earlier.

When she returned to the Indies, Neumann had been posted elsewhere in the field, and he was to be replaced by a new missionary, Hermanus van Beek. This presented a delicate situation to the board in that Van Beek, as the missionary in charge of the post, was technically Wynekes's supervisor but would be the newcomer, with everything to learn about the language and the people. Fresh from the missionary training program, Van Beek, in his early twenties, was considerably younger than Wynekes. To the board's credit it determined that Wynekes should be allowed to work independently as much as possible and that Van Beek would be her "mentor and support rather than her chief" (NZG Archives, Board to Wynekes, 21 May 1920).

In the same letter the board informed her of a new regulation stating that personnel who performed specialist's tasks such as hers were now permitted to attend the missionary conferences, although without voting rights. "Sister Wynekes, much to her pleasure, has attended the missionary conferences," one of her colleagues wrote some months later. "With 'manly courage' she followed the discussion about the various matters" (NZG Archives, Van den Berg to Board, October 1921). The board invited her to write something about her work for the NZG's publications, and two years later Neumann recommended that she be given full responsibility for managing the hospital's finances.

Just as Wynekes began to gain greater respect from and parity with her colleagues, she again experienced some frustrations in her work. Attendance in the clinic and the hospital were down in 1922 compared to 1920, and on many days she felt "useless." The slump continued into the next year, hitting its low point in 1923, when there was a total of only seventy-five patients in the hospital for the year. In that year, however, two Karo "girls" came to her asking her to teach them nursing. Six months later both were still there, taking lessons in reading, writing, and arithmetic three days a week in addition to working in the hospital. Sometime later Wynekes took in a third student, and a year later all three apprentice nurses were still working in the hospital, and a fourth had joined them. By that time the patient load was again picking up, and everyone was so busy that sometimes there was little time for the reading and writing lessons. By 1926 the hospital had opened a facility to care for orphaned newborns, women were sometimes coming to the hospital to give birth, and the hospital was equipped with a telephone, with which Wynekes could call a doctor for consultations.

She went to Holland for a second furlough in 1927 and served only a few years after she returned, when she was forced to retire for medical reasons. In contrast, Smit, who had come with Wynekes in 1915, had been discharged in 1918. The missionaries had judged Smit to be "extremely stupid" and "too old," almost upon their first meeting with her. The board failed to build a house for her as they had promised and failed to inform her, finally, that she was being replaced by a male missionary as director of the leprosarium. She left embittered, saying that the experience had taught her "not to trust people." Actually, Smit's experience was more typical than that of Wynekes, who worked in the Karo field from 1915 to 1931. As one of the first two women recruited to work in this colonial mission field, Wynekes served longer and more successfully than any who came after her.

Linda Wilkens

At a meeting of the conference in 1924 the missionaries discussed doing something to answer the disquiet or ambition that they sensed among young Karo women, especially the daughters in more "developed" families. A pagan headman beat them to it, however, setting up a finishing school under the directorship of a Muslim, and this competition pushed the missionaries into action. They sought permission of the board to open a Christian school for girls that would teach reading and writing, Malay, home economics, religion, music, nutrition, and health. They planned a boarding school to which girls from all over the Karo Plateau might come, and the missionaries felt it was essential (especially in the light of their competition) that the leader be a European woman. Because of financial constraints, the board vetoed these plans.

There were already a number of schools in Kabanjahe, the Karo district capital, in the 1920s, but it was not always easy for families to find accommodations for their children in that town. In 1928 the missionaries opened two small hostels for students, one in which twenty-one boys lived under the supervision of a Karo evangelist and his wife and one in which ten girls were crowded into a small and rather primitive house near the missionary's house. In early 1929 the board received this telegram: "Heathen headman Kabanjahe opens February own girl's hostel. Mission hostel requires European leader otherwise cannot keep up with competition urgent signal answer." When the board again determined that it had no money for an expanded hostel project, the missionaries canvassed the European community in the lowlands around Medan and received a 10,000 guilder donation from a planter family that had long been one of the mission's major patrons. The board, feeling now "forced" by the planter's beneficence, approved hiring a European woman as supervisor.

The buildings were completed by the end of the year, "three exquisite buildings, entirely free of debt, and an ornament for the mission yard at Kabanjahe." While the squeeze at the girls' hostel had prompted the new building, the conference decided to move the *boys* into the new buildings and let the girls take the one the boys had been using. There were now sixty-seven boys and twenty-seven girls in these two facilities, for the most part students at a Dutch-Native School and a government secondary school but also some small children who came to Kabanjahe for education from villages without elementary schools. Because of space problems, twenty-five of the very small boys were moved into the girl's hostel, although the number of girls had then climbed to forty (Van den Berg 1931; NZG Archives, Neumann, ms. Semi-annual Report 1930; Van den Berg to Board, January 1931).

With the buildings completed, E. J. van den Berg did not wait for the board to find someone for the leadership post but telegrammed the board that he had found a woman for the girl's hostel himself, a New Zealander named Linda Wilkens whom he had known from a period when she had worked in Medan.

Linda Wilkens, thirty-four years old, was broad through the arms and chest, with short graying hair parted on the side, and she wore glasses. Her parents were of Dutch origin. At age seventeen she had been "converted" in a Salvation Army meeting, and she came to the Indies as an officer in the Salvation Army, serving in Medan. After some years, finding that she could not agree with some of the army's teachings, she left that organization and joined the Gereformeerd Church, the orthodox branch of Dutch Reformed Christianity. She volunteered to work in missions for the Gereformeerd Church and took a place in Jogjakarta, where she was working when she decided to take the position in the Karo field. Wilkens was effusive in contrast to her staid Dutch colleagues in the Hervormd tradition, both in the way she expressed affection for others and her own feelings and in the way she spoke of her religious convictions (NZG Archives, Board to Van den Berg, 25 February 1931; Board to Van den Berg, 15 February 1931; Wilkens to Board, 10 April 1931; Wilkens to Van den Berg, 12 January 1931).

Wilkens was hired to administer both hostels, although a Karo evangelist, Pa Rembak, was to remain as housefather at the boy's hostel. Pa Rembak was subordinate to Wilkens; he was to turn to her for "support and leadership." Wilkens in turn answered to the missionary supervisor, (i.e., the missionary resident in Kabanjahe), at that point Van den Berg. In addition to these duties, her job description included giving sewing lessons and seeking contact with women in the congregation in Kabanjahe, or, as the board broadly phrased it, "the education and training of the female side of the populace." In addition, Van den Berg wanted her to give the wives of the evangelists a month-long course in "household training," presumably so their households would more approach a European or developed form as befitting their position (NZG Archives, Van den Berg to Board, January 1931; Rijnders and Brouwer to Wilkens, 26 March 1931).

Van den Berg met her at the port in Belawan in March 1931, welcomed her, and solemnly read her the official instructions from the board. Of this he wrote: "We have tried to make her feel that her task is an important one and not just a pastime," saying that he hoped this reception and little installation ceremony substituted for what other sisters in the NZG got when they met the board and received their commission to go to the Indies (NZG Archives, Van den Berg to Board, 10 April 1931). After only a few months in her new position she wrote the board, whom she had never met, a ten-page letter in English:

> You wrote, in your first letter to me, that you would be glad to hear from me regularly, not only about the blessings experienced in my work, but also about the disappointments and difficulties. I am afraid that the latter far outnumber the former. Blessings there are, certainly. The fact that the people have accepted me in their midst, and that the girls seem to like me, is proof of this, as is also the fact that my days are full to overflowing with opportunities for service.

Too full, to be exact. Wilkens's unhappiness stemmed from the sense that she did not know what her priorities should be, going on to describe in detail her daily and weekly schedule. Arising at 5:30 A.M., she treated any sick children, supervised breakfast and morning prayers, inspected dress, and accompanied the littlest ones to school. On it went through the week, her mundane routine punctuated by walk-in visits of parents (especially on market days), shopping, sick visitations, prayer meetings, church services, and "those hundred and one 'odd jobs' that fall to the lot of the mother of the family." In the evenings she gave sewing lessons to girls and women, some of whom came in from surrounding villages. She felt that she was neglecting the work with the older girls and the women and that she did not give the boy's hostel and its supervisor enough attention and direction either. She felt pulled in too many directions and requested that she be responsible only for the girls in the hostel.

> Forty girls is, after all, a big enough proposition, if one is going to accomplish anything worthwhile. I want to teach them sewing and mending, first aid, child welfare, gardening, gymnastics and a lot of other things that a womanly woman needs to know, but there is neither time nor opportunity at present . . . It makes me so sad to see and expe-

> rience that this big work is being only half done because the line of attack is too extensive . . . And the difficulties that I mentioned at the beginning of this letter have arisen from the fact that I do not know which part of all this work I ought to do and which I ought to leave undone. It all seems so very necessary and *is* necessary, but not as it is done now . . . I hope that you all will be able to find some way out, so that God's work in Kabanjahe may advance, to His glory. It is His work! If I were not so sure of that I would not be so anxious to have it well done. (NZG Archives, Wilkens to Board, 9 October 1931)

The board responded that her feeling that she had too much to do was normal but also that, "You should strive more, above all, to make giving leadership your task, and entrust the carrying out of it into other hands as much as is possible." Along with delegating authority over the household details, the board encouraged Wilkens to act less like a real mother to the children and to assume a superior relationship with the woman who worked in the hostel.[11] Wilkens had described an almost equal relationship, in which she and the Nora (a Karo term for native evangelist's wife) took turns minding the smallest children at home while the other went to the church services. Admitting that such a relationship *was* "in the right spirit of missionary work," the men of the board still found it inappropriate. Leave more work to your helper, the board encouraged Wilkens, but not finances or other administrative work, "for the Nora is not capable of that. But you do not, for example, have to go with the little ones to the bath place!" (NZG Archives, Board to Wilkens, 21 December 1931).

Through this exchange with the board Wilkens learned other lessons about how authority flowed in the Dutch Missionary Society. In a conference in January 1932 the missionaries objected to the way she had written asking the board to alter her assignment without first discussing it with them, her immediate superiors, who were in a better position to judge whether or not she had too much to do. She suspected that the missionaries were worried about what the board might have written back to her and in her next letter to the board admitted that she was now "a little afraid of what I can and cannot write." Still she was unclear about her priorities and felt stretched too thinly. Her colleagues seemed to think that her main work was in the hostels, but the board had written that her time should be given "in the first place to the women and girls," that is, outside as well as within the hostels. In fact, many of her colleagues felt that she did not do enough and that she was incapable of managing both hostels (NZG Archives, Wilkens to Board, 12 February 1932; Notes of the Deli Zending Conference, 27 January 1932).

As the numbers grew at the hostels, overcrowding and deteriorating conditions prompted one of Wilkens's colleagues to write to the board asking them to approve a plan for building a new girl's hostel and expanding the work with women and girls in general. In this proposal he criticized Wilkens, saying that he would like to see her lead mealtime discussions, for example, and to direct more of the children's free time than she did. When a member of the NZG board visited in 1932, he met with the voting members of the conference and evaluated Wilkens's work. Only one of her four colleagues approved of her performance, saying that she was energetic and the children loved her. The other three judgments of her work were not positive (NZG Archives, Notes of the Deli Zending Conference, 24 November 1932). Wilkens asked for another six months to prove that she could do more and, shortly afterward, started a Bible club for girls and began holding prayer meetings in her quarters on Saturdays. She took ten of the oldest girls on a field trip to Medan and directed a conference for the wives of Karo evangelists, successful events that she repeated the following years (NZG Archives, H. Vuurmans, Jaarverslagen ms. 1932).

In 1934 the numbers at the hostel started to decline, the result of the world depression, but Wilkens continued to ask the board to relieve her of some of her work outside the hostels so that she had more energy and time to devote to the children. In that same year she discovered that she was an incipient diabetic, and she contracted amoebic dysentery, which required hospitalization. In February 1935 she gave the board notice that she was resigning, blaming not her health and the declining state of the hostels but, rather, the constant bickering that characterized the missionary community in Kabanjahe in those years. "There is always fighting here, and inwardly I am broken from it." But when Karo Christians in Kabanjahe learned of her plan to leave they begged her to stay, and she retracted her resignation, despite the fact that one of her colleagues, a nonmissionary school administrator, advised her to resign. Some members of the conference remained unhappy with her work, she knew. They thought she showed too little self-sufficiency. One had told her straight out that she should proceed with "less love, more intellect." Hospitalized again with chronic amoebic dysentery and diabetes, she finally did resign in September 1935, saying, "I only want to return to my own country in order to recover there" (NZG Archives, Wilkens to Board, 8 January 1935, 18 February 1935, 23 April 1935, 6 July 1935; Wilkens to Fischer, 30 September 1935). The board, however, understood that Wilkens's problems in this assignment were more than personal. At her resignation the board wrote the colleague who had been most critical of her, blaming him in part for her decision to leave and expressing reluctance to send someone to replace her, "who, as a single woman, will again run up against these same difficulties" (NZG Archives, Board to Stad, 17 April 1935).

Conclusion

Dutch women, socialized to nurture and to anticipate self-sacrifice, were attracted to the opportunity to serve in missions in the Indies. Yet the Protestant missionary movement in Holland was unusually slow to utilize women, and editorials anticipating this event agonized over the possibility that such women, instead of remaining "genuinely feminine," would be tempted to act like "half-men." These essays, while making a strong case for the urgent necessity of sending women missionaries, tried at the same time to forestall the image of women *competing* with men by envisioning a separate sphere for them. These published discussions anticipated some of the problems women actually did encounter when, at last, they began to work in mission installations in the Indies.

Limiting women's entry into missionary work was an implicit hierarchy of callings available to women. The opportunity to work in missions was open only to single women, and, indeed, marriage necessarily resulted in the resignation of women already so employed. While everyone assumed that male missionaries required the support of a wife to maintain their effectiveness in the field and that a missionary wife would quite naturally follow her husband wherever his superiors decided to place him, no one in that era could have imagined that a husband might follow a wife who was responding to a higher spiritual calling. There was not, to my knowledge, a formal policy against the NZG's employment of married women. Rather, the taken-for-granted gender hierarchy operating within marriage precluded the need for any such official statement.

The first female employees of Dutch mission installations worked in medicine, their spheres of responsibility carefully circumscribed from the purely ministerial sphere of the male missionary. They were hired as specialists, but their expertise, unlike that of their male colleagues, did not include education for work in an intercultural setting or for the challenges of translating Christianity across great cultural and linguistic gaps. The lack of education or orientation pointed specifically to the challenge of working in the colonial Indies goes a long ways toward explaining why so many women who accepted these positions were unhappy in them, why colleagues often found their work unsatisfactory, and thus why their tenures were so often brief and stormy. Symbolic of their lack of credentials and secondary status, no laying on of hands marked their commissioning ceremony, not even when finally responding to a long-standing popular demand for missions "by and for women" the NZG commissioned the first woman to work in a fully evangelistic role in 1935.

The genuinely feminine aspects of some women's behavior—diffidence, nurturance, and deference—resonated with Christian ideals of humility, compassion, and sacrificial service. But these feminine traits had to be unlearned on the job or at least tempered with behaviors deemed suitable for exercising authority and operating efficiently within the missionary organization. To be deemed successful women missionaries had to take charge in the spheres in which they were granted responsibility. The criticisms leveled against women who worked in this field—that they showed too much love and not enough intellect and initiative—suggest, perhaps, that these women had not discerned how to change their behavior to fit the standards of the organization in which they were employed. Perhaps they just did not yet know how to "dress" themselves, as it were, for success. On the other hand, the women's struggles hint that the missionaries could not easily measure or predict the technical competence of *anyone wearing a dress.*

Gender is not merely fixed in society and then imported into bureaucracies as an attribute of persons (Savage and Witz 1992) but is embedded in the formal/legal bases of bureaucratic authority. Bureaucracies themselves are among the sites where gender is reproduced and sometimes contested. While the older missionaries to the Karo were particularly ambivalent about the new bureaucratic character of the missionary society and the growing impersonality of their relationships with superiors (e.g., NZG Archives, Van den Berg to Board, 29 November 1920), they participated, at the same time, in building the very iron cage that constrained them, pulling rank on their female underlings, who joined the organization as their junior colleagues.

Gender surely interferes with realizing the bureaucratic ideal of a hierarchy based strictly on competence. The ideal that bureaucratic placement and advancement are gender blind is like the Christian ideal that "in Christ, there is neither male nor female." Neither is there, in Christ, White and Brown, as the missionaries themselves would have been the first to acknowledge. Yet, just as European women were always placed subordinate to particular male supervisors and to the collective male authority of the conference that managed each field, they were always placed *above* indigenous male helpers. The professional women and eventually the missionary wives attended the conferences with voice but no vote, but indigenous helpers, who were mostly male, did not attend at all, no matter how long they had served the mission or how well they proved themselves to be effective evangelists and leaders. These patterns of race and gender within this little bureaucracy belie the formally rational ideal that technical competence determines placement, through judgments unencumbered by traditional survivals or the dynamics of interpersonal politics.

Contemporary Christian Karo cringe at memories of the colonial mentality, both that of the Dutch, whom they now remember as imperious and authoritarian, and that of themselves and their forebears, whom they suspect were too often accommodating and passive. In August and September 1983 I interviewed a man born in 1898 who had attended mission schools, including a boarding school for aspirant teachers. He recounted vividly the way bells had punctuated his days at the boarding school—from waking to meals to classes and finally bedtime. And he still remembered how the boys' rotation of the maintenance chores had worked. Although he admired the school's director, Gezinus Smit ("when he prayed, it sounded like the voice of God coming through him"), he and the other students also feared and respected Smit as a tough disciplinarian. Smit entrusted him with the important role of "key keeper," meaning he was responsible for locking the sleeping rooms during the day, unlocking them at night, and returning the key where it hung on a nail behind the director's desk. If Smit were busy working, he was not to greet or disturb him, he recalled, but simply slip quietly past. "If he was silent, I had to be silent. Sometimes he (Smit) would get it. Sometimes, if he looked at me, I could speak. We [students] had to think to determine just what he wanted" (interview with Bapa Rakut Sinulingga, 6 September 1983, Kabanjahe).

It is sometimes useful to imagine radical alternatives. What if the carriers of the Gospel in Karoland had all been women? How then would Karo remember the colonial era and the colonial mission? Would people tell stories about how the missionaries cared for them and loved them, instead of stories about uncompromising "fathers" who lived by the clock and introduced to them the word *discipline* (*disiplin*)? Would the unspeakable gulf between White and Brown have been smaller?

Had the personnel in this mission been entirely female, that racial gulf separating them from the Karo would have still been there, as would basic cultural differences such as attitudes toward time, work, and bodily hygiene. Women in colonial mission fields generally shared their male colleagues' imperialist assumptions (Bowie et al. 1993). Dutch women not connected with missions in the Indies were no more exempt from racism than their husbands, and, while they were seldom in a position to inflict bodily harm or to subject workers to inhumane conditions as their husbands sometimes were, they certainly played their part in protecting the privileges that marked racial boundaries (Gouda 1995, 186). I have no evidence that the two women described here or others who worked in the Karo field in this era ever questioned the goodness of Dutch empire, based as it was on a presumed racial superiority and a God-given responsibility. Still, imagining the Karo Mission as an all-female organization, composed exclusively of persons socialized to expect self-sacrifice and valorize love, is to imagine a very different history. Although the Karo today are predominantly Christian, they largely resisted conversion throughout the colonial era (Kipp 1995; Rae 1994, 92–94). We can only wonder if Christianity's most elemental message—"For God so loved the world, that he gave his only begotten son"—might not have rang quite as hollow in the ears of colonial Karo if more women had been there to proclaim and enact it.

NOTES

1. Research for this essay was carried out for the most part in the Netherlands at the archives of the NZG, which are housed at the Hendrik Kraemer Instituut (HKI) in Oegstgeest. It was supported by a fellowship from the National Endowment for the Humanities. I wish to thank Mary Huber, Nancy Lutkehaus, Richard Kipp, and Margaret Jolly, whose critiques improved the argument and the exposition, and M. C. Jongeling, formerly head of the HKI library, who read a draft of this essay and saved me from some embarrassing errors and who contributed useful references and biographical details.

2. Compare, for example, Beidelman in this volume, who reports that the CMS sent its first woman missionary in 1820 (n. 6). Predelli and Miller, also in this volume, report that the Basel mission placed its first independent woman missionary in 1857, and between 1870 and 1910 sent seventy such women into service.

3. For other studies of missionaries that address bureaucratic contradictions, see also Miller 1994, on the management of religious zeal in the Basel Mission, Huber's (1988) work on the Society of the Divine Word in New Guinea, and Beidelman 1981. Klein (1994) deals also with gender contradictions in a mission in southeastern Alaska.

4. A study of women executives was reported recently in the press. One executive advised other women aspiring to emulate her success: "Don't be attractive. Don't be too smart. Don't be assertive. Pretend you're not a woman. Don't be single. Don't be a mom. Don't be a divorcee" (Grimsley 1996).

5. I am not clear on the extent to which the women's support groups in the Netherlands could be construed as a device for achieving racial solidarity across class lines, as Thorne, in this volume, suggests for Britain. Certainly, these organizations of women from the "lower classes" were usually led by women who were married to men who served on the boards of directors of the missionary societies, to pastors, or to doctors (pers. comm., M. C. Jongeling), that is, women of the middle or upper classes.

6. The social structure of the NZG compares more closely to the Basel mission than to the more egalitarian Norwegian Missionary Society, as described by Predelli and Miller in this volume.

7. See also Huber, in this volume, on the idea of separate spheres.

8. The Nederlands Hervormde Kerk first ordained single women as full-fledged ministers beginning in 1968 but stipulated that in case of marriage they had to resign, without receiving even the designation and rights of an emeritus pastor. A few years later this ruling was rescinded under pressure (M. C. Jongeling, pers. comm.).

9. Mrs. A. Vermeer was Maria Magdalena Vermeer-Hilekes, who had been trained as a deaconess and worked for the Gereformeerd Church in Batavia from 1898 to 1904 as a social worker among Indo-Europeans. She married missionary A. Vermeer in 1902 (pers. comm., M. C. Jongeling).

10. A survey sent in 1930 to 1931 to 312 women working primarily in mission installations in the Netherlands and its colonies asked about respondents' educational background and their advice about what training would be appropriate for women in their positions. The 62 who answered overwhelmingly called for language training. Bible study, group leadership, missions and theology, history and ethnology of the area, childcare, medicine, sewing, and other household arts were also named. These desires for education and training were frustrated in this era by the prevailing sense among the male leadership of the NZG that such training was not necessary for women employees (Jongeling 1985).

11. Compare this to what Predelli and Miller (in this volume) describe about Wilhelmina Mauer's experience as a teacher and her conflict with another female colleague over matters of leadership style and discipline.

REFERENCES

Barker, John. 1995. "We are *Ekelesia*": Conversion in Uiaku, Papua New Guinea. In *Conversion to Christianity: Historical and Anthropological Perspectives on a Great Transformation,* ed. Robert W. Hefner, 199–230. Berkeley: University of California Press.

Beidelman, T. O. 1974. Social Theory and the Study of Christian Missions in Africa. *Africa* 44:235–49.

———. 1981. Contradictions between the Sacred and the Secular Life. *Comparative Studies in Society and History* 23:73–95.

———. 1982. *Colonial Evangelism: A Sociohistorical Study of an East African Mission at the Grassroots.* Bloomington: Indiana University Press.

Bowie, Fiona, Deborah Kirkwood, and Shirley Ardener, eds. 1993. *Women and Missions: Past and Present—Anthropological and Historical Perceptions.* Oxford: Berg.

Brubaker, Rogers. 1984. *The Limits of Rationality: An Essay on the Social and Moral Thought of Max Weber.* London: Allen and Unwin.

Carone, Pasquale A., Sherman N. Kieffer, Leonard W. Krinsky, and Stanley F. Yolles. 1977. *Women in Industry.* Albany, N.Y.: SUNY Press.

Clegg, S. 1989. *Frameworks of Power.* London: Sage.

———. 1990. *Modern Organizations.* London: Sage.

Cockburn, Cynthia. 1994. Play of Power: Women, Men, and Equality Initiatives in a Trade Union. In *The Anthropology of Organizations,* ed. Susan Wright, 95–114. London: Routledge.

Crozier, Michael. 1964. *The Bureaucratic Phenomenon.* Chicago: University of Chicago Press.

Dauber, Kenneth. 1995. Bureaucratizing the Ethnographer's Magic. *Current Anthropology* 36, no. 1: 75–95.

Douglas, Ann. 1977. *The Feminization of American Culture.* New York: Knopf.

Dreyfus, Herbert L., and Paul Rabinow. 1982. *Michel Foucault: Beyond Structuralism and Hermeneutics.* Chicago: University of Chicago Press.

Extract Acten. Various years. Abstracts of the Minutes of the Nederlands Zendelinggenootschap.

Ferguson, Kathy E. 1984. *The Feminist Case against Bureaucracy.* Philadelphia: Temple University Press.

Fields, Karen E. 1985. *Revival and Rebellion in Colonial Central Africa.* Princeton: Princeton University Press.

Gouda, Frances. 1995. *Dutch Culture Overseas: Colonial Practice in the Netherlands Indies, 1900–1942.* Amsterdam: Amsterdam University Press.

Grimsley, Kirstin Downey. 1996. No Easy Path to the Top. *Washington Post.* National Weekly Edition. March 4–10, 37.

Harragan, Betty Lehan. 1977. *Games Mother Never Taught You: Corporate Gamesmanship for Women.* New York: Warner Books.

Haslett, Beth J., Florence L. Geis, and Mae R. Carter. 1992. The *Organizational Woman: Power and Paradox.* Norwood, N.J.: Ablex.

Hennig, Margaret, and Anne Jardin. 1976. *The Managerial Woman.* New York: Pocket Books.

Hill, Patricia R. 1985. *The World Their Household: The American Woman's Foreign Mission Movement and Cultural Transformation, 1870–1920.* Ann Arbor: University of Michigan Press.

Hoekendijk, C. J. 1905. De Arbeid der Vrouw op het Zendingsveld. *De Opwekker* 439.

———. 1914. De Vrouw en de Zending. *De Opwekker* 650.

Huber, Mary Taylor. 1988. *The Bishop's Progress: A Historical Ethnography of Catholic Missionary Experience on the Sepik Frontier.* Washington, D.C.: Smithsonian Institution Press.

Hunter, Jane. 1984. *The Gospel of Gentility: American Women Missionaries in Turn-of-the-Century China.* New Haven: Yale University Press.

Hyatt, Irwin T. 1976. *Our Ordered Lives Confess: Three Nineteenth-Century American Missionaries in East Shantung.* Cambridge: Harvard University Press.

Jongeling, M. C. 1985. Op Ieder Zendingsterrein een Vrouwelijke Zendeling. *Allerwegen* 16, no. 2: 8–44.

Kanter, Rosabeth Moss. 1977. *Men and Women of the Corporation.* New York: Basic Books.

Kennedy, Marilyn Moats. 1980. *Office Politics: Seizing Power, Wielding Clout.* New York: Warner Books.

Kipp, Rita Smith. 1990. *The Early Years of a Dutch Colonial Mission: The Karo Field.* Ann Arbor: University of Michigan Press.

———. 1995. Conversion by Affiliation: The History of the Karo Batak Protestant Church. *American Ethnologist* 22, no. 4: 868–82.

Klein, Laura. 1994. "Timid Women Do Not Make Good Missionaries in Alaska": Gender and Mission in Southeastern Alaska. In *The Message in the Missionary: Local Interpretations of Religious Ideology and Missionary Personality,* ed. Elizabeth Brusco and Laura F. Klein, 23–42. Studies in Third World Societies, no. 50. Williamsburg, Va.: Department of Anthropology, College of William and Mary.

Kwolek-Folland, Angel. 1994. *Engendering Business: Men and Women in the Corporate Office, 1870–1930.* Baltimore: Johns Hopkins University Press.

Maandberichten. (Anon.) 1891. Ons Zendelinghuis, nos. 8–9: 137–40.

McCabe, Joseph. 1905. *The Religion of Woman.* London: Watts.

Meerwaldt, J. H. 1905. De Vrouw in den Dienst der Christelijke Liefde op het Terrein der Zending. *Mededeelingen NZG* 48:436–46.

Miller, Jon. 1994. *The Social Control of Religious Zeal: A Study of Organizational Contradictions.* New Brunswick, N.J.: Rutgers University Press.

Montgomery, Helen Barrett. 1911. *Western Women in Eastern Lands: Fifty Years of Women's Work in Foreign Missions.* New York: Macmillan.

Neumann, H. 1966. Gegevens over het Zendingswek in the Karo-Bataklanden van 1890 tot 1943. NZG. MS.

Neurdenburg, J. C. 1879. *Proeve eener Handleiding bij het Bespreken der Zendingswetenschap.* Rotterdam: Wyt en Zonen.

NZG Archives. Hendrik Kraemer Instituut (HKI), Oegstgeest.

Pringle, Rosemary. 1994. Office Affairs. In *The Anthropology of Organizations,* ed. Susan Wright, 115–23. London: Routledge.

Rae, Simon. 1994. *Breath Becomes the Wind: Old and New in Karo Religion.* Dunedin: University of Otago Press.

Rauws, Joh. 1922. Het Vrouwen Hulp-Genootschap te Rotterdam, 1822–1922. *Mededeelingen* (NZG) 66:220–32.

Roper, Michael. 1994. Gender and Organizational Change. Introduction to *The Anthropology of Organizations,* ed. Susan Wright, 87–94. London: Routledge.

Savage, Mike, and Anne Witz, eds. 1992. *Gender and Bureaucracy.* Oxford: Blackwell.

Thoburn, James. 1893. *The Deaconess and her Vocation.* New York: Hunt and Eaton.

Van den Berg, E. J. 1931. Het Tweede Internaat te Kabanjahe. *Zendingsblad* 3:35–36.

Van Randwijck, S. C. Graaf. 1981. *Handelen en Denken in Dienst der Zending.* 's Gravenhage: Boekencentrum.

Vermeer, A. 1905. Het Inwonen van de Zendingzuster bij de Zendings Familie. *De Opwekker* 441.

Weber, Max. 1947. *The Theory of Social and Economic Organization.* New York: Free Press.

———. 1954. *Law in Economy and Society.* Cambridge: Harvard University Press.

———. 1958. *The Protestant Ethic and the Spirit of Capitalism.* New York: Charles Scribner's Sons.

The Dangers of Immorality: Dignity and Disorder in Gender Relations in a Northern New Guinea Diocese

Mary Taylor Huber

> The general policy in our Mission will be to have separate schools for boys and girls who reach the age of puberty or are getting near to it . . . In all of our schools whether boarding or others where bigger pupils are in attendance, the dangers of immorality are quite great. All teachers and directors are therefore asked to keep the pupils busy.

> In Papua New Guinea, the relationships between the sexes are different from those in Europe or America . . . It seems priests [here] would be wise not to give too much social attention to women . . . We must exercise caution in these matters, because scandal is easily given in New Guinea, and we also know the dangers to the priest himself.

Thus wrote Leo Arkfeld, bishop of Wewak, to his staff in the East Sepik Province of Papua New Guinea, the first in a 1959 circular *The Church on Coeducation* and the second in a circular entitled *The Priest in the Diocese of Wewak* in 1973. The purpose of the earlier message was to remind his priests of the Vatican's instructions restricting coeducation and noting that in his territory mission schooling should be separate for "boys and girls who are near or at the age of puberty, probably 11 to 14 years of age." Indeed, teachers were advised to keep the bigger pupils busy in all mission schools, because the "dangers of immorality" were "quite great."[1]

The bishop expressed a similar view about "relationships between the sexes" among adults, including missionary priests. To safeguard their "priestly image" and "personal reputation" priests should not drive women around too often in their cars, especially after dark, they should not dance with women, and they should employ only men as domestic servants in their homes. These cautions are attributed to local sensibilities but not entirely: the circular ends with a warning of the "dangers to the priest himself." And the issue did not concern local women alone. A few years earlier, in 1969, an official observer from the Society of the Divine Word had remarked to the missionary priests and brothers about their work with lay volunteers from Europe, Australia, and the United States: "though true cooperation, Christian charity, and mutual confidence are essential elements in living and working together, human weakness and our status as religious make prudence and due precautions indispensable and especially in dealing with women." In these messages from their bishop and their missionary society, mission men were reminded that reputation and morality are at risk when contact between the sexes is not carefully controlled.

This vision of dignity and disorder in gender relations has had deep resonance in the history of the Catholic mission along the north coast of New Guinea, underwriting significant areas of mission practice and teaching, even though the separation it recommends has not always been easy to establish or maintain. The predominantly German priests, brothers, and sisters who first arrived in New Guinea in 1896 came with clear ideas about the proper arrangement of relations between men and women. Like any ideal, this model of gender relations did not so much summarize experience as outline what Raymond Williams calls "some higher or better state . . . projected as a way of judging conduct or of indicating action" (1983, 152). Yet, even more than in Europe, conditions on the north coast of New Guinea did not lend themselves readily to the institution of the missionaries' concepts of gendered order, and they found that practical work in the region challenged their understanding of gender, along with other basic categories of spiritual and material life (Huber 1987; 1988a).

Many recent studies in history, anthropology, and literature have explored how the cultural dislocations of colonial societies have shaped the experience of colonizers as well as the colonized (Beidelman 1982; Huber 1988a; Stoler 1989a–b, 1991; Dirks 1992). As Stoler notes: "We are beginning to sort out how Europeans in the colonies imagined themselves and constructed communities built on asymmetries of race, class, and gender—entities significantly at odds with the European models on which they were drawn" (1991, 51). European men typically had a wider range of opportunities in the colonies for economic and social advancement, not to mention sexual adventure, than they would have had at home (Hyam 1990). For European women colonial experience was often less liberating (Suleri 1992, 75–110). Stoler observes: "the majority of European women who left for the colonies in the late nineteenth and early twentieth centuries confronted profoundly rigid restrictions on their domestic, economic, and political options, more limiting than those of metropolitan

Europe at the time and sharply contrasting with the opportunities open to colonial men" (1991, 52).

Whether their situation offered additional liberties or further constraints, most colonial actors remained acutely aware of differences between life in the colonies and life "at home"—often to the disadvantage of the colony. Indeed, an idealized concept of "home"—where things were done right—was frequently used to legitimate the subjugation of places "abroad," where it was not possible for things to be properly arranged.[2] In the Pacific Islands, for example, it was quite common for colonists to view their own society as comprised of discrete occupational groups, each performing its rightful tasks: missionaries, government officials, miners, planters, traders, labor recruiters, and the like (Huber 1988a, 47–54). Yet experience typically belied the model, not only because people shifted from one group to another but also because—given what colonists saw as "primitive" conditions—work tended to overlap. In frontier regions the slippage was especially notable. Instead of performing complementary functions, government officers, missionaries, and planters might all be engaged in a similar range of activities. Colonial politics in such circumstances were frequently fractious, conducted in a discourse of sector impurity with each group loudly arguing that the others should not be involved in competing enterprise but should stick to their own proper tasks.

Within groups, too, the division of labor was subject to confusion. Responsibilities might be neatly attributed to native and European staff, junior and senior officers, outstation and central station personnel, or, of course, women and men. But experience was often not so tidy. The missions may have been especially vulnerable to tensions around gender roles, because they more than other organizations employed women professionally. Yet, even when European women were officially relegated to the confines of domesticity, circumstances could conspire against it—an experience not uncommon among missionary wives (Grimshaw 1985; Langmore 1989; Beidelman, in this volume). Such issues were seldom seen as neutral by those involved: politics within as well as between groups often spun around contradictions between official expectations and local needs.

For Christian missions deflections in the field from official models could be understood as temporary if necessary detours in the progress from mission to church. Nonetheless, these areas of dislocation brought about a certain instability in their collective identity, providing space for the play of power and potentially becoming sites for social and cultural change. In this essay I examine some of the historical and institutional contexts in which Catholic gender ideology came into play in one mission field. Yet, as McDonough has noted more generally, "the rate of change in institutional Catholicism has varied across domains . . . but change has been tortuous when it comes to sexuality, the role of women, and the ecclesiastical hierarchy" (1990, 351). In this mission, I argue, conventional hierarchies were challenged during the colonial experience but, especially in the realm of gender, were not truly overturned.

Separate Spheres

The profound influence of patriarchal models of family life to Roman Catholic concepts and experience of Christian community is well-known (Troeltsch 1981, 280–302; McDonough 1990). Still, religious orders and congregations have long offered Catholic women the opportunity for life and work largely separated from, if still subordinated to, the rule of men. During various periods of European history women in religious communities had attempted to engage in charitable social service. But during the Counter-Reformation these efforts were suppressed as dangerous and unseemly, and nuns were confined to cloistered communities where religious life did not permit the mobility that active work in the community required (Liebowitz 1979; Monter 1987). Although these restrictions were gradually removed, the idea that male and female "religious"—subject, by definition, to the vow of chastity—should pursue their work separately remained firm. Sisters (nuns) were only introduced into Roman Catholic missions about the middle of the nineteenth century, when modern systems of transportation and supply had lessened "the perils and hardships of traveling and living in foreign countries" (Fischer 1925, 436; cf. Hobsbawm 1987, 13–14).[3] But the plans for their participation in foreign missionary work maintained, to a greater or lesser extent, the idea that even if men and women should have to work side by side, it should be in separate spheres.

The Society of the Divine Word (Societatis Verbi Divini, or SVD) was one of several Catholic mission-sending societies founded in Europe during the revival of Catholic foreign mission work in the second half of the nineteenth century (Schmidlin 1933). Established in 1875 as a seminary for training German priests for mission work, the institute's statutes were revised ten years later to establish the group as a full-fledged religious congregation, including priests, brothers, and a related order of sisters, dedicated to serve and staff Catholic missions in foreign lands (Bornemann 1975, 166–75). Although the SVD was separated in matters of spirit and organization from the larger ecclesiastical and secular societies of which it formed a separate part, its conception of an "orderly" life as a religious community drew on the social and cultural resources of these larger communities, especially those related to the division of labor by gender and by class.

From the start priests had a valorized role in the SVD, just as they had in the Catholic Church at large and just as educated, cultured men enjoyed in the Germanic societies of Europe during the late nineteenth century. All administrative and supervisory offices were reserved for priests, while the brothers were servants who were to provide material labor to enhance the spiritual services such as teaching, preaching, and administration provided by the priests. A few years later the society's founder, Arnold Janssen, created a separate organization of nuns, with one branch cloistered for prayer and contemplation and another branch, the Servants of the Holy Spirit (SSpS), for active sisters who would both pray and do "work appropriate to their sex" in the society's various establishments.[4] A complete community consisted of each of these types—priests, brothers, and active sisters—performing their respective tasks, with the cloistered sisters at home and, eventually, also in the United States, Germany, Philippines, and China, praying for their consociates' success in the mission fields.

In mission territories the priests of the Society of the Divine Word—like those of many other mission societies—formed, or augmented, the clerical staff of the local bishop, who in many cases was appointed by the Vatican from the ranks of the society "entrusted" by the Vatican with the territory concerned. The organizational goal was to create a mature diocesan structure in which the bishop and his priests would all be recruited from the local population, and the mission society would no longer be needed. In the meantime the missionary bishop and priests worked as something of a "shadow" church, attempting to create the conditions by which the mature church—with its full complement of locally recruited personnel—would gradually come into being. Missionary priests were expected to serve as pastors in proto-parishes and to administer the mission's major institutions, while the brothers were to keep the mission running with their manual skills.

Sisters, like brothers, were important to the task of establishing the church less in their own right than as facilitators of the activities of the priests. As the plan for the women's congregation clearly stated: "the missionary sisters are needed to supplement the work of the missionaries." In part this involved domestic work for the priests and brothers, to which some sisters devoted their efforts in the field. But this was not by any means the sisters' raison d'être. The sisters' aid was considered most valuable in the one area forbidden to priests and brothers by the people among whom they worked (or so it was widely thought at the time)—the evangelization of women. The expense and risk of sending sisters to work abroad were justified by the professional tasks they were expected to do: establishing schools for girls, orphanages, hospitals, and dispensaries and instructing women in catechism and in visiting "pagan" homes (Fischer 1925, 436).

The importance of these roles in the eyes of the mission's founder derived, again, less from their intrinsic worth than from the position of women in the ecclesiastical economy of the still highly clerical Catholic mission and church. Local women were the mothers of sons who might become priests. Celibate sisters were understood to play a maternal role, too, through their special contributions to the welfare and spiritual renewal of missionary priests and to the recruitment of local priests. In this task of social reproduction both cloistered sisters at home and missionary sisters in the field took part. "It might appear," founder Arnold Janssen wrote, that the cloistered nuns "ought to pray most for the propagation of the faith," but "they should pray first for the priesthood, because through the holy priesthood, Christian families also would be sanctified and the vocations for the priesthood and the missions be increased" (Fischer 1925, 442).

The active sisters, in Janssen's plan, would also pray for the priesthood but, in addition, would contribute to the formation of priests in practical ways. In his early articles exploring the desirability of including sisters, Janssen pointed out:

> sisters would have much easier access to and greater influence upon the female portion of the pagan population than priests can hope to exert; and that consequently, they could in an eminent degree become helpful in transforming pagan women into Christian mothers. And without these Christian mothers, truly Christian families are impossible. Again, without numerous Christian families there can be no native clergy, and without a native clergy, no permanent establishment of the Christian Faith in pagan countries . . . [T]he priestly calling is a grace of God: and only rarely does God work a *miracle* of grace. As a rule, He allows good to come out of the Church in a slow and natural way: but it is to be observed of nearly all periods that priestly vocations thrive only in the bosom of good Christian families. Especially do pious mothers, through their prayers and virtue, receive priestly sons. Therefore, we need in the missions many pious mothers . . . and it is the nuns in the missions who can cause them to flourish. (Qtd. in Fischer 1925, 428–29)

The SVD's rather conventional division of labor among priests, brothers, and sisters was accompanied by some fairly innovative practices and a self-consciously modernizing and progressive spirit at least in comparison to other Catholic religious orders of the day. The ideal type for a mission brother remained that of a "simple, natural, prayerful" man engaged in "manual labor and farming," but the SVD was in fact attracting highly skilled craftsmen using the most up-to-date processes, equipment, and tools. Priests responsible for the spiritual development of the missions were expected to use modern sciences to aid in the task. The most talented, in fact, were sent to the best German universities to study the branches of knowledge that could contribute to missionary work. For women, as with men, a similar combination of conventional spirituality with modern techniques prevailed. Active nuns were rigorously selected for intelligence and health, with the more talented among them receiving a three-year course of teacher training to suit them for their principal task in the mission fields (Fischer 1925, 434–35; Bornemann 1975, 237–39).

The Society of the Divine Word's programs proved popular indeed. With the aid of revenues and publicity generated by the sale and circulation of magazines and pamphlets published and printed by the mission's own press, the society expanded rapidly. From 1875 to 1909 its number of priests rose from 2 to 48, its brothers from 0 to 301, and its candidates for the men's divisions increased from 4 to 293. During the same time the number of sisters, including candidates, grew to 558. Part of the reason for the SVD's rapid growth may have been a certain national pride, because the SVD was the only specifically German mission-sending society at that time. Indeed, Arnold Janssen was intent upon involving German Catholics in missionary work. He wrote early on: "May the time soon come when Catholic Germany will contend in sacred rivalry with France for the cause of the foreign missions . . . Let us not say: we have missionary work enough to do in Germany. The Lord said: Go out to all peoples. Though these words may not be a mandate for each individual, they are directed nevertheless to all large Catholic nations as a whole. We must implore the grace of a mission vocation for many of our people" (Bornemann 1975, 43).

Janssen added a note of gender rivalry for women. The SVD was founded at a time when Bismarck, in an ill-considered bid to make Germany a Protestant country, was threatening to expel all Catholic religious orders established within German borders (Sperber 1984, 207–52).[5] Arnold Janssen hoped the misfortune (were it to actually occur) might be used to the benefit of the missions. According to Herman Fischer: "Even before he himself thought of founding a missionary society, he published, in the second and third numbers of his *Little Messenger of the Sacred Heart* (1874) an invitation to the women orders of Germany to participate in the work of the missions." It is interesting to note, in particular, Janssen's use of gender pride as a means of persuasion:

> The following lines are directed to the superioresses and members of religious communities. A danger is threatening them all,—the danger of exile. Whither will they go when the blow falls? Will the missions have a chance to give them a hearty welcome? Or will they only wait for bet-

> ter days in the frontier countries [Holland, for example], or go to North America, where practically European conditions prevail? They will be useful everywhere. But they should ask themselves where they will be *most* useful. They should try to make their lives as serviceable as possible to God. Neither is it well to choose what is easiest to do. In a time when bishops and priests make such great sacrifices, nuns should not lag behind. Or is only man capable of heroism? (Qtd. in Fischer 1925, 427).

Part of the SVD's appeal for women, then, was that in the 1870s and 1880s foreign mission work was an adventurous direction for Catholic women inclined toward social service and religious life.[6] But, in considering the SVD's appeal to women, one must also consider the dignity with which the SVD endowed women's separate sphere. German women had been permitted little role in public charity prior to the early nineteenth century (Prelinger 1987, 1) But in the mid- to late nineteenth century women throughout the world were making use of the ideology of "moral motherhood" to enter public life (di Leonardo 1991, 16). Although Arnold Janssen's vision of women in the missions was certainly not grounded in the contemporary discourse of German feminism, it is still worth noting that a similar but secularized ideology of "maternalism" was opening doors to public life for German lay women at about the same time (Allen 1991). German missionary nuns and their secular sisters both had gendered missions. Through teaching and social work feminists hoped to foster the sense of community and cooperation necessary for the new national state in Germany. Through similar modes of female professionalism the Servants of the Holy Spirit were to build the Christian families essential for the Catholic Church in mission lands.

Blurred Boundaries

A "frontier" by definition is a place where things are out of place, where order is a goal to be achieved rather than an accomplishment to be maintained. Frontiers are quintessentially found in territory that is distant from the "centers" of an expanding civilization. But they need not be so far away. Frontier conditions also have a temporal dimension and can be experienced at the beginning of virtually any human project, especially those that involve building new institutions. Weber's description of the routinization of charisma provides the classic sociological description of the changes that can accompany a vision when it is organized to last (1958, 262). Yet even in less dramatic circumstances, like getting the work of the sisters going, boundaries that appear clear in the conception can blur, and detours can obscure the route.

One condition for successfully fulfilling the gendered missions that Janssen had planned for the sisters on the one hand and the priests and brothers on the other was a certain degree of autonomy for the groups concerned. This was made clear to mission society leaders by confusion over the sisters' role in society projects, even before they set foot in mission lands. To be sure, a certain amount of manual labor was expected of the sisters, both for the practical purposes of maintaining their own community and by continuing their traditional work in the men's laundry, with which the first women hoping to become sisters had begun. Yet, as the society historian notes, "this tradition does not explain why other manual work was done, even on an unusually large scale, especially when one recalls the lofty goals the Superior had set for the training of the missionary Sisters" (Bornemann 1975, 240). In fact, it turns out that the sisters were totally dependent financially on the men's divisions and spent much time folding and trimming and stitching pages for the publications that supported them. Bornemann's conclusion alludes to what must have been a divisive quarrel:

> It seems that this helping one another, which was natural enough in the beginning, became excessive in the course of time. The situation was remedied only when the Sisters became completely independent both juridically and economically. Thereafter the number of Sisters working for the mission seminary and the press gradually decreased. (1975, 245)

In New Guinea, as the priests, brothers, and sisters would find out, boundaries were in danger of being further blurred because conditions were more extreme. As I have elsewhere described, one of the first victims was the division of material and spiritual labor between brothers and priests. Arriving in a region of the country where colonial activity had only just begun and where a modern infrastructure of transportation, supply, and communication did not yet exist, the mission's first leader decided to do everything himself. Under his direction the mission built an impressive array of stations along the north coast and became the most active economic agent in the region, providing not only sermons and schools for the natives but also sawn timber for government stations and private establishments, transportation services on its steamer, agricultural experimentation, and coconut plantations for its own financial support. Although this program successfully established the mission on a firm economic base, it was highly controversial because it required the involvement of priests in such "material" tasks as plantation management and limited their engagement in preaching, teaching, and delivery of the sacraments—the very activities that defined "spiritual" work (Huber 1988a, 61–74).

Not only did this shift toward the material side of mission work blur boundaries between priests and brothers; it also—especially from the perspective of colonists in other sectors—moved the mission into the borderland between religious and secular institutions. As one traveler in the region observed, one might admire the efficacy with which missionaries ran their stations and plantations but still question the propriety of a religious institution with *Ltd.* following its name (Marshall 1938, 225). Missionaries themselves worried that natives might misinterpret their cooperation with the administration. They might, for example, loan horses to the government officer or carry him part way on the mission steamer but preferred to avoid the appearance of involvement in a government patrol (Townsend 1968, 95).

Despite the political dangers to which their economic and political enterprise exposed them, these activities also brought the missionaries grudging respect in the rough colonial world. To outsiders the practical skills possessed by some of these missionaries were an unexpected point of contact, distinguishing them from a stigmatized "otherworldly" missionary stereotype. Indeed, these missionaries' practical expertise transported them from the vaguely feminine realm of religion into the clearly masculine secular sphere. As the naturalist, A. J. Marshall reported of the mission's second bishop, ship captain Father Joseph Loerks:

> On steamer days, so the story runs, you'll see him there on the beach checking the mission cargo, lending a hand, shifting the cases, coatless, in shirtsleeves. Perhaps the South Seas is the only place where you can see a bishop's shirt sleeves. But it makes little difference what Bishop Lorks [*sic*] wore, for he has a noble bearing, a fluent scholarly tongue, and the look of the man of the world in his frank direct eyes. (1938, 221)

Bishop Loerks needed his noble bearing because central authority, as well as work, became confused in New Guinea conditions. By the early 1920s the mission had seventeen main stations and thirty-one auxiliary stations scattered along the islands, rivers, and coast from the Dutch border in the west to Astrolabe Bay (Madang), a stretch of some 375 miles. Transportation by boat, horse, and foot was time-consuming, and communications were slow. Further, in a region known for the small political scale of its societies and for cultural and linguistic diversity, a premium was placed on the local knowledge of the resident priest, confounding efforts to centralize mission policy.[7] The early mission's position on clothing provides a good example. The SVD missionary anthropologist Georg Höltker wrote that in the years between World War I and World War II most of the missionaries—especially at the older mission stations—preferred native Christian men to wear an ordinary, short lap-lap (waistcloth of imported fabric) to mass and to receive the sacraments. "However, a general and explicit order of this type on the part of the Mission leaders could not long endure. So the decision in practice was left to the separate missionaries. At the newer inland stations European clothing, especially long women's garments, were no longer introduced." And in the footnote accompanying the passage Höltker is critical of an earlier scholar who claimed that missionaries wished natives to wear European clothing whenever in touch with the mission. "It could be correct for at best, perhaps, one or the other station, but not for all or even most stations" (1946, 48 n. 9).

With only weak centralization possible, priests tailored their message to what seemed most important around their particular station and a variety of approaches to native social and religious practices bloomed. For these German Catholics this was a situation that challenged the very nature of the church they were attempting to build (Huber 1988a, 75–92). It spoke also to the isolation of mission personnel and the difficulties of building and maintaining fraternity when a priest's confreres were so far away and their pastoral concerns so different from his own. As Bruno Hagspiel, an official visitor to the mission in 1921, remarked: the "very lack of any universal binding characteristic among the people . . . sets up real barriers of difficulty among the Fathers and Brothers themselves . . . What is meant here is that each mission [station], being so entirely segregated from the others, has its own distinct problems to such an extent as to be almost a distinct mission by itself" (1926, 69).

For missionary women, as for missionary men, conditions along the north coast of New Guinea blurred the boundaries that defined their special identity as a separate community within the mission field. Only three years after the founding of the mission by the pioneer contingent of six brothers and priests, the first three sisters, Servants of the Holy Spirit, arrived. Bringing along much equipment and European domestic animals "to conduct an experiment of acclimatization," the pioneer sisters joined the men at the mission's first headquarters, hundreds of miles up the coast from the nearest colonial settlement of any size (K.H.J.B. 1898–99, 94). As the mission expanded its base, the sisters expanded theirs. By 1900 sisters accounted for nearly one-third of the fifty-nine Catholic missionaries then in northern New Guinea, and by 1921 the thirty-eight sisters constituted nearly half the missionary force. But they were not as scattered as the men: seventeen were working at the new headquarters of Alexishafen, and three each at seven of the main stations—Bogia, Monumbo, Wewak, Boiken, Yakamul, Ali, and Tumleo (Fischer 1925, 400; Hagspiel 1926, 207).

Like the priests and brothers, the sisters' work became exceedingly diverse. Charged with the women's equivalent of both material (housekeeping) and spiritual (teaching, nursing) tasks, they struggled to keep the former from swamping the latter and to keep relations with local people within the bounds of traditional churchwomen's work. Summarizing the sisters' activities in 1921, Hagspiel observed:

> Most of the Sisters are active as teachers and nurses. A number of them do splendid work as catechists: accompanied by one or two native girls, they go out, every week, either on foot or on horseback, to the neighboring villages to instruct the little ones and the adults in the truths of our holy religion. Upon such occasions they go about to the thatched huts of the natives, seeking to help the needy and suffering. Sometimes they prepare the dying; frequently they baptize those in danger of death . . . Wherever there are Sisters in a station, they as a rule conduct classes in domestic economy, composed of native girls who board with them and who thereby come speedily to learn the various branches of housekeeping, such as cooking, sewing, mending, and even gardening. With the help of these girls, the sisters also take care of the church and the sacristy, do the washing, and prepare the meals for the priests and the Brothers. (1926, 206–7)

"Without the sisters," Hagspiel effused, "all the priests' missionary activities in New Guinea would be . . . incomplete and, in the long run, doomed to failure." He praised highly the sisters' influence on the native women, recapitulating official views: "Not until a mission can, through a band of sisters, exert its influence on the pagan women, will it succeed in attaining to great growth or real, solid development" (1926, 207). And he took special note of the domestic comfort the sisters provided to the priests: "Any visitor of the mission will be struck at once with the noticeable difference that exists between those stations where the priest is assisted by a number of Sisters and those where all the work devolves upon the priest alone" (206):

> What this last service means for every priest and Brother only those will be able to appreciate who, like the majority of our New Guinea missionaries, have to do all the washing and cooking themselves, or are obliged to depend on some native boy who hardly knows the rudiments of the culinary art, and, as for the laundry work, has (that is to say, generally speaking) received a diploma for his cleanliness! (207)[8]

Still, beneath all the praise there was something about the diversity of the sisters' tasks that troubled this official observer, for he took care throughout his discussion to emphasize the sisters' role not as independent actors but as helpmates to the men. One may note in particular a certain hesitancy over the sisters' more spiritual, or priestly, work—their visits to the villages, where they "sometimes . . . prepare the dying" and "frequently . . . baptize those in danger of death." Hagspiel felt obliged to explain that "in such cases, upon their return to the station, they report to the missionary observations made which may be useful to the Father on his next visit to the place" (1926, 206). As Hagspiel's comment suggests, the slippage in the division of labor between priests and nuns could be a problem for the men upon whose spiritual territory it encroached.

Yet the situation also posed problems for the women parallel to those faced by priests. Like the fathers, whose time for spiritual work could be diminished by the material tasks frontier life appeared to require, the sisters' special calling in regard to teaching women and children could be diluted by excessive household or garden tasks. In addition to the domestic services they supervised and/or directly provided, sisters often had associated farm responsibilities as well. Wewak, for example, was a major agricultural station with a coconut plantation, farm, banana plot, and a few hundred head of cattle in the interwar years. In a 1982 interview with Karol LaCasse, Brother Leonard Althoff recalled that, when he was sent there for training in 1938, he was struck by the sight of the six resident sisters working in the garden "in their long dresses and veils." The sisters were also in charge of milking cows, which clearly was a time-consuming task:

> In those years, the Sisters did the milking. One supervised and they had boys and girls who helped. They didn't milk like they do in America or at home [Germany] in those days. A boy would have to catch the cow and bring the calf along. The calf would start to suck, then the milk would flow, and the Sister could start the milking. The boy takes the calf away and maybe the milk stops coming, so he has to bring it back and the whole thing starts over again. It took a long time sometimes.

If sisters, like priests and brothers, found themselves engaged in a wider variety of work than initially planned, they were somewhat differently affected by the political economy of the mission arrangements. The mission's policy of assigning groups of sisters to the most accessible and developed coastal stations protected them from some of the forces of fragmentation that beset the men. But the conditions that made every station "almost a mission unto itself," thus enhancing the autonomy of individual priests, could compromise the autonomy of the sisters. Like the French Daughters of Our Lady of the Sacred Heart on the south coast of Papua in the 1890s, whose "identity was threatened by interference from some of the younger priests who, in their immature zeal, exceeded their authority in relation to the sisters" (Langmore 1989, 181), the small communities of sisters at the isolated stations on the north coast of New Guinea were subject to the personality or style of the particular priest in charge.

In Papua the bishop attempted to relieve the state of constant conflict between priests and nuns by "a complete separation according to canonical law" between the sisters and priests, making the sisters responsible to their own superior instead of the priest. The bishop of Papua also decided early on to sever the "close working relationship that since the beginning had existed between the priests and the sisters," building their convents further from the local priest's residence and relieving them from daily responsibility for his cooking and laundry (Langmore 1989, 181). Relations between priests and nuns on the north coast do not appear to have been this troubled, perhaps because the Servants of the Holy Spirit and the Society of the Divine Word arrived in New Guinea with legal separation and separate superiors already in place. Yet, as long as the priests and sisters continued to work closely together, identities initially imagined as separate and complementary remained in some danger of blurring if special efforts were not made to keep them properly aligned and apart.

Gender Alignment

For mission priests and sisters the conditions that might allow specialized work and a surer control of its shape and direction improved after World War II. The mission suffered greatly during the war. Most of its establishments on the north coast were devastated by bombing, and, of the 230 priests, brothers, and sisters "active in New Guinea before World War II, 122 (or 53 percent) lost their lives during the war" (Divine Word Missionaries 1969, 55). The period that followed, however, was one of unprecedented building and expansion, and communications and supply between stations and headquarters were much improved by the introduction of aviation and the shortwave radio into mission work. Missionaries still spent much of their time traveling by foot, canoe, or small motor boat to the villages in their station region. But they had more opportunities to visit their fellow missionaries once aviation was well established, more opportunities for overseas leave, and—with their bishop a pilot—more chance to see him as well (Huber 1988a, 137–48).

These postwar years were a time when the mission no longer had to be quite so self-sufficient in order to feed and clothe its personnel. It was a time when mission personnel became more diversified in terms of national origins, with Americans, especially, coming to dominate the priestly ranks. During the 1950s and 1960s the mission was rebuilding its old stations and establishing new ones at a fast pace. And during this era priests' ideas about what constituted "spiritual work" shifted from the more generalized pastoral work of earlier times, to include development projects of various kinds (Huber 1988a, 156–65). Small or large, these projects consumed much priestly effort and enormous amounts of time. A 1976 report on a "Self-Study" conducted by the Catholic Church in New Guinea in the early 1970s observed that "business and building occupied the time of many a priest."

For some years the mission on the north coast of New Guinea was even more a man's world than the prewar mission had been. Descriptions and photographs of mission life during the 1950s and 1960s emphasize tractors and radios and airplanes and cars. In 1962 Father Karsten, the Society's Regional Superior, felt impelled to call his priests' attention to "our whole approach to parishioners." In this special *Society Newsletter on Mission Problems* Karsten noted again the old theme of each priest developing his own private mission methods and resisting suggestions to reflect critically upon them. In particular, Karsten suggested that personal, pastoral contact with local people was impeded by unwise use of technology:

> The accoutrements of civilization, mechanized transport, machines of all kinds, etc. can certainly contribute to a better and more intensive ministry. But the danger is that we use them too much for other things than our pastoral work. Bishops and superiors complain that some fathers spend too much time repairing their vehicles, take too many pleasure trips, and that outstations beyond the reach of vehicles are too often neglected. Gadgets contribute to fruitful mission work only if that is what we use them for.[9]

Mission women appear only sparsely in accounts of these years, in part because there were in fact very few sisters present at all. Throughout the 1950s there were only a dozen or so Servants of the Holy Spirit in the Diocese of Wewak. These sisters still laundered and cooked for the men at a few stations and were much appreciated, to be sure. There were nuns on the station next door to that of Father Hughes, for example, and he described himself as "always a recipient of their benevolence." The sisters were simply too few in number, however, to look after the diocese's growing need for teachers and nurses as development goals quickly rose. In a letter home in 1950 Father Francis Swift wrote about his hopes for the newly founded congregation of indigenous sisters:

> The Lord knows how badly they are needed: for the schools, for medical work, for the women and children, and for the many other tasks for which the priest is not suited. The [SSpS] nuns are too few in number to

> begin to take care of all the needs. For the most part, they are kept in Alexishafen and Wewak to do the cooking and laundry for the priests and brothers. If I had sisters here at Timbunke, I would be the happiest priest in the mission, and I would make sure that their only work would be in the schools and hospitals. (Swift 1989, 40)

By the mid-1960s, however, the situation had improved, and the mission staff in the Diocese of Wewak included fifteen sisters of the SSpS, thirty-one indigenous Rosary Sisters (a diocesan congregation founded in 1951), and twenty-three Sisters of Mercy from Australia, whose first members began work in the diocese in 1957. Each group worked separately at schools, hospitals, and clinics at nine or ten of the mission's approximately forty stations. And, while the balance between men and women was still uneven, with fifty-seven missionary priests and twenty-four missionary brothers scattered throughout the province, the participation of women was enhanced by the arrival, beginning in the 1950s, of lay missionaries from around the world—including women teachers and nurses who agreed to work without real salary for a period of time.

This was a "boom" time for the Catholic mission. The bishop was receiving money from large overseas foundations for major development projects; priests were improving their stations with new churches and new buildings; a hundred small projects were under way as missionaries tried to find ways for people in their station areas to engage in the modern economy as well. The air strip at the mission's headquarters in Wewak during the late 1960s was reputed to be the busiest in the southern hemisphere—a boast that was somewhat tongue in cheek, given the small single-engine planes it served.

Mission women, too, caught the spirit. Many of the more domestic and manual tasks they had undertaken before were no longer necessary or could be turned over to local workers. Sisters could now focus on teaching and nursing, endeavors that were themselves becoming professionalized in the modernizing rush of the postwar years. The new congregations of sisters and brothers invited to work in the diocese were specialized in teaching: the Christian Brothers ran the boys' high school on Kairiru Island, and the Mercy Sisters were engaged both in primary schooling and in secondary education for girls. Even the indigenous Rosary Sisters were brought up to date. In the mid-1970s the congregation was in crisis, and after a year of spiritual renewal an intense period of educational renewal took place. The rules were changed to admit only women who had completed at least eight years of schooling, and the older sisters, many of whom had training only as domestics, were given a chance to complete their primary education and to train as teachers, nurses, and secretaries.[10]

Bishop Leo Arkfeld, Sr. Eurista, SSpS, and Sisters of the Rosary, Wewak, Papua New Guinea (ca. 1954)

Missionary maternalism was modernized through professionalism and modified through the distinct character of the diocese's different congregations of nuns. But some things remained the same. Sister Nikola, SSpS, who came from Germany to New Guinea in 1913, represented the old maternal ideal: "She is one who combines motherly care and kindness," according a mission public relations piece of 1963, "with the firmness of the woman in the Gospel in charge of her household. During her many years in the Mission fields, in her own way she introduced many young Fathers into mission life." One of Sister Nikola's golden rules, we are told, was: "If you want to get somewhere in the Mission, if you want to get something done, you have to be 'anstandig frech'—persistent in a nice way." Although the Australian Mercy Sisters were believed to have a warmer approach to mission work than the older German SSpS sisters, they needed to be equally persistent in pursuit of their projects, for the conditions of their autonomy did not much change.

Cooperation between priests and sisters remained essential, a point well illustrated by the history of the diocese's high school for girls. The original plan had been for the Mercy Sisters to open this school at Ulupu, but, because the station priest had not yet completed the necessary facilities, the school accepted an invitation from the priest at Torembi to locate the school there. According to Sister Maureen Grant, who joined the staff in 1964, "it was really through [the Torembi station priest] that we were able to get this start, because he was tremendous in his support . . . spiritual support and monetary support with the food." Later, when it became clear that Torembi was too isolated a place for the high school and that the interest of the Ulupu priest had further waned, the sisters found an appropriate site near the town of Wewak, with a parish priest who was enthusiastic about the project. In addition to helping organize the necessary political and logistical support, this priest was responsible for much of the site design and building. He was, Sister Maureen recalled, "the brain behind it all."[11] He did not, however, involve himself in setting education policies or in the daily routine of the school.

Sisters' independence was enhanced by government funding for mission-run schools and clinics during the postwar years. By accepting such funding, the mission facilities gained resources with which to expand and pursue their goals, but these goals were no longer set solely by the mission. The sisters' projects thus became even further separated from the general run of pastoral work conducted by the mission's priests. The lives of men and women on the same station no longer intersected so often, especially when the women were running a government-funded school or health center. In a 1982 interview recalling her sixteen years' experience at the Timbunke health center on the Sepik River, for example, Sister Mary Anthida Kueckmann, SSpS, mentioned hardly any priests as crucial to her work.[12]

This was not, of course, the only way to conduct such relationships, even within the limited domain of Roman Catholic mission societies. These societies each have their own separate style, reflective of their own spirituality and their different national roots. Consider the local contrast provided by Australian Franciscan missionaries who took over the western section of the Sepik diocese after World War II. The Franciscans, like the SVDs, ran into difficulties establishing themselves in a way appropriate to their ideals (Duggan 1983; Huber 1988b). But the two groups' ideals were different. Unlike the individualistic SVDs, the Franciscans were dedicated to fraternity among themselves and with the Papua New Guineans around them. This ideal involved both men and women Franciscans and contrasted notably with the relations that came to characterize the Society of the Divine Word and the congregations of sisters who came to work in the Diocese of Wewak after the war. As one SVD priest told me in the late 1970s, the Franciscan priests and sisters are friendly and work together on projects, while in SVD territory priests and sisters work apart.[13]

It is certainly notable that society newsletters during this period contain little news of the sisters, who were working at the same stations as the SVD's brothers and priests. One reason for this was that mission life was dominated by congregational affiliations, and the newsletters circulated to SVD members carried little news of sisters in part because they were not SVDs. For the missionary sisters of the SSpS in New Guinea and for other groups of sisters working on the north coast, however, congregational membership was extremely important in helping their members maintain a separate identity in the field. This is not to say that confusion about women's roles or authority over their work no longer occurred. Indeed, the bishop felt it necessary to remove one priest from his station in the early 1960s, when it turned out that he could not get along with the Papua New Guinean Rosary Sisters, who had been posted there and who had threatened to run away. On the whole, however, during the busy years of the 1960s and early 1970s sisters appear to have been sufficiently well protected by their separate organizations and discrete projects to avoid serious conflicts with the men over their work.

Lay missionaries, especially women, were much more vulnerable to adverse conditions in their life and work than sisters who were backed by their congregations and the traditions these congregations upheld. During my fieldwork in Wewak in 1976–77 and in interviews conducted in the early 1980s by Karol LaCasse it was clear that lay women stationed at the diocesan headquarters had long-standing grievances among themselves stemming from the small annoyances of living in close quarters, rivalry for responsibility and recognition, and real differences in styles of spirituality and missionary approach. It is also worth recalling the warning (noted at the beginning of this essay) that an official observer to the mission in 1969 gave to priests to avoid too much socializing with these lay workers. Given the "dangers of immorality" believed to come from too close an association between men and women, it is notable that rumors about illicit liaisons between male and female missionaries tended to concern priests or brothers with lay missionary women rather than with nuns.[14]

Separation between male and female mission workers and complementarity between their tasks appears to have been partially achieved during the years following World War II, but the era was short-lived. Colonialism proper ended suddenly in Papua New Guinea, with a rush toward self-government and independence in the early 1970s that caught most expatriate communities in the country unprepared. The Catholic mission on the north coast was no exception. There, despite nearly eighty years of mission work aimed at producing sufficient numbers of male clerics to man a local church, the mission found itself facing the political imperative of localization with extremely few Papua New Guinean priests and a sudden excess of expatriate sisters displaced from their government-funded schools and clinics by local personnel. Along with the grave decline in the numbers of men in Europe and America entering the priesthood, this imbalance appears to have precipitated a small gender crisis in the Roman Catholic mission and set the stage for a new "ecclesiastical" or institution-building frontier.

The old pattern of separating the work of male and female missionaries was again placed in question in the 1970s. Certainly there appeared to be room for women in general parish work. As the 1976 report on the Church's Self-Study in Papua New Guinea phrased it, "with both business and building on a downward trend in the early seventies, it was an opportune time to reopen channels of communication with the people . . . It was a good time to bury the ghost of that haunting complaint voiced so frequently . . . 'Father doesn't visit us or talk to us very much. He's too busy. It was not like that in the old days.'" But could the declining number of expatriate parish priests be persuaded to let displaced expatriate sisters take over some of their pastoral responsibilities? And would the church be able to rely more on local women in such traditionally male roles as catechist?

In the Diocese of Wewak in 1976 a letter was sent from the Bishop's House to the parish priests asking them to fill out a questionnaire concerning their willingness to have sisters perform pastoral work in their parishes. The letter explained:

> As is well known, localization has been taking place at a rapid rate in the teaching and medical profession and so more and more sisters are being released from their positions in these professions. Many sisters, in line with instructions from Rome which propose a more active *pastoral* apostolate for women, feel that there is such an apostolate for them here in [Papua New Guinea].

The letter noted that some pastoral work was already being carried out by sisters, who were giving retreats to teachers, prayer leaders, and villagers; taking parish censuses; supervising teaching of religion in schools; leading religious discussion groups with women in the village ("keeping in mind the role of a Christian woman in the family"); engaging in social and family counseling; giving instructions for marriage, baptism, and family planning (ovulation method); and preparing people for First Communion and confession.

By the mid-1970s Papua New Guinean laymen and laywomen were also being seen as a new resource. Before Vatican II Catholic laity in Papua New Guinea, as elsewhere, had only limited access to formal pastoral roles. Catechists, who were responsible for elementary religious instruction and observance in the villages, could achieve considerable local influence. But it was not until after the status of the laity was enhanced, in the 1960s, that other formal positions were created, especially for men. The mission in Wewak began to experiment with a married deaconate, ordaining married men who could, in conditions of necessity, perform certain priestly functions like administering holy Communion and baptisms. In some areas of the diocese laywomen were invited to take up nonordained roles. When I was doing my fieldwork in 1976–77 women were performing as "church leaders" and "prayer leaders." Later it appears that women were being accepted into the ranks of catechist—a role that was elevated in the 1980s to include vestments and ceremony marking the dignity with which the mission hoped modern catechists would be received.[15]

By the time of national independence, then, the maternalism that had historically underwritten a degree of autonomy for missionary women by marking out separate spheres for women's work was beginning to appear confining in the circumstances facing the emerging Papua New Guinean church. First, the old racial/imperial maternalism that had given European women a special role vis-à-vis indigenous women was fraying as educated Papua New Guinean women—lay as well as religious—moved into the ranks of professional roles alongside and even supplanting Europeans. Second, the old maternalism that gave women in religious orders a special place in the mission was beginning to blur as European and Papua New Guinean laywomen took on professional and pastoral roles. Finally, and most important for this essay, were the pressures to involve women, lay and religious, in the kinds of pastoral work previously seen as appropriate to the priesthood—an order that has remained, of course, reserved for men.

Suggestive though this moment appeared to be, it was nonetheless the case that changes in roles for women in the Diocese of Wewak were taking place more in a spirit of expediency, given urgent mission tasks, than from the conviction that the place of women vis-à-vis men should or even could be fundamentally changed. As the 1976 questionnaire about expanding the role of nuns conceded, "But of course, pastoral work for sisters will be impossible without full cooperation of the parish priests in our diocese." And as the bishop later wrote in regard to his vision for a viable local church:

> It seemed to me that if a diocese is to become a real family working together with the bishop, there should be local priests for pastoral work and sisters and brothers for the many tasks associated with the work of the priests. There is of course always plenty to do in the schools, hospitals, and family ministries. (Arkfeld 1992, 24)[16]

The nature of women's work might have shifted toward the pastoral end of the spectrum, but on the whole the social and symbolic grounding of the church in male clerical authority had not shifted much at all.[17]

Conclusion

Clearly, the roles for women missionaries envisaged by the founder of the Society of the Divine Word and the Servants of the Holy Spirit were consistent with the gender ideologies predominant in Germany (and elsewhere in Europe and America) by the late nineteenth century—ideologies that posited a "polarization of the 'character of the sexes'" and assigned to men work in the world and to women work at home (Hausen 1981, 63). Patricia Grimshaw cites a similar ideology as background to the work of American Protestant missionary women in Hawaii. In the Great Awakening women had been represented as having a special role in creating the home as a "haven of domesticity." According to Grimshaw, "The elevation of women's nature inherent in these fresh definitions of femininity contained within it the seeds of change in women's social and political roles. Women's supposed moral and spiritual value was used to stress a new competency for women in the public arena, initially within the orbit of social reform" (1985, xx).

As we have seen in the Catholic missionary experience in New Guinea, frontier circumstances could place a premium on women's "new competency" in the public sphere and blur the boundaries between male and female work. Not surprisingly, there appears to be a parallel in the early medieval church, when the more formal separation of male and female members of religious communities recommended by Scripture and tradition was simply not followed as Christianity expanded into northern and eastern Europe. As Suzanne Wemple notes: "Saint Paul's injunction that it was improper for women to teach men was ignored through the eighth century because of the demands of the frontier situation in most of Europe" (1991, 138). Studies of missionaries in the modern era show too that such "confusion" was common, regardless of denomination: frontiers invited—demanded—a relaxation, sometimes even a reversal, of the rules (see essays by Miller, Beidelman, and Kipp, in this volume). This blurring of boundaries often contributed to the liberating quality of frontier experience in the missions and in other colonial institutions as well.

In colonial circumstances, however, hierarchies that colonizers could not express in conventional ways were often re-expressed through other means. As we have seen, the Catholic mission's experience along the north coast of Papua New Guinea made negotiable the role of women vis-à-vis men. As we have also seen, however, what the situation permitted for

Catholic missionary sisters in regard to pastoral work was usually paid for in risks to their autonomy. In this mission, convergence in the tasks performed by men and women missionaries was being accompanied by new reminders from those in authority of the continuing necessity for the social and symbolic subordination of women if the mission community were to be a "real family"—that is, an authentic diocese of the Roman Catholic Church.

NOTES

1. This essay is based in part on my own fieldwork and historical research and in part on a private collection of documents, interview manuscripts, photographs, and notes assembled in the 1970s and 1980s by Karol LaCasse for a biography of Archbishop Leo Arkfeld. Unfortunately, Ms. LaCasse died before she could fully use these materials, and they were donated to me for use in my scholarly work by Archbishop Arkfeld and Robert LaCasse. These documents, together with my own collection of similar material, are housed in my home. My fieldwork in Wewak, Papua New Guinea, in 1976–77 was funded in part by the National Science Foundation (BNS-15269) and by a Mellon predoctoral fellowship from the University of Pittsburgh. I would like to express my gratitude to Angelica Striegel, librarian at the Society of the Divine Word's Missiological Institute in St. Augustine, Germany, for her assistance during my visit in July 1992. I also thank Linda Layne and the University of Michigan Press reviewer, Margaret Jolly, for insightful remarks on earlier drafts. Translations from German are my own.

2. This argument has been made for literature as well. For example, Edward Said argues that Jane Austen uses the beauty and order of Mansfield Park to validate its extension to Sir Thomas Bertram's overseas properties in the Caribbean (1993, 79). Said has been criticized, however, for his reading of Austen on this issue (Fraiman 1995, 810). Fraiman also points out that Said does not address the argument made by his student, Suvendrini Perera (1991), "whose book on empire and the English novel . . . [argues] that 'home' was a construct policing British women as well as colonial 'others'" (816).

3. In this the church was not alone. Colonial governments and private trading companies placed severe restrictions on the importation of European women to colonial countries from the sixteenth century to as late as the early twentieth century. They, too, cited dangers to the health and welfare of European women as a prime reason for these restrictions, although some scholars have argued that the restrictions also served the political and economic interests of colonial powers (Stoler 1991).

4. Fritz Bornemann, biographer of Arnold Janssen, founder of the Society of the Divine Word, emphasizes Janssen's steady faith in the importance of women to the missions, amid many vicissitudes of vision and plan. At first the concept for the sisters moved between the poles of contemplation and action and between

joined and separate groups. First, Janssen thought of missionary sisters who would be part of the SVD, like the priests and brothers. Then a plan for a separate congregation of "praying" sisters gained sway. When the group was actually founded in 1889, the idea was for the two branches to belong to one organization with relations between them represented as like the biblical sisters Martha and Mary. But all the applicants accepted were taken as active sisters at the start, and it was not until after the first missionary sisters had made their profession, in March 1894, that Janssen began preparation for the cloistered branch. The cloistered "Adoration Sisters" later became independent from the active Servants of the Holy Spirit. Although they were at first restricted to a convent in Steyl, Holland (where the Society of the Divine Word was founded), they subsequently established a second convent in Holland, two convents in Germany, two in the United States, two in the Philippines, and one in China (Bornemann 1975, 339).

5. It was necessary for Janssen to found the Society of the Divine Word in Steyl, Holland, just across the border from Germany, because the repressive laws in force during the *kulturkampf* forbade the establishment of new Catholic orders in the German empire.

6. The dangers were political as well as physical. Janssen was willing to send sisters to Argentina, Togo, and New Guinea, although he did not consider the SVD's first mission field in South Shantung, China, suitable for its new congregation of missionary sisters, because the stations all were inland and the sisters could not be assured of a safe evacuation if trouble ensued.

7. The geographical spread of mission stations also limited the application of centralized policy in the Church Missionary Society among the Ukaguru (see Beidelman, in this volume). Paradoxically, the spread itself was part of central policy for the Catholic Mission, whereas the drive to build new stations among the CMS prior to World War I appears to have been fueled by dissension and disagreement among the missionaries. Beidelman notes that the "usual solution to differences was for each to work at his or her own outpost. Under such circumstances it mattered relatively little what a putative local head tried to enforce, since the relative isolation of stations allowed each person to pursue what she or he wanted." Elsewhere in East Africa, geographical expansion in CMS territory was driven partly by status concerns. Lay missionaries, Strayer observes, soon realized that the quickest way to ordination and its associated benefits was to start a new station some distance away from the others (1978, 30–51).

8. Speaking about work in the region from 1938 to 1941, Brother Leonard Althoff recalled: "To Mass every day we wore the long cassock. You could tell the ones from the bush because their cassocks were all yellowed . . . no Sisters to wash them" (interview with Karol LaCasse, 1982).

9. Karsten was concerned that the misuse of technology contributed to priestly neglect of traditional catechetical work and to the lack of an "organic adjustment of the church in the New Guinea culture"—by which he meant the practice of "proclaiming the culture of the white man as higher and better than theirs and forcing them to follow it—also in religious matters." The danger, Karsten concluded, was that the missionaries would "only bring about an inferior-

ity complex among [local people]; we ask from them what they cannot master as yet. We see the precise result of this already in the economic field, the cargo cult mentality, a symptom of their unhappiness of mind" (Society Newsletter on Mission Problems, 1962).

10. In the early 1970s most girls in Papua New Guinea finishing grade eight would have been able to go into teacher training, nursing school, or secretarial college and get a job. According to Sister Maureen Grant, headmistress of the mission's high school for girls and leader of the Rosary Sisters' year of renewal, this standard soon changed. By around 1980 grade ten was the effective cutoff for further education and careers of this type, and by 1982 "there was a big drop and only 72 percent to 73 percent of the grade ten graduates got a position" (interview with Karol LaCasse, 1982).

11. Sister Maureen Grant said she did not know why the priest at Ulupu lost interest, but it is worth noting that in the early 1960s there was opposition to the very idea of a girls' high school among a number of priests. These priests preferred to send intelligent girls who had completed grade six at their station primary school to teacher training or nursing courses, for which they were then eligible. Sister Maureen attributes this attitude to "a bit of a misunderstanding of what we were trying to do for the girls" in high school (interview with Karol LaCasse, 1982).

12. This is not to say that Sister Mary Anthida Kueckmann did not have to work for her autonomy. As she said obliquely: "I make a point to understand different people. I've been with very many different types of people. While I try to respect different peoples' opinions as such, sure there have been difficult times in different ways. It has been quite an experience in many ways, but I don't think it has influenced my work very much. I must say that Father Ben has respected my health work for the most part" (interview with Karol LaCasse, 1982).

13. These differences may also relate to the national origins of the two groups, the SVD representing a more Germanic view of patriarchy and the Australian Franciscans a more Irish view. As McDonough notes: "One puzzle concerns the extent to which the presumed need to subjugate women gets at the pith of traditional Catholicism and possibly kindred patrimonial arrangements. While the outcomes might be much the same from the perspective of excluded women, there probably are significant differences between cultural institutions in which males prevail through displays of outright aggression and those in which domination reflects sexual abnegation and intragender bonding. The control mechanisms are neither mutually exclusive (as both occur in Catholicism), nor are they equally prevalent across cultures. The active pattern seems to be common in Mediterranean and Latin settings; the indirect seems to have been widespread in Ireland and the Irish religiosity that has shaped American Catholicism. The simplest implication of this variation is that patriarchy cannot be construed as unitary" (1990, 355).

14. It is interesting to recall that many SVD missionaries believed that local sensibilities called for an even stricter separation between the sexes than either they themselves or other Europeans were wont to follow. In addition to the views of the bishop and the official mission observer cited in the beginning of this essay, con-

sider the conclusion of an unpublished manuscript by Reverend J. M. Noss, SVD on "Womanhood in New Guinea" (1968). After reviewing the separation of the sexes in local village life, including eating habits, the etiquette of staring, the consequences of being seen with a woman not one's wife, or accepting food or a smoke or betelnut from the younger opposite sex, and negative attitudes toward holding hands, loud laughing, and joking between men and women, the author asks: "Well, what do we whites look like in their eyes in this regard for manners?"

15. These, plus other lay positions, continued to gain importance in the eyes of many missionaries. Sister Maureen Grant, speaking to Karol LaCasse in 1982, voiced her opinion that "this whole catechist, pastor, deacon program is really getting somewhere and I think it is tremendous, and I think this is going to be the Church in the years to come. The PNG Church."

16. Arkfeld mentions this vision in regard to his controversial but forward-looking decisions to establish an indigenous sisters' community in the early 1950s and an indigenous brothers' community in the late 1950s.

17. This is not to say that when the church is further localized such shifts will not occur. The relations between Papua New Guinean men and women in contemporary society have become a public issue, debated in the media and in a variety of public forums. It remains to be seen how these gender questions, along with associated ideas of "Christian community," will be handled by Papua New Guinean Catholics—churchwomen and churchmen (Huber 1988a, 179–98).

REFERENCES

Allen, Ann Taylor. 1991. *Feminism and Motherhood in Germany, 1800–1914.* New Brunswick, N.J.: Rutgers University Press.

Arkfeld, Archbishop Leo, S.V.D. 1992. The Short Story of a Long Life. MS.

Beidelman, T. O. 1982. *Colonial Evangelism: A Socio-Historical Study of an East African Mission at the Grassroots.* Bloomington: Indiana University Press.

Bornemann, Fritz. 1975. *Arnold Janssen; Founder of Three Missionary Congregations, 1837–1909: A Biography.* Manila: Arnoldus Press.

di Leonardo, Micaela. 1991. Gender, Culture, and Political Economy: Feminist Anthropology in Historical Perspective. Introduction to *Gender at the Crossroads of Knowledge: Feminist Anthropology in the Postmodern Era,* ed. Micaela di Leonardo, 1–48. Berkeley: University of California Press.

Dirks, Nicholas. 1992. Colonialism and Culture. Introduction to *Colonialism and Culture,* ed. Nicholas Dirks, 1–25. Ann Arbor: University of Michigan Press.

Divine Word Missionaries. 1969. Divine Word Missionaries in New Guinea. In *The Word in the World 1969. Divine Word Missionaries: New Guinea: A Report on the Missionary Apostolate.* Techny, Ill.: Divine Word Publications.

Duggan, Stephan. 1983. In the Shadow of Somoro: The Franciscan Experience in the Sepik Region, 1946–1975. Master's thesis, La Trobe University.

Fischer, Herman. 1925. *Life of Arnold Janssen: Founder of the Society of the Divine Word and of the Missionary Congregation of the Servants of the Holy Ghost.* Techny, Ill.: Mission Press.

Fraiman, Susan. 1995. Jane Austen and Edward Said: Gender, Culture, and Imperialism. *Critical Inquiry* 21:805–21.

Grimshaw, Patricia. 1985. New England Missionary Wives, Hawaiian Women, and "The Cult of True Womanhood." *Hawaiian Journal of History* 19:71–100.

Hagspiel, Bruno. 1926. *Along the Mission Trail,* vol. 3: *In New Guinea.* Techny: Mission Press.

Hausen, Karin. 1981. Family and Role Division: The Polarization of Sexual Stereotypes in the Nineteenth Century—An Aspect of the Dissociation of Work and Family Life. In *The German Family: Essays on the Social History of the Family in Nineteenth- and Twentieth-Century Germany,* ed. Richard J. Evans and W. R. Lee, 51–83. Totowa, N.J.: Barnes and Noble Books.

Hobsbawm, Eric. 1987. *The Age of Empire: 1875–1914.* New York: Vintage Books.

Höltker, Georg. 1946. Die Kleiderfrage in den beiden Vikariaten Ost- und Zentral-Neuguinea. *Neue Zeitschrift fur Missionswissenschaft* 2:43–55.

Huber, Mary Taylor. 1987. Constituting the Church: Catholic Missionaries on the Sepik Frontier. *American Ethnologist* 14:107–25.

———. 1988a. *The Bishops' Progress: A Historical Ethnography of Catholic Missionary Experience on the Sepik Frontier.* Washington, D.C.: Smithsonian Institution Press.

———. 1988b. Service and Solidarity: Colonial Contradictions and Community Ideals. Paper presented in the session "Studies in Historical Anthropology," Eighty-seventh annual meeting of the American Anthropological Association, Phoenix, Ariz.

Hyam, Ronald. 1990. *Empire and Sexuality: The British Experience.* Manchester: Manchester University Press.

K.H.J.B. (Kleine-Herz-Jesu-Bote). 1898–99. The First S.Sp.S. Sisters for New Guinea. *The Little Messenger of the Sacred Heart,* no. 26. Trans. Fr. John J. Tschauder. MS.

Langmore, Diane. 1989. *Missionary Lives: Papua, 1874–1914.* Center for Pacific Islands Studies: Pacific Islands Monograph Series, no. 6. Honolulu: University of Hawaii Press.

Liebowitz, Ruth P. 1979. Virgins in the Service of Christ: The Dispute over an Active Apostolate for Women during the Counter-Reformation. In *Women of Spirit: Female Leadership in the Jewish and Christian Traditions,* ed. Rosemary Ruether and Elaine McLaughlin, 131–52. New York: Simon and Schuster.

Marshall, A. J. 1938. *The Men and Birds of Paradise: Journeys through Equatorial New Guinea.* London: William Heinemann Ltd.

McDonough, Peter. 1990. Metamorphoses of the Jesuits: Sexual Identity, Gender Roles, and Hierarchy in Catholicism. *Comparative Studies in Society and History* 32:325–56.

Monter, William. 1987. Protestant Wives, Catholic Saints, and the Devil's Handmaid: Women in the Age of Reformations. In *Becoming Visible: Women in European History,* ed. Renate Bridenthal et al., 2d ed., 203–19. Boston: Houghton Mifflin.

Perera, Suvendrini. 1991. *Reaches of Empire: The English Novel from Edgeworth to Dickens.* New York: Columbia University Press.

Prelinger, Catherine M. 1987. *Charity, Challenge, and Change: Religious Dimensions of the Mid-Nineteenth-Century Women's Movement in Germany.* New York: Greenwood Press.

Said, Edward. 1993. *Culture and Imperialism.* New York: Vintage Books.

Schmidlin, Joseph. 1933. *Catholic Mission History.* Techny, Ill.: Mission Press, SVD.

Sperber, Jonathan. 1984. *Popular Catholicism in Nineteenth-Century Germany.* Princeton: Princeton University Press.

Stoler, Ann. 1989a. Rethinking Colonial Categories: European Communities and the Boundaries of Rule. *Comparative Studies in Society and History* 13:134–61.

———. 1989b. Making Empire Respectable: The Politics of Race and Sexual Morality in Twentieth Century Colonial Cultures. *American Ethnologist* 16:634–60.

———. 1991. Carnal Knowledge and Imperial Power: Gender, Race, and Morality in Colonial Asia. In *Gender at the Crossroads of Knowledge: Feminist Anthropology in the Postmodern Era,* ed. Micaela di Leonardo, 51–101. Berkeley: University of California Press.

Strayer, Robert W. 1978. *The Making of Mission Communities in East Africa: Anglicans and Africans in Colonial Kenya, 1875–1935.* Albany: State University of New York Press.

Suleri, Sara. 1992. *The Rhetoric of English India.* Chicago: University of Chicago Press.

Swift, Fr. Francis P. 1989. *Greetings from the Land that Time Forgot: Letters from Rev. Francis P. Swift, S.V.D.,* ed. Mary Hartig. N.p.: Hartig Publications.

Townsend, G. W. L. 1968. *District Officer: From Untamed New Guinea to Lake Success, 1921–46.* Sydney: Pacific Publications.

Troeltsch, Ernst. 1981. *The Social Teaching of the Christian Churches,* vol. 1. Trans. Olive Wyon. Chicago: University of Chicago Press.

Weber, Max. 1958. *From Max Weber: Essays in Sociology.* Translated by H. H. Gerth and C. Wright Mills. New York: Oxford University Press.

Wemple, Suzanne F. 1987. Sanctity and Power: The Dual Pursuit of Early Medieval Women. In *Becoming Visible: Women in European History,* ed. Renate Bridenthal et al., 2d ed., 131–51. Boston: Houghton Mifflin.

Williams, Raymond. 1983. *Keywords: A Vocabulary of Culture and Society.* Rev. ed. New York: Oxford University Press.

Missionary Maternalism: Gendered Images of the Holy Spirit Sisters in Colonial New Guinea

Nancy C. Lutkehaus

> In many parts of New Guinea the priest and brother missionaries found that customs sometimes prevented them from helping the women. The Holy Spirit Sisters consider the education of women and the forming of Christian families one of their special aims.
>
> It wasn't long after the Sisters had come to New Guinea that children were sitting on a long log or on the beach learning to read and write and finding out about the world outside their village. They learnt to pray to God and praise him with songs.[1]

In this essay I describe the gendered dimensions of the work of the Holy Spirit Sisters (also known as the Servants of the Holy Spirit, or SSpS), a German Catholic order of missionary nuns who arrived in colonial New Guinea in 1899. I use the term *maternal* to describe the predominant character of the Holy Spirit Sisters' relationship to and engagement with New Guinea women and children. I also examine multiple meanings of *maternalism* with regard to three areas: the role of missions in New Guinea within a colonial division of labor, the formal goals and stated ideology of the Holy Spirit Sisters, and the sisters' actual behavior, as recorded in official chronicles from two convents in New Guinea and from personal interviews and my own participant observation. I discuss the different meanings of missionary maternalism in relationship to social, political, and economic conditions in both the metropole and colonial New Guinea. In conclusion, I suggest that, while maternal activities and maternalism remain important aspects of the Holy Spirit Sisters' present-day identity, postcolonial political and social changes in the now independent nation of Papua New Guinea, as well as Australia, Europe, and North America, have led to the Holy Spirit Sisters' constitution of themselves as a multicultural institution and to concomitant shifts in their relationships with Papua New Guinea women.

Missions as "Maternal" Colonial Institutions

Recently anthropologists interested in colonial studies and the role of missionaries in the colonial enterprise have increasingly challenged the prevailing sentiment among many Western scholars that missionaries simply reproduced the hegemonic values and roles of the colonizer (see Comaroff and Comaroff 1991; Kipp 1990).[2] We are beginning to acknowledge that the mission of missionaries has sometimes put them at cross-purposes with colonial officials, plantation owners, traders, and, in some instances, other missionary organizations.

As historian R. L. Lacey has noted, "a . . . common source of suspicion of missionaries stemmed from their educational work. To Europeans who recruited or employed labour, mission educated people were shrewd and untrustworthy" (1972, 776).[3] This attitude was not always the case, however; initially missionaries were welcomed to the colony *precisely* because of their willingness and ability to teach. In many missions teaching women and children, in particular, was seen as the responsibility of women, whether missionaries themselves, wives of missionaries, or lay religious personnel (Langmore 1989). For the Holy Spirit Sisters, who were affiliated with the Society of the Divine Word (SVD), the education of children and women was one of their primary tasks (see Huber, in this volume). While SVD priests and brothers proceeded to establish mission plantations and to build churches, the SSpS Sisters quickly organized schools.

For the sake of analysis and discussion I propose to characterize the initial role of missions in the colonial enterprise in New Guinea as "maternal," as opposed to the "paternal" roles of the colonial state and the plantation system, the predominant economic base of colonial New Guinea. This designation may go against the grain of how many of us commonly think of missions in general and Catholic missions in particular, that is, as institutions that replicate the hegemonic values, beliefs, and practices of the patriarchal Western societies and churches of which they are a part. I suggest, however, that maternalism—used here in the sense of a focus on caregiving and nurturance, on the upbringing and socialization of children, and on the development of "inner" qualities of morality and spirituality, all pursued in a compassionate manner—may be a useful trope through which to analyze the missionary endeavor in general and the SVD and SSpS missions in particular within the context of colonial New Guinea.

I suggest this in part because of the emphasis placed on the role of the missions in the education of indigenous men, women, and children by both the missionaries themselves and the colonial government in New Guinea. In contrast to the economic, military, and political activities pursued by planters and government agents, the spiritual and material educational tasks performed by the missionaries were deemed of necessary, but subordinate, value. This attitude was much like the then current perception in Germany of the role of the mother within the family in the socialization of children as well as the contribution of motherhood to the nation-state.[4] In general, according to nineteenth-century middle-class European thought, women were better suited to socializing children than men.[5] As students of colonial culture remind us, colonizers (including missionaries) often referred to local people as "children" who needed to be socialized into the customs of Western society. Thus, by analogy missionaries were like mothers preparing their children to become good citizens and laborers.

My comments will be limited largely to a discussion of the role of the Holy Spirit Sisters prior to 1945 in what was initially the German Territory of New Guinea (1884–1914). After World War I this region became part of the Australian Territory of Papua and New Guinea.[6]

Germans in New Guinea: "Internal" versus "External" Education

Several years before Germany's annexation of northeastern New Guinea in 1884, Friedrich Fabri, director of the Rhenish Mission Society, described the potential role of missions in the German colonial project in an influential pamphlet entitled, *Does Germany Need Colonies?* (1879). According to Fabri, successful colonization depended upon missionaries, since they alone were capable of "regenerating the uncivilized, still barbaric peoples" through their ability to influence natives' "mentality, intelligence and moral and religious conceptions" (Fabri, qtd. in Firth 1983, 136). While planters, traders, and officials would undertake the "external" education of the colonized people, the missionaries would work "internally" to insure a ready acceptance of European values (Firth 1983). Fabri suggested the complementarity between missionaries and secular actors in the colonial division of labor, a marriage of mutual convenience between representatives of the church and the (colonial) state.

In 1885, after having investigated the impact of the British Australiasian Methodist Mission in the islands of German New Guinea, the imperial commissioner Gustav von Osertzen told Otto von Bismarck that he agreed with Fabri. He cautioned, however, that church, school, and language would eventually become such important factors that they should be exclusively in the hands of German missionaries (Firth 1983). This recommendation opened the door for the arrival of two groups of German missionaries to the northeast coast of New Guinea: the Catholic order of the Society of the Divine Word (SVD) and the Neuendettelsau Lutheran Mission. The two organizations proceeded to divide the north coast mission field between them. The SVD missionaries arrived in 1896, and the SSpS sisters joined them three years later.

The separation Fabri identified between external and internal education can, I suggest, also be thought of in gendered terms: the external, or public work—that of the planters, traders, and government officials—being more "masculine," while the internal work, whether performed by male or female missionaries, because it related to spirituality and the inner dispositions of the villagers, more "feminine."

An additional value of the missionaries to the German colonial administration was that they achieved their conversions and socialization peacefully, in contrast to the sometimes violent disciplinary force exhibited by the colonial state (Firth 1986, 136). Here is another way in which the missions can be considered maternal, for, according to gender stereotypes of the time, men—and by extension, such male institutions as the colonial state—were viewed as more inherently aggressive and violent in nature than women (Hausen 1981, 56).[7]

While this metaphoric extension of gender is my own designation, it reflects notions about the differences between the sexes (*Geschlechtscharakter,* or "the character of the sexes") current in nineteenth-century Germany (Hausen 1981). For example, Meyer (1848) describes the disposition of the sexes in these terms:

> In relation to . . . women, sympathy, love prevail; in man, due to his predominant individuality, antagonism, hate—and thus the former is more sympathetic, kinder, more moral, more religious than the rougher, often hard-hearted man. (Qtd. in Hausen 1981, 54)

If it was the missionaries' primary task to civilize the inner dispositions of the unruly savage, to socialize the barbarian into the customs and beliefs of Western culture, they were more maternal in character than other externally focused colonial institutions.

This gendered characterization of colonial institutions and the colonial division of labor also reflects past and present Western images of the Christian church and religion. Within Catholicism itself, for example, the Jesuit scholar Walter J. Ong has written that "the Church is sexually defined. To the psyche, the Church is always feminine, the Holy Mother Church. Psychoanalytically as well as theologically there is no way to have a 'Father Church.'"[8] He goes on to suggest that in patriarchal societies "even an all-male clergy is likely to be regarded by other males as somewhat feminine because of the close alliance with the feminine church" (1981, 178).

Blurred Categories: Missionaries and Plantations

In reality, of course, the boundaries between the work of the missionaries and other colonial actors was more blurred than either dichotomy (internal/external, maternal/paternal) implies. And, precisely because of this inevitable blurring, tensions arose between the missions and other colonial institutions.[9] There was no doubt in the eyes of the German colonial government that evangelization was a means to a practical end: the preparation of natives as a willing and docile labor force. There was also no doubt that the missionaries were to teach the villagers practical as well as spiritual skills. Both colonial administrators and representatives of the Neu Guinea Compagnie (the latter, the dominant economic *and* political presence in the colony) considered the missionaries' purpose to be to serve *German* as well as Christian aims. According to them, German aims included teaching villagers manual skills, horticulture, and farming as well as preparing them for plantation work (Firth 1983).

As Huber (1988) points out with regard to the Society of the Divine Word, the SVD missionaries themselves made a distinction between "spiritual" and "practical" work. Ironically, despite the mission's own emphasis on spiritual work, the ability of the missionaries to accomplish their spiritual work in New Guinea meant that initially they spent much of their time on material matters, both in terms of the physical establishment of the mission in New Guinea and in the education of laborers:

> Of all the missions in German New Guinea . . . the SVD was the least in a hurry to save souls. "We have to be farmers and planters, we have to import, care for and breed cattle. For sea journeys we must understand sailing and steering," wrote Father Eberhard Limbrock, the leader of the first group of SVD missionaries, in 1902. (Firth 1983, 153)

The governor of German New Guinea thought Limbrock the ideal missionary, "a man of action committed to the economic development of the colony and to the spread of German language and culture" (154). According to the colonial government, the more "masculine" a mission was in its activities, it seems, the better—as long as the missionaries performed their tasks in a maternal (i.e., nonviolent) manner.

This benign attitude toward the missionaries changed, however, after

World War I, when Australia took control of the Territory of New Guinea from the Germans. Then, according to Lacey, not only were Australian settlers in New Guinea suspicious of the missionaries' educational work, but "there was also the suspicion that with such a large number of German personnel in some missions the local people might be under the influence of seditious ideas."[10] Thus, for example, the immediate reaction in the press and the public to the Rabaul labor strike of January 1929 was that the missions were behind the affair, a suspicion that was later proved to have no foundation (1972, 780). Here we see metropolitan political issues reflected in the colony, as the enmities of World War I still reverberated five years later in remote New Guinea.[11]

Why, despite the public's suspicions—and, most likely, possible resentment of German mission plantation holdings—were German missionaries allowed to stay? As Lacey points out, prior to 1945 the Australian colonial administration relied heavily on the German missions for the provision of educational and medical services to the territory (1972, 779). Thus, it appears that the primary reason the Australian government allowed the German missionaries to remain was because of the usefulness of their nursing and teaching activities, much of which were in the hands of women.[12]

Maternalism Extended: The Holy Spirit Sisters and Social Motherhood

A second meaning of *maternalism* refers specifically to the work of the Holy Spirit Sisters and their gendered missionary roles as nurses, teachers, pastoralists, and domestic helpmates to the priests and brothers on mission stations worldwide.[13] As has often been noted, during the nineteenth and early twentieth centuries middle-class European and North American women were commonly seen as having a special role to play in missionary endeavors that was justified on the basis of the "natural" tendencies of their sex. These tendencies included maternal nurturance and women's exalted role in Christian societies as the bearers of moral uplift, in contrast both to men and to the role of women in "heathen" societies (Beidelman and Thorne, both in this volume; Grimshaw 1989; Flemming 1992).

This attitude toward women was no less prevalent in North America and Britain than in Germany (Allen 1991; Frevert 1993). The SSpS order was founded in 1889, a period in German history in which feminists and other groups of women were articulating a new notion concerning the value of motherhood: an extension of woman's biological nature into the realm of public good known as *Mütterlichkeit,* or social motherhood.

Mütterlichkeit and the Notion of Social Motherhood

According to nineteenth-century sexual stereotypes prevalent in Germany, physiological distinctions between the sexes were used to describe the mental characteristics distinctive of men and women. These stereotypes mixed biology, social destiny, and inner nature and were intended to form a typology of the characteristics of men and women. Reduced to their essential contrast, men's nature destined them to be concerned with social production, while women were destined for the private world of reproduction (Hausen 1981, 55). These stereotypes, or character of the sexes (*Geschlechtscharakter*), formed the basis for a debate at the turn-of-the-century about the relationship of motherhood, child rearing, and family life to the welfare of the state (Allen 1991).[14]

While many contemporary feminists have argued that a woman's biological role as childbearer has been used to limit women's social and economic possibilities, in the context of nineteenth-century Germany motherhood provided a model of empowerment and ethical autonomy. During this period in Germany the mother-child bond became the basis of a concept of social morality that linked the individual woman to the larger community. Feminists, in particular, citing the importance of child rearing and maternal duty, argued that these functions should be incorporated into public policy, creating a role of "public motherhood" based on the notion of "extended motherliness" (*Mütterlichkeit*) (Allen 1991, 2; Frevert 1993, 126). (The creation of *kindergartens*—or "children's gardens" / play areas—was one lasting result of this movement.) Moreover, they continued, because women were best suited for the maternal role, logically they should also be responsible for fulfilling the role of public mother.

The idea of motherhood as a source of ethical authority, although derived from a biological model, was not merely a product of biology; it was adopted by many women who were not biological mothers, "sometimes in order to avoid biological motherhood" (Allen 1991, 12). The characteristics of maternalism (nurturance, emotional empathy, compassion) and other female characteristics, bourgeois German women argued, were important antidotes to the masculine characteristics of modern technology and industry. Society as a whole was thus seen as needing "feminine cultural influence" in order to mitigate various deleterious effects of the modern world, such as housing shortages, the breakup of the family, alcoholism, and prostitution (Frevert 1993, 126–27).

Although Catholic women were underrepresented in the German feminist movement (Allen 1991), it is not unreasonable to see young Catholic women's attraction to newly established missionary societies such as the

Holy Spirit Sisters, or to convents in general, as a product of this larger cultural climate.[15] Both local Catholic convents and women's mission orders could be seen as the spiritually inflected institutionalization of the practice of "social motherhood" promoted by secular women's organizations in nineteenth-century Germany.

Missionary Maternalism

As Huber mentions in her essay in this volume, Father Arnold Janssen, the founder of the Society of the Divine Word mission, recognized early on the special need for women in his mission endeavor. According to the story that the Holy Spirit Sisters recount of the origin of their order,[16] two German women, Hendrina Stenmanns and Helena Stollenwerk, who had come to work for Father Janssen as kitchen staff for the SVD mission in Steyl, Netherlands,[17] were catalysts in getting Janssen to found a women's missionary order. Wanting to play a more important and immediate role in the missionary project than that of menial assistants to the priests and brothers, they begged Janssen to allow them to perform missionary work too. Janssen conceded to their request, and, after first considering incorporating women into the Society of the Divine Word itself, by 1889 he had established two separate female orders at Steyl. The Contemplative Nuns (or "pink nuns," as they are often called in reference to the color of their robes) were to remain cloistered in the home country and to pray for the success of the SVD and SSpS missionaries' endeavors, while the Servants of the Holy Spirit were to go abroad to actively work with women and children as teachers, nurses, and pastoralists. The same complimentarity of female tasks—the active and the passive, the cloistered and the worldly—continues at present.

Today Mother Josepha (Hendrina Stenmanns) and Mother Maria (Helena Stollenwerk) are recognized as the First, or Founding, Mothers of the SSpS order, and a Holy Mass is celebrated annually to honor each of them. Similarly, an annual Holy Mass is celebrated to honor Father Arnold for his role in the establishment of the order. These three celebrations thus ritually acknowledge the dual origins—female and male—of the SSpS order.

On the one hand, we see in the origin story of the SSpS nuns evidence of the historically subordinate relationship of Catholic women to men. As women did not have the authority to create a mission order themselves, they were dependent upon Janssen to establish an order for them. The story is also a charter for the principle of separate but complementary spheres and a gendered division of labor in the mission culture of the SVD and SSpS orders. Finally, the story contains within it a seed of female autonomy, for ultimately Janssen decided to create an affiliated yet structurally independent female organization.

The Mission Calling

At the end of the nineteenth and the beginning of the twentieth centuries it was unusual for a woman not to marry and more unusual yet for her to become a nun, let alone a missionary sister.[18] What might have motivated a young Catholic woman around the turn of the century in Germany to become a Holy Spirit Sister, and how might she have expressed and acted upon her desire? As the following excerpts from an interview with Sister Maria suggest, a spiritual calling—in her case, one made manifest by a family crisis—lies at the heart of her decision.

I spoke with Sister Maria, born in Germany between 1907 and 1911, at the Holy Spirit Sisters convent at Alexishafen in Papua New Guinea in 1992:[19]

> *Being the eldest daughter in a rural family of four children, Maria's decision to join the Holy Spirit Sisters at Steyl was precipitated by what she felt to be the impending death of her mother. She had been thinking about dedicating her life to Jesus, she said, ever since she had been confirmed, at age 11. When she was 18 her mother nearly died of cancer. While her mother lay in the hospital, Maria prayed to the Lord and asked him to help her mother to live at least another year. If her mother lived, she prayed, she would enter the convent. When her mother recovered, Maria took her recovery as a sign that the Lord had answered her prayers and that she was to become a nun.*
>
> *Around the time of her mother's illness, Maria happened to read a copy of the* Steyler Missionsbote *that her grandmother received from the SVD mission.*[20] *The description of the missionaries' work in far-off China, Africa, and New Guinea caught her imagination. Although she could have gone to one of the five convents in the area near her home, a rural farm community in Westphalia, Maria decided to go to Steyl, instead, because it was a missionary sending order.*
>
> *What had clinched the matter for her was that the SSpS sisters would accept her even though she was only 19. She was impatient and did not want to wait until she was 20, the age required by some of the other convents.*

Maria's narrative tells us that, even prior to the crisis of her mother's illness, she had been contemplating the idea of "dedicating her life to Jesus." As the Holy Spirit Sisters sometimes express their commitment to their vows of chastity, poverty, and obedience in terms of their dedication, or marriage, to Jesus, Maria is indicating that since her confirmation she had been interested in the possibility of becoming a nun. That initial spark of interest became transformed into a spiritual calling that permitted, indeed required, that she become a nun. In a time of personal crisis—the serious illness and potential death of her mother—Maria prayed to God for his help. She told herself and God that if He answered her prayers—if her mother lived another year—out of gratitude she would dedicate her life to serving God by becoming a nun.

Looking beyond Maria's own words, we might also see in this story a young girl fearful that if her mother died duty would require her, as the eldest daughter in the family, to assume her mother's role as the female head of her father's household. Her mother's premature death might prevent her from leaving home and pursuing her desire to become a nun. But, if her mother lived, her family might well understand the nature of her gratitude and her spiritual motivation to leave home to join a convent. Fear of her mother's imminent death, despite her recovery, might also explain Maria's eagerness to enter a convent as soon as possible. Indeed, her mother died two years later, after Maria had already become a novice, and her father allowed her to remain at Steyl.

Several years later, sometime in the early 1930s, Maria was sent to southern China as a missionary teacher, where she learned to read and write the local Chinese language. When the political climate made it no longer feasible for the SVD and SSpS missionaries to remain in China, she was sent to New Guinea. There she continued to work as a teacher and became renowned among the SVD priests for her success in establishing the first primary school on the Middle Sepik River, in an area where the priests had failed to get the local Iatmul parents to send their children to school. She claims she succeeded where the priests had failed because, unlike them, she was willing to live alone out in the bush in a small house built close to the school, thus allowing the school to be built near the village.

Maria's story is typical of several of the accounts I heard from SSpS Sisters her age and younger who came to New Guinea prior to and immediately after World War II. In these narratives the sisters decide to leave home either because of a strong spiritual calling or because of a desire to be trained as a teacher or nurse, or both. For example, several of the sisters commented that becoming a nun was the only way in which they could receive training in medicine and nursing. As others have noted of the female missionary role, at the time it offered women opportunities for work, travel, and independence that they would not have had if they had remained at home.[21]

For many of the SSpS Sisters I spoke with, reading accounts written by missionary sisters in the *Steyler Missionsbote* while growing up had fueled their imagination and stirred their desire to travel to foreign lands rather than enter convents in Germany. Several of the sisters also spoke of their fondness for the sisters' role as caregiver and mother to many children. They expressed this maternal role, however, in relationship to Jesus: "Like Jesus, the Sisters recognize the special needs of women," "Like Jesus, the Sisters were teachers," "Like Jesus, the Sisters help the sick."[22] Thus, they subscribe to a notion of maternalism based upon the model of Jesus as the caretaker of humanity in general.

Reality versus Rhetoric: Negotiating Maternalism

In this section I describe some of the activities of the Holy Spirit Sisters at mission stations in colonial New Guinea, where they lived in close proximity to SVD priests and brothers. I recount several incidents of the sisters' interactions with local women, in particular with mothers, that they recorded in the chronicles they kept at the outstation on Manam Island and at Alexishafen, the missions' headquarters in New Guinea.[23] As these incidents show, the sisters' behavior was more varied and nuanced than that delineated by either the rhetoric of social motherhood (*Mütterlichkeit*) or nineteenth-century German notions of the character of the sexes (*Geschlechtscharakter*). Instead, aspects of nationalism, race, sex, and religion are intertwined in the context of colonial New Guinea to allow for and necessitate different modes of behavior than those prescribed by the ideologies of the time.

Following Jolly (1993) and Ramusack (1992), I use the term *maternalism* here not as a female-centered substitute for the male-centered concept of paternalism nor simply as the internal/external or gentle/violent contrast in orientation and demeanor suggested in the previous discussion of missions but, rather, to indicate a different construction of sociality based on the different ways that race, class, and gender intersected for European women and, in particular, for the Holy Spirit Sisters, who were embedded within the patriarchal structure of the Catholic Church and the German Society of the Divine Word.

Missionary Maternalism in Practice

The sisters believed strongly that good Christian families, from which religious vocations would grow, could not develop if the women were neglected (SSpS Manual n.d.) In 1899, only three years after the arrival of the first SVD priests and brothers in New Guinea, four sisters came to assist them.[24] By the eve of World War I there were almost equal numbers of nuns in northern New Guinea as priests and brothers combined. Of the ninety-one SVD missionaries and SSpS nuns in German New Guinea in 1913, forty-three were sisters, twenty-six were priests, and twenty-two were brothers (Sack and Clark 1980, 144).

The following entry from 1907 in the chronicle kept at the Holy Spirit Sisters' convent at Alexishafen gives some idea of what the sisters' living quarters were like and what was involved in the establishment of a new convent during their first years in New Guinea.[25]

> November 29th, 1907 we reached Doilon [the former name of Alexishafen] on board the boat "Raphael." Our reverend Fr. Prefect traveled with us. Fr. P. Loerks, SVD, the manager of Doilon [plantation] welcomed us warmly. After we had been shown the carpentry shop and various other installations, Fr. Prefect brought us to our new home, about ten minutes away. Our convent has two rooms downstairs, a work room and the dining room. Upstairs is the chapel and four cells. Everything was ready for our moving in. Close to the convent is a kitchen with store room and adjoining it the dormitory of our domestic girls. We had been allowed to bring four girls along from Ali [Island]. They should help us with the necessary work in the convent and the garden, with the planting of fruit trees. The convent was within a coconut plantation and we soon started with the making of a vegetable garden close to our convent.

In this short passage we gain a glimpse at the sisters' relationship with the SVD missionaries, get a sense of the hum of activity around a successful mission station run as a plantation, can envision the simplicity and functionality of the sisters' living quarters, and learn that they are assisted in their work by village girls, who do much of the daily subsistence work of housekeeping and gardening.

On lengthy trips, such as the one described here in which the sisters traveled from Tumleo Island on the Aitape coast a hundred or so miles by sea to Alexishafen, near Madang, the sisters were always accompanied by at least one of the fathers. At a mission station the sisters lived in proximity to the SVD priests and brothers (at Alexishafen, because of the large size of the mission plantation, they were a full ten minutes away), yet were independent of them, having their own convent house with chapel, kitchen, and gardens. Not all mission stations were as extensive as Alexishafen (especially those not located on or near a mission plantation), which, complete with printing presses and a book bindery, stables, a wharf, a carpentry shop, and other facilities necessary to the operation of

The first four Holy Spirit Missionary Sisters to be sent to New Guinea in 1899. *Left to right:* Sister Fridolina Voegt, Sister Valeria Dietzen, Sister Ursula Sensen, Sister Martha Sieferding. Photograph courtesy of the Holy Spirit Sisters (SSpS). Reprinted from *The History of the Holy Spirit Sisters in Papua New Guinea.*

a large plantation, soon became the mission's main headquarters on the north coast.

The sisters' living quarters were quite simple, however, with the upstairs devoted to private space for sleeping (the four cells) and prayer, while the downstairs space was for communal and public use. Gardens and fruit trees, along with hen houses and enclosures for a few pigs and head of cattle, were necessary to provide for subsistence needs. Horses were also kept as the main means of transportation when visiting villages in the jungle. The village girls who accompanied the sisters—both to work for them and to attend classes in cooking, sewing, housekeeping, singing, and Bible study—lived in separate quarters. Eventually, a boarding school was set up at Alexishafen for girls brought from villages up and down the coast, and an orphanage was established, primarily for mixed-race children.

In contrast to the sisters' relatively substantial dwelling and other facilities at Alexishafen, some eighteen years later, when the first mission outstation was established further up the north coast on Manam Island, the sisters described their situation in these terms:

> On Ash Wednesday, February 25, 1925 the much longed for [mission boat] "Gabriel" took us and all our belongings from Monumbo to the Fire Mountain Manam[26] . . . The first company included three Monumbo maid servants, my humble self, and Karo, our faithful companion. In addition, there were twelve to fourteen *sumatin* [schoolchildren], boxes, and various pieces of furniture, most of them old and dilapidated, but since no replacements had arrived yet, we had no choice but to take them along to Manam.
>
> The house was more or less completed, but there was much to clean and sweep. The Reverend Father saw to it that the kitchen was finished and built a brick stove for us. There was no hen house yet either . . . As a sign of friendship, some women brought us bowls of cooked taro, etc. during the first weeks which we accepted gratefully and in return for which we gave them rings and fishing hooks.
>
> The first three sisters on Manam are Sister Gertrud, who is our Superior, Sister Hermegilde, our schoolteacher, and Sister Vintiana, our cook. Just before Easter, on April 7, 1925, Sister Cunera arrived as our second schoolteacher.[27]

Throughout their presence in Papua New Guinea the primary tasks that have concerned the SSpS Sisters have been teaching (reading, arithmetic, geography), nursing, domestic training, and religious education. Additional responsibilities have included cooking, washing, and housekeeping for SVD priests and brothers living in separate quarters on the mission station. Depending upon the size of the mission station, like traditional wives, the sisters have often been expected to perform both sets of duties, although they were often assisted in all these tasks by local girls. On smaller mission stations, those with only three or four sisters, at most, it was not uncommon for a nursing or teaching sister to return to the convent at the end of the day and help prepare dinner for the priest(s), brothers, and other sisters. At the larger convents there was a division of labor among the sisters such that one or two were designated as "kitchen," or "domestic," sisters, whose main responsibilities were cooking or housekeeping chores. Local girls always lived in a separate dormitory in the convent compound or came to work daily from nearby villages. They were either paid wages or received their board and lodging plus some clothes in exchange for their labor.

Under the often trying conditions of an unhealthy climate,[28] lack of supplies, and dependence upon their own subsistence gardens for fresh food, the sisters pursued their primary work as teachers and dispensers of medical aid. They were particularly concerned with maternal and infant care, traveling by boat or horseback to conduct open-air baby clinics:

> The Sisters not only visited the sick, the needy and mothers with newborn babies in the villages, but there were always crowds of sick people who flocked to the clinics, dispensaries and small hospitals run by the Sisters on the mission stations.[29]

While they were intently focused on providing children with some education, they were also equally intent on teaching as a means of recruiting new members to the Catholic Church:

> A small *garamut* [slit drum] called the children to classes in the morning. Instructions lasted half a day. In the afternoon, the Sisters left the classrooms and became teachers on horseback. They visited the villages, preaching the "Good News" wherever they went.[30]

Maternalism Imposed

At mission outstations such as Manam Island, where the following incident took place, the sisters' attempts at eliminating local customs such as the practice of infanticide posed a quandary for them: local beliefs prohibited village women from raising a newborn baby when a mother died in childbirth, yet the sisters were not able to assume the role of surrogate mother themselves.[31] For example, several months after their arrival on Manam the sisters were faced with a difficult situation:

> In October [1925] . . . [a] woman from Boda [village] became very sick during labor, but she was lucky to receive holy baptism. Her only request to me was to take the child, otherwise it would be buried with her. We had no choice for we had tried in vain to get some women to feed it.
>
> "We will die if we touch it," they said.[32]
>
> So we took mercy upon the poor orphan and cared for it as well as we could. Tea, a little bit of canned milk, and a flour mix kept it just barely alive.
>
> "We'll take care of it after a few months," the women told me. But as we were approaching Christmas still no one would have the little one. I can't blame the women, however, because they all have plenty to do taking care of their own children.
>
> Fourteen days later a woman from Kuluguma [a village adjacent to Boda] accepted the little worm with much love, which made us very

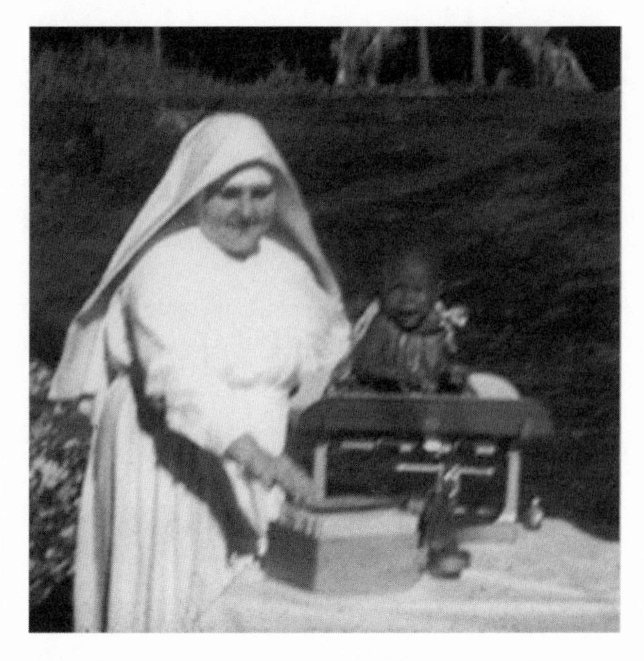

Sister Leowina, SSpS, conducting an open-air infant clinic on Manam Island, New Guinea (ca. 1959). Photograph by Father Böhm, courtesy of Sister Leowina.

> happy indeed, because it takes much work to raise such small children at the station, not to mention the worry about the right food for such a small child.[33]

Given the exigencies of life on a small mission outstation, the sisters' attitude is understandable: they did not have the resources to set up an orphanage on Manam nor to become surrogate mothers themselves.[34] The dilemma they faced pitted their maternal Christian values against the constraints of their local environment: although they abhorred the practice of infanticide—in this case, the practice of burying the newborn with its mother when she died in labor—they were not capable of taking care of infants on a long-term basis. Their inability to care for the abandoned infants points up the limits to their maternal role and the conflicts and contradictions caused by their moral beliefs regarding motherhood.

Like impassioned mothers attempting to save their threatened young and unflinchingly convinced of the morality of their actions, as the following incident reveals, the sisters could also act aggressively in order to impress upon villagers the need to stop infanticide. In this case the object of the sister's aggression was the birth mother herself. The text is from the sisters' chronicle from Manam and was recorded in 1931, six years after the missionaries had settled on the island:[35]

> In Oaia [village], there was a young woman who had an illegitimate child.[36] We tried to get her to keep the child and not kill it. We baptized it, but a short while later on, the child was dead. We do not know whether the child's mother had killed it or not. I went over to the village to get her. I went into the house after her, but she ran away. I threw bowls and pots after her, which all broke to pieces.
>
> During the night I went there again, accompanied by some girls. Again, the young woman saw me too soon and was able to escape. So I kicked down the little birth house [*boaruku*] and destroyed it.[37] "Come now and sleep in your destroyed house, if you like!!" I called out after the woman.

The entry ends with the following statement:

> The [Oaia] people were very subdued. They do seem to understand after all what is right and what is not. If I had burnt down their entire village they would not have dared to turn me in because they know very well that they must not kill their children. At last we made headway here by the Grace of God.

Here we have a dramatic example of the manner in which the sisters gradually began to change Manam attitudes toward childbirth and infanticide, not simply by preaching tolerance and respect for human life but also by forceful demonstrations of their belief in the validity of their convictions. It also reveals that they could be far from docile women when faced with what they suspected to be a violation of the Lord's word. Like the priests, who also found themselves sometimes forced to use violence to insure order on the mission station, as well as to secure their authority, the sister showed no hesitancy in using physical force to impress upon the wayward woman—and the other villagers—the strength of her moral convictions.

The sister's comment at the conclusion of the incident that the villagers know that they must not kill their children perhaps confuses the villagers' knowledge that infanticide was not permitted by the colonial government with a hopeful belief that they comprehended the moral implications of the act. The fact that the villagers would not have reported the sister to the colonial authorities even "if I had burnt down their entire village" may demonstrate their acknowledgment of the political power of the mission rather than having been a sign of their comprehension and acceptance of the sister's moral authority.

These two incidents highlight some of the contradictions and ironies the Holy Spirit Sisters faced when trying to enact their Christian beliefs about children and maternal behavior in the context of local customs and conditions in New Guinea.

Protection of Local Women and Girls

The Holy Spirit Sisters began almost immediately to teach catechism to girls and women as well as to instruct them in hygiene and infant care. In addition to hiring local girls to help them with cooking, housework, and gardening, the sisters invited the girls to join them on trips to other mission stations. For many young village women working for the sisters provided them with new opportunities for independence from their parents, and the trips allowed them to see the north coast and visit with girls—and boys—from other parts of the region. Village men, however, were not always pleased with the women's new opportunities, especially for travel away from the village, as one such incident in the sisters' chronicle from Manam Island recounts:[38]

> In August [1927] our Mother Superior and Sister Hermegilde traveled to Alexishafen for spiritual exercises. Several Manam girls went along as working girls. The *luluai*'s[39] son from Baliau, Oswald Karam, tried to keep one Baliau girl back, but Father Hubers intervened by chasing away the impertinent fellow. All of Baliau was excited by the incident, the son of the Big Man [i.e., the *luluai*] had been beaten, even worse, he had been mistreated, so they lied to themselves. Two saucy women destroyed the garden of the catechist, others destroyed the school. The schoolchildren were kept away from the Sunday service as well as from school by the offended Father, until the defiance had calmed down somewhat.

In this incident the sisters and the Baliau girl are dependent upon the aid of the SVD father. In order for the girl to travel with the sisters he must assert his authority against the traditional authority of village leaders. On the one hand, we see the depth of the Baliau villagers' resentment of the father's challenge to their *luluai.* On the other hand, we see how the nuns—and the priests—worked at challenging local traditions that circumscribed women's autonomy.

As another incident from the Manam sisters' chronicle reveals, the sisters also offered village girls the option of temporary sanctuary at the convent, helping to protect them from arranged marriages with unsuitable partners or as second wives:[40]

> On November 13 and 14 [1931], the *Kiap* was here.[41] They took away our little Maria from Kuluguma [village]. She was barely fifteen. The *Tanepoa* from Kuluguma has promised her to Paisi, a relative of his, who works as a Police Boy in Madang [the Provincial capital].[42] But Maria did not want to go. For this reason she came to us six months ago, hoping that we would help her. She went to mass and communion almost every day, even when she was still living in the village.
>
> Now the villagers have come and said that she has to come home. The Kiap was in a hurry, waiting on the beach at Baliau for her. What is Maria to do? Is she supposed to go with Paisi? Maria's first words were: "I don't want to." She began to cry bitterly, which the people could see.
>
> I said that Paisi himself should come and that I wanted to speak with him. "He has no time," they said. Then I said to Maria, "If you want, you may go and marry him for he has no other wife so far." She went to a corner of the garden and continued to weep. When we saw that she did not want to go, we let her be.
>
> In the evening, around nine o'clock, two police boys along with several men from Kuluguma were in front of our house. "Paisi wants to get Maria now," they said, adding that they had been sent by the Kiap. "Do you have a piece of paper from him?" we asked. "No, Paisi said, 'The Kiap said that if I want to get the girl who was bought[43] for me, then the Sisters have to give her to me. If the Sisters hold her back or in case the girl does not want to come, just carry her off.'"
>
> We tried to convince him with all kindness to leave, but he said no. Then they went to the house to speak to Maria. When they asked her whether she wanted to come along, she said very timidly, "No." They commanded us to open the door, but of course we did not do that . . . "We shall knock down the door," was the answer of the hothead fellows. "Go," I said, "this is not the manner in which kiaps behave, sending police boys in the middle of the night to bother Sisters and young girls. You may not do that anywhere else and you cannot do it here either."
>
> "I'll go straight to the Kiap to ask for a paper," one of them said. They returned at eleven. "We have a paper from the Kiap," they said. I sent them to the Father with it . . . The entire letter was a threat taken from the book of statutes . . . The lawful punishment is three years imprisonment and hard labor. We were accused of having robbed the

> girl of her freedom because we had not let her go with the police boys during the night . . . Since there was no summons for Maria, we still did not let her go.
>
> At 5:30 in the morning the impertinent police boy came with a gun and an official piece of paper. This contained an accusation against us . . . and a summons for Maria . . . The Kiap was on his pinnace. Maria was brought aboard first. We also asked to be brought aboard . . . We wanted to defend ourselves against unjust accusation and if possible help Maria in her predicament. They accused us once more of having held the girl back, to which we answered that we had given her complete freedom . . . Then [the kiap] asked the girl what kind of work she was doing. She said that she was working in the garden . . . "I know what kind of work she is doing at the Sisters'," he said, "and that's supposed to be education!" Then he made us read several passages in the book of statutes about how the mission had to treat workers and educate children. If we were to pay attention to these laws, we might as well let all the girls go. Then he asked Maria whether she was attending school. She answered, "Every day, " at which he was surprised . . .
>
> . . . The length of the lawful conversation gave the people enough time to frighten Maria. Finally, Maria was asked once more if she wanted Paisi, to which she answered, "Mi laik" ["I like" or "I want"] and she began to cry loudly. At that time she was ordered to go to Paisi's relatives in the village. Her mother, who had begged us in tears to keep Maria back, went home crying loudly. Once again injustice was victorious. We could do no more but to pray for the girl.

At the heart of this complicated story is a tale of a young woman's struggle to avoid an unwanted marriage. In the end she is unsuccessful and is forced to go live with her future parents-in-law. Stories like this were probably not uncommon on Manam at that time, since young women had little say in their marriage arrangements. What is different about this particular case is the role the Holy Spirit Sisters played, or attempted to play, in altering the outcome. The sisters' account reveals the constraints they faced in their struggle to support Maria in her desire not to marry Paisi. On the one hand, they were able to offer her a temporary haven away from home as well as their backing of her choice not to marry and thus the hope of success. These offers of support were probably not of insignificant value to young Manam women, as many of them sought out the sisters' aid. Yet we also see the limits to the sisters' (and father's) effectiveness in confrontation with the Kiap, the local Australian government official. He, too, had to keep his indigenous officers content, thus his support of the Police Boy, Paisi. Although the sisters could offer Maria support—and demonstrate to her and her family the lengths they would go to help her, in the end they could not overturn local male hegemony when coupled with the authority of the colonial state.

Conclusion

As the incidents involving the Holy Spirit Sisters in colonial New Guinea show, many unexpected factors constrained and shaped the nature and effectiveness of these missionary nuns' goals and behavior. Most important among these factors were the strength of indigenous customs and beliefs, the limitations posed by the physical constraints of a rugged tropical frontier environment, and the subordinate position of missionaries (particularly German missionaries) within the colonial social structure of Australian New Guinea.

I have characterized many of the Holy Spirit Sisters' aims and aspects of their behavior, as well as the character of missions in general within the colonial enterprise, as maternal: that is, showing concern for the care and nurturance of children, for the education of girls and women, and for expressing a focus on the creation of good (Christian) families. As Stoler (1991) and other scholars of colonial culture have demonstrated, these maternal aims were not solely the concern of colonial missions.[44] Both the SVD and the SSpS missionaries, however, felt that women were best suited to these tasks. Hence, early on Holy Spirit Sisters came to New Guinea to work in tandem with the SVD priests and brothers.

Once in New Guinea the sisters experienced a greater personal freedom than they would have had if they had remained at home, where they would have faced pressure to conform to the traditional role of domestic maternalism expected of them in their Catholic communities in Germany at the time. Yet, while conditions in New Guinea allowed SSpS Sisters unanticipated opportunities for personal independence (e.g., several of them commented on the pleasure they took in going off on clinic patrols on horseback by themselves, usually accompanied by at least one local girl) and achievement (Sister Maria's success, e.g., in setting up a viable primary school among the Iatmul), as Huber also points out (in this volume), the gendered division of labor within the allied SVD and SSpS organizations still hove to the nineteenth-century model of men's and women's appropriate gendered roles. This gendered dichotomy also replicated the subordinate role of women within the hierarchy of the Catholic Church.

The education (as well as the opportunities for work and travel) that the sisters provided local women and children did not simply reproduce hegemonic ideas and values; it was also the source of new ideas and concepts of the self and of self-worth. Although Maria from Kuluguma village failed in her attempt to avoid an unwanted marriage, other Manam girls were able to use successfully the sanctuary and support of the sisters. Moreover, although the sisters encouraged local women in the development of Christian families, they had themselves rejected marriage and biological motherhood. Thus, simply by the example of their own lives, the sisters were an alternative model of womanhood for New Guinea women.

I suggest that one of the consequences of the presence of the Holy Spirit Sisters in Papua New Guinea has been to create a space for indigenous women to experience new female roles, celibate and otherwise. This knowledge and the opportunity to gain new skills (reading, writing, arithmetic, sewing, cooking, etc.) opened several new directions—both secular and spiritual—for women to pursue besides the traditional role of village wife and mother. On the one hand, many New Guinea women who have continued their education beyond primary school have, like the sisters, been trained to work as teachers or nurses. Unlike the sisters, however, they are able to marry and raise families while pursuing their own careers.

On the other hand, there is a steadily increasing, although relatively small, number of young Papua New Guinea women who have chosen the role of sister as their vocation. Although the SVD mission created an order of indigenous sisters, the Rosary Sisters, in the 1950s, it was not until 1984 that Papua New Guinea women were invited to become members of the SSpS order itself.

In the aftermath of Vatican II and the decolonization of the former Third World, the Holy Spirit Sisters have in recent years become an increasingly international order, with members from former missionized countries such as the Philippines, India, Indonesia, and Brazil. Almost half of the sisters working in Papua New Guinea today and almost all of the sisters under 40 are from countries other than Europe, Australia, or the United States. Papua New Guinea has recently sent its first indigenous Holy Spirit Sister on a mission assignment outside of her own home country. In 1994 Sister Agnes, originally from the Iatmul village of Tambunam, where Sister Maria had established an elementary school, took up her new mission assignment in Ghana. From the standpoint of the Holy Spirit Sisters, almost 100 years later, the circle has now been completed in New Guinea as they bear witness to the fruit of their labor: a new indigenous SSpS sister on a foreign mission of her own.

NOTES

The research for this essay was conducted under grants from the Wenner-Gren Foundation for Anthropological Research (grant no. 5569) and a Zumberge Faculty Research Stipend from the University of Southern California (USC). Translation from German into English of the Servants of the Holy Spirit (SSpS) "Chronicle from the Herz Jesu Convent, Bieng Catholic Mission, Manam Island, Papua New Guinea: 1924–1974" was supported by a Faculty Grant from the Gender Studies Program (formerly the Program for the Study of Women and Men in Society) at USC.

I would like to thank the Holy Spirit Sisters on Manam Island and at Bogia and Alexishafen in Papua New Guinea, especially Sisters Leowina and Christophilda who generously gave of their time and hospitality to talk with me, as well as the SSpS Sisters in Steyl, the Netherlands, Wimbern, Germany, and Rome, who allowed me access to their archives and their memories. Thanks also to Mary Huber, Margaret Jolly, Jim McBride, Ann L. Stoler, and the graduate students in the 1995 seminar on "The Colonial Order of Things in Southeast Asia," Department of Anthropology, University of Michigan, for their insightful comments and criticisms. Finally, special thanks to Jim McBride for his help with the archival photographs.

1. *The History of the Holy Spirit Sisters in Papua New Guinea* (pamphlet, n.d.).

2. Anthropologists, however, are not the only scholars to complicate our stereotypes of missionaries. See, for example, the work of historians Hunt (1990) and Thorne (1997).

3. See also the work of Burridge (1960) on the relationship between government officials, planters, and missionaries in post–World War II New Guinea as well as Huber (1988) with reference to the SVD mission in particular and its relations with other colonial actors in New Guinea.

4. There is a burgeoning literature on motherhood and nationalism as well as the role of motherhood as perceived by the colonial state. See, for example, Davin 1997; and Stoler n.d.

5. See, for example, Grimshaw 1989; and Allen 1991.

6. In 1884 Germany and Britain initially annexed the northeastern and southeastern portions, respectively, of the island of New Guinea. The western portion of the island was subsequently annexed by the Dutch as an adjunct to the Dutch East Indies. The German colony was called the Territory of New Guinea, or Kaiser Wilhelmsland, while the British colony was known either as British New Guinea or Papua.

7. Hausen arranges a set of contrasting terms found in nineteenth-century texts describing the differences between the sexes (1981, 55–56). Among these sets of contrasting terms are the following:

Man	*Woman*
Social Destiny: External Life	Social Destiny: Inner Life
Public Life	
Doing: Acquisitive	Being: Protective
Forceful	Love, Goodness
Antagonism	Sympathy
Ability to get his own way	Self-denial, adaptation

8. Ong goes on to say that "the overwhelming femininity of the Roman Catholic Church from the human side suggests that a male clergy is basically not a characteristic of the Church so much as a countervailing feature" (1981, 178). Ong's work is analyzed by Peter McDonough in an article that discusses gender roles and hierarchy in contemporary Catholicism. McDonough suggests that one of the reasons Catholicism has struggled to maintain a hiearachical structure of male dominance is that "male domination and masculine stoicism have served as a protection against the feminization of charity" (1990, 326). Implicit in this statement is the idea not only that the feminization of charity would somehow diminish the value of charity as a (male) activity but also that charity itself is susceptible to "femininization," or perhaps is seen by many as fundamentally a "feminine" activity.

9. See Huber 1988, for a detailed discussion of the tensions between the SVD mission and the colonial government in New Guinea.

10. During the 1930s Germans constituted the largest number of expatriate missionaries in New Guinea outside of Australians (Lacey 1972, 779).

11. Another contributing factor to the antipathy Australian settlers felt toward German missionaries after World War I was that not only were the missionaries allowed to remain and carry on their work in New Guinea, but they were not forced to relinquish their landholdings (unlike other individuals and enterprises of German nationality). In some parts of the territory these holdings were extensive. Because of the great distance from Europe, the Lutheran and SVD missionaries had been allowed to develop coconut plantations as the economic base for their local mission economy (Wiltgen 1969; Huber 1988).

12. Vocational training in skills considered appropriate to men, such as carpentry, printing, shipbuilding, and seamanship, were taught, for the most part, by the brothers.

13. Although in this essay I concentrate on a discussion of the work of the SSpS sisters in New Guinea, sisters were also initially sent to Argentina and Togo.

14. During this time there was a deeply held conviction, among men and women alike, that males and females were different beings with naturally diverse functions (Laqueur 1990). According to Frevert, "Even in the late 19th century women who subscribed to the bourgeois movement [in Germany] firmly believed that the female sex was without exception 'destined for motherhood,' and that their destiny determined women's physical and psychic constitution" (1989, 126).

15. See, for example, Prelinger 1987.

16. This story has been published in several languages as an illustrated storybook that is readily available through the SSpS convents. See, for example, "Das Leben ist Mission, Helena Stollenwerk, Mutter Maria, Mitgrunderin der Steyler Missionsschwestern" and "Die Mission des guten Herzens, Hendrine Stenmanns, Mutter Joseph, Mitgrunderin der Steyler Missionsschwestern," both in the magazine *Geist und Auftrag* (February 1984) (Wickede-Wimbern: Karitative Vereinigung der Steyler Missionsschwestern).

17. Due to Bismark's anti-Catholic policy (*kulturkampf*) in Germany at the time (Blackbourn and Eley 1984), Father Arnold had been forced to locate his

fledgling mission order across the border from his native Westphalia to Steyl, Netherlands. Steyl became the mission headquarters of both the SVD and the SSpS orders. The mother house of the SSpS has subsequently moved from Steyl to Rome.

18. As the German feminist historian Ute Frevert points out (1989), it was less unusual for young women to work for a number of years as a factory or clerical worker prior to marriage. If a woman wanted to be a teacher, it was tantamount to deciding not to marry. Of course, she always had the option of marrying and leaving the teaching profession, an option that was not open to sisters, whose vows of celibacy, poverty, and obedience were taken for life.

19. Sister Maria died at Alexishafen in 1993.

20. The *Steyler Missionsbote,* a magazine published by the SVD mission from its publishing house at Steyl, was one of the primary means through which Catholic parishoners learned about the activities of the SVD and SSpS missionaries abroad. It contained articles written "from the field" by priests, brothers, and sisters, along with photographs of their mission stations or the local population.

21. See Ramusack 1993, for an example of a similar set of reasons British women who were not missionaries gave for their decisions to go to India to work among Indian women.

22. *History of the Holy Spirit Sisters in Papua New Guinea,* 1–2.

23. The chronicles are official documents that the sisters are required to keep as a record of important events in the life of the convent. A copy of the chronicle was, and is, sent annually to the provincial superior and to the SSpS headquarters.

24. By 1907 there were Holy Spirit Sisters at Tumleo and Ali Islands, Monumbo, Bogia, and Alexishafen.

25. "Chronicle of the Servants of the Holy Spirit, Alexishafen, Madang Province, Papua New Guinea: 1907–1974" (MS, 1907), 1.

26. Manam Island was, and is, an active volcano. See Lutkehaus 1995.

27. "Chronicle of the Servants of the Holy Spirit, Herz Jesu Convent, Bieng Catholic Mission, Manam Island, Papua New Guinea: 1924–1974" (MS), 1–2.

28. In addition to the work of establishing a new convent from scratch, in the early years of the sisters' presence in New Guinea their health was a constant concern. While the climate on Manam Island was relatively healthy because of the temperate winds, mosquitoes and heat were constant problems on the mainland.

29. From *History of the Holy Spirit Sisters in Papua New Guinea,* 1.

30. Ibid.

31. For more detailed information about the presence of the SVD and SSpS on Manam Island, see Lutkehaus 1983, 1995.

32. Another entry in the sister's chronicle explains the cultural rationale behind this Manam belief: "On Ascension Day we received another little orphan. If we had not taken it in, they would have buried it alive. This is the sad fate of newborn children here whose mothers die within the first fourteen days of their birth. Such a child may not be touched by anyone. During the first days one may hardly come close. Whoever touches it pronounces his own death sentence according to their tradition" ("Chronicle of the Servants of the Holy Spirit, Herz Jesu Con-

vent," 1925, 3). There are strong taboos surrounding birth that concern pollution beliefs and pertain to both the mother and newborn child. For more detail, see Böhm 1983; Lutkehaus 1995; Wedgwood 1934.

33. "Chronicle of the Servants of the Holy Spirit, Herz Jesu Convent," 4–5.

34. From a later entry in the sister's chronicle, it appears that they would like to have been able to establish an orphanage on Manam, in part because children raised in an orphanage were thought to grow up to be especially loyal to the mission.

35. "Chronicle of the Servants of the Holy Spirit, Herz Jesu Convent," 28.

36. The incident begins with the comment: "It is of great disadvantage for good family life that many eligible young men or married young men go away. The girls and women become tired of waiting and go off as second wives. Illegitimate children are born and buried immediately . . . it is a disgrace, people say, for a young [unmarried] girl to walk around with a child" (ibid.).

37. Manam women are confined to the *boaruku,* or birth hut, for the first month after having given birth until pollution taboos surrounding childbirth have been ritually removed. By destroying the *boaruku,* the sister had effectively made the mother "homeless," as she would not be welcome in her own, or any other woman's, house. Men still slept in separate dwellings from women at the time of this incident.

38. "Chronicle of the Servants of the Holy Spirit, Herz Jesu Convent," 6–7.

39. *Luluai* is a Melanesian Pidgin term used to describe a local village leader appointed by the colonial government. In Manam society the village *luluai* were usually men of high status (*tanepoa*) or even the traditional Manam village leader, or Big Man (called *Tanepoa Labalaba* in Manam), himself. See Lutkehaus 1995, for more detail.

40. "Chronicle of the Servants of the Holy Spirit, Herz Jesu Convent," 30–34.

41. *Kiap* is the Melanesian Pidgin term used to describe a local government officer.

42. Manam village leaders, or *Tanepoa,* traditionally had the right to designate that local women marry specific men. See Lutkehaus 1995.

43. Apparently, Paisi had already given a bridewealth payment to Maria's family in exchange for her, as was the local custom. See Lutkehaus 1995.

44. In fact, after World War II, as the Australian colonial government became more concerned with the development of citizens of the potential new independent state of Papua New Guinea who would be loyal to their former Australian protectors, rather than simply concerned with the cultivation of a cheap labor force, they argued for a shift in the locus of control over education from the missions to the government itself (Wetherell and Carr-Gregg 1990).

REFERENCES

Allen, Ann Taylor. 1991. *Feminism and Motherhood in Germany, 1800–1914.* New Brunswick, N.J.: Rutgers University Press.

Beidelman, T. O. 1982. *Colonial Evangelism.* Bloomington: Indiana University Press.

Blackbourn, David, and Geoff Eley. 1984. *The Peculiarities of German History.* Oxford: Oxford University Press.

Böhm, Karl. 1983. *The Life of Some Island People of New Guinea.* Trans. Karl Böhm and Nancy Lutkehaus. Berlin: Reimer Verlag.

Bowie, Fiona, Deborah Kirkwood, and Shirley Ardener, eds. 1993. *Women and Missions: Past and Present. Anthropological and Historical Perceptions.* Oxford: Berg.

Burridge, K. O. L. 1960. *Mambu: A Melanesian Millenium.* New York: Harper Torchbooks.

Comaroff, Jean. 1985. *Body of Power, Spirit of Resistance: The Culture and History of a South African People.* Chicago: University of Chicago Press.

Comaroff, Jean, and John L. Comaroff. 1991. *Of Revelation and Revolution: Christianity, Colonialism and Consciousness in South Africa,* vol. 1. Chicago: University of Chicago Press.

Cooper, Frederick, and Ann Laura Stoler. 1989. Tensions of Empire: Colonial Control and Visions of Rule. Introduction to a special issue of *American Ethnologist* 16, no. 4: 609–21.

———, eds. 1997. *Tensions of Empire: Colonial Cultures in a Bourgeois World.* Berkeley: University of California Press.

Davin, Anna. 1997. Imperialism and Motherhood. In *Tensions of Empire: Colonial Cultures in a Bourgeois World,* ed. Frederick Cooper and Ann Laura Stoler, 87–151. Berkeley: University of California Press.

Firth, Stewart. 1983. *New Guinea under the Germans.* Victoria: Melbourne University Press.

Flemming, Leslie A. 1992. A New Humanity: American Missionaries' Ideals for Women in North India, 1870–1930. In *Western Women and Imperialism: Complicity and Resistance,* ed. Nupur Chaudhuri and Margaret Strobel, 191–206. Bloomington: Indiana University Press.

Frevert, Ute. 1989. *Women in German History: From Bourgeoisie Emancipation to Sexual Liberation.* Oxford: Berg. (Original German edition, 1986.)

Grimshaw, Patricia. 1989. *Paths of Duty: American Missionary Wives in Nineteenth Century Hawaii.* Honolulu: University of Hawaii Press.

Hausen, Karin. 1981. Family and Role-Division: The Polarization of Sexual Stereotypes in the Nineteenth Century—An Aspect of the Dissociation of Work and Family Life. In *The German Family,* ed. Richard J. Evans and W. R. Lee, 51–83. Totowa, N.J.: Barnes and Noble Books.

Hill, Patricia R. 1985. *The World Their Household.* Ann Arbor: University of Michigan Press.

History of the Holy Spirit Sisters in Papua New Guinea (pamphlet, n.d.).

Huber, Mary Taylor. 1988. *The Bishop's Progress: A Historical Ethnography of Catholic Missionary Experience on the Sepik Frontier.* Washington D.C.: Smithsonian Institution Press.

Hunt, Nancy Rose. 1990. Domesticity and Colonialism in Belgian Africa: Usumbura's Foyer Social, 1946–1960. *Signs* 15, no. 3: 447–74.

Hunter, Jane. 1984. *The Gospel of Gentility.* New Haven: Yale University Press.
Jolly, Margaret. 1991. "To Save the Girls for Brighter and Better Lives": Presbyterian Missions and Women in the South of Vanuatu, 1848–1870. *Journal of Pacific History* 26, no. 1: 27–48.
———. 1993. Colonizing Women: The Maternal Body and Empire. In *Feminism and the Politics of Difference,* ed. Sneja Gunew and Anna Yeatman, 103–27. Boulder: Westview Press.
Jolly, Margaret, and Martha Macintyre, eds. 1989. *Family and Gender in the Pacific: Domestic Contradictions and the Colonial Impact.* Cambridge: Cambridge University Press.
Kipp, Rita Smith. 1990. *The Early Years of a Dutch Colonial Mission: The Karo Field.* Ann Arbor: University of Michigan Press.
Lacey, R. L. 1972. Missions. In *Encyclopedia of Papua and New Guinea,* ed. Peter Ryan, 772–82. Melbourne: Melbourne University Press.
Langmore, Diane. 1982. A Neglected Force: White Women Missionaries in Papua, 1874–1914. *Journal of Pacific History* 17:138–57.
———. 1989. *Missionary Lives: Papua, 1874–1914.* Honolulu: University of Hawaii Press.
Laqueur, Thomas. 1990. *Making Sex: Body and Gender from the Greeks to Freud.* Cambridge: Harvard University Press.
Lutkehaus, Nancy. 1983. Introduction to *The Life of Some Island People of New Guinea,* by Karl Böhm, 13–70. Berlin: Reimer Verlag.
———. 1995. *Zaria's Fire: Engendered Moments in Manam Ethnography.* Durham, N.C.: Carolina Academic Press.
McDonough, Peter. 1990. Metamorphoses of the Jesuits: Sexual Identity, Gender Roles, and Hierarchy in Catholicism. *Comparative Studies in Society and History* 32, no. 2: 325–56.
Ong, Walter J. 1981. *Fighting for Life: Contest, Sexuality and Consciousness.* Ithaca, N.Y.: Cornell University Press.
Prelinger, Catherine M. 1987. *Charity, Challenge, and Change: Religious Dimensions of the Mid-Nineteenth Century Woman's Movement in Germany.* New York: Greenwood Press.
Ramusack, Barbara N. 1992. Cultural Missionaries, Maternal Imperialists, Feminist Allies: British Women Activists in India, 1865–1915. In *Western Women and Imperialism: Complicity and Resistance,* ed. Nupur Chaudhuri and Margaret Strobel, 119–36. Bloomington: Indiana University Press.
Sack, Peter, and Dymphna Clark, eds. 1980. *German New Guinea: The Draft Annual Report for 1913–14.* Trans. Peter Sack and Dymphna Clark. Canberra: Australian National University.
Servants of the Holy Spirit (SSpS). N.d. *The History of the Holy Spirit Sisters in Papua New Guinea.* Printed Pamphlet. Papua New Guinea.
Stoler, Ann L. 1989. Making Empire Respectable: The Politics of Race and Sexual Morality in Twentieth Century Colonial Cultures. *American Ethnologist* 16, no. 4: 634–60.
———. 1991. Carnal Knowledge and Imperial Power: Gender, Race and Morality

in Colonial Asia. In *Gender at the Crossroads of Knowledge: Feminist Anthropology in the Postmodern Era,* ed. Micaela di Leonardo, 51–101. Berkeley: University of California Press.

———. N.d. The Racial Politics of Mothercare: Poor Whites and the Subversion of the Colonial State. MS.

Thorne, Susan. 1997. "The Conversion of Englishmen and the Conversion of the World Inseparable": Missionary Imperialism and the Language of Class in Early Industrial Britain. In *Tensions of Empire: Colonial Cultures in a Bourgeois World,* ed. Frederick Cooper and Ann Laura Stoler, 238–62. Berkeley: University of California Press.

Wedgwood, Camilla. 1937. Women in Manam. *Oceania* 7:401–28; 8:170–92.

Wetherell, David, and Charlotte Carr-Gregg. 1990. *Camilla: A Life. Camilla Wedgwood, 1901–1955.* Kensington: New South Wales University Press.

Wiltgen, Ralph. 1969. Catholic Mission Plantations in Mainland New Guinea: Their Origin and Purpose. In *History of Melanesia,* 329–62. Proceedings of the Second Waigani Seminar, Port Moresby. Canberra: Australian National University Press.

Unpublished Material

Chronicle of the Servants of the Holy Spirit, Herz Jesu Convent, Bieng Catholic Mission, Manam Island, Papua New Guinea: 1924–1974. MS. Archives of the Holy Spirit Sisters, Rome.

Chronicle of the Servants of the Holy Spirit, Alexishafen, Madang Province, Papua New Guinea: 1907–1974. MS. Archives of the Holy Spirit Sisters, Rome.

Contributors

T. O. Beidelman is Professor of Anthropology at New York University. Among his publications on missionaries are "Social Theory and the Study of Christian Missions in Africa" (*Africa,* 1974) and *Colonial Evangelism: A Socio-Cultural Study of an East African Mission at the Grassroots* (1982). His most recent book on the Kaguru of Tanzania is *The Cool Knife: Imagery of Gender, Sexuality, and Moral Education in Kaguru Initiation Ritual* (1997).

Mary Taylor Huber is a Senior Scholar at The Carnegie Foundation for the Advancement of Teaching. Her writings include *The Bishops' Progress: A Historical Ethnography of Catholic Missionary Experience on the Sepik Frontier* (1988) and "Missionaries" (*Encyclopedia of Social and Cultural Anthropology,* 1996). She is working on a biography of Leo Arkfeld, SVD, retired bishop of Wewak and archbishop of Madang, Papua New Guinea.

Rita Smith Kipp is Professor of Anthropology at Kenyon College. She is author of *The Early Years of a Dutch Colonial Mission: The Karo Field* (1990) and "Conversion by Affiliation: The History of the Karo Batak Protestant Church" (*American Ethnologist,* 1995). She is working on a book tentatively called "Rethinking Divide and Rule: Missionary Effects in Indonesia," about the response of Indonesian Christians to the nationalist movement.

Nancy C. Lutkehaus is Associate Professor of Anthropology at the University of Southern California. Her essay on "Missionaries as Ethnographers" is the introduction to the English translation of *The Life of Some Island People of New Guinea* by Fr. Karl Böhm (1983). She is the author of *Zaria's Fire: Engendered Moments in Manam Ethnography* (1995) and is working on a film about SSpS nuns in Papua New Guinea.

Jon Miller is Professor of Sociology at the University of Southern California. His recent publications include "Missions, Social Change, and Resistance to Authority: Notes toward an Understanding of the Relative Autonomy of Religion" (*Journal for the Scientific Study of Religion,* 1993) and *The Social Control of Religious Zeal: A Study of Organizational Contradictions* (1994).

Line Nyhagen Predelli is a sociologist and political scientist wih the Norwegian Institute for Urban and Regional Research (NIBR) in Oslo. Her dissertation for the Department of Sociology, University of Southern California is entitled "Contested Patriarchy and Missionary Feminism: The Norwegian Missionary Society in Nineteenth Century Norway and Madagascar" (1998).

Susan Thorne is Assistant Professor of History at Duke University. Her publications include "The Conversion of Englishmen and the Conversion of the World Inseparable": Missionary Imperialism and the Language of Class in Early Industrial Britain" (In *Tensions of Empire,* ed. Frederick Cooper and Ann Laura Stoler, 1997) and *Congregational Missions and the Making of an Imperial Culture in Nineteenth-Century England* (forthcoming).

Index